The *Prose Solomon and Saturn* and *Adrian and Ritheus*

MCMASTER OLD ENGLISH STUDIES AND TEXTS I

JAMES E. CROSS
AND THOMAS D. HILL

The *Prose Solomon and Saturn* and *Adrian and Ritheus*

EDITED FROM
THE BRITISH LIBRARY MANUSCRIPTS
WITH COMMENTARY

University of Toronto Press
Toronto   Buffalo   London

©University of Toronto Press 1982
Toronto   Buffalo   London
Printed in Canada

Canadian Cataloguing in Publication Data

Solomon and Saturn.
The Prose Solomon and Saturn and Adrian and Ritheus
  (McMaster Old English studies and texts; 1)
  Old English text with notes and commentary in English.
  ISBN 0-8020-5472-2 (bound); ISBN 0-8020-6509-0 (pbk.)
  I. Solomon and Saturn. 2. Adrian and Ritheus.
  I. Adrian and Ritheus. II. Cross, James E.
  III. Hill, Thomas D., 1940–   . IV. Title. V. Series.
  PRI770.AI 1980   829'.8   C79-094885-0

Publication of this book was made possible by grants from
McMaster University and from the Publication Funds of
University of Toronto Press.

To Joyce Cross and Carol Hill

Contents

Preface

The two question-and-answer lists presented here, the *Prose Solomon and Saturn* and *Adrian and Ritheus*, have attracted the attention of some well-known names in Anglo-Saxon studies. Franciscus Junius transcribed *Adrian and Ritheus* on two occasions and Thomas Wright was the first to print the text, while Benjamin Thorpe first printed the *Prose Solomon and Saturn* and John Kemble was the first to consider the content of the two pieces. But since 1848 when Kemble used, and speculated on, Thorpe's text for the *Solomon and Saturn* and also transcribed *Adrian and Ritheus* there has been no study of the two texts, although Max Förster's printed corrections to Kemble's *Adrian and Ritheus* indicated that a new printing of that text was needed. Our reading of the manuscript against Thorpe's printing of *Solomon and Saturn* and Kemble's emendations also suggested that a new text of this piece was necessary, especially since the Thorpe/Kemble text produced some false entries for Bosworth's *Anglo-Saxon Dictionary*.

We were drawn separately to the study of the pieces, however, by the content, for James Cross as supervisor of an undergraduate thesis by Valerie Hill at the University of Bristol in 1962, for Thomas Hill as part of his Cornell University doctoral dissertation: 'Old English Poetry and the Sapiental Tradition,' presented in 1967. The friendly advice of R.E. Kaske of Cornell University brought us together in 1968, at first in discussion by correspondence, then, in person in the spring semester of 1975.

We had realised that, despite the delightful essay by F.L. Utley in 1957, there was much to be done in attempting to trace the ideas which informed these questions and answers. We had the advantage, denied to Kemble, of thorough discussions of similar lists in other languages in two monographs by W. Suchier which, particularly, allowed comparisons for the detection of corrupt transmissions. But no one, including Utley and Suchier, had attempted to face all the subtle problems presented by the ideas in the pieces. For this two heads have proved better than one, and although some explanations in our commentary will no doubt appear obvious, they do not record the abortive reading done before the simple answer appeared. We have not been able to explain everything in the lists, possibly because of some unfathomable corruption in the textual transmission but probably because our reading has not been in the right area. But we now feel that reliable texts (we trust) and our attempts at explanation should be presented to other scholars who may be able to suggest better solutions or to fill the gaps in our knowledge. Our confessions of failure are not, we believe, so many.

Suchier's work showed that these Old English texts are of value to scholars of medieval literature in other languages and for this reason our commentary includes translations of the Old English, and, normally, of the parallels to the questions in other languages.

The interest shown by our friends and colleagues over a comparatively lengthy period has encouraged us and might have delighted the ancient question-masters. When we were writing our material in the spring of 1975 we had the benefit of discussions in a knowledgeable luncheon-group including R.E. Kaske, Arthur Groos, and Giuseppe Mazzotta. We owe gratitude for help to many others. The late F.L. Utley had generously offered to read the commentary and encouraged us from the outset. The late C.L. Wrenn identified a Junius transcript for us (see 'Manuscripts and Transcripts'). Angus Cameron of Toronto read the texts against the Toronto photostats for slips in transcript and edition. At different stages individual experts answered questions on the varied material. John Vigorita of Cornell and N.J.A. Williams of Liverpool checked printed translations and offered new translations (as cited) of the Irish vernacular quotations. Andrew Hamer of Liverpool read through the Norse quotations, while Joyce Bazire of Liverpool read text and glossary with her alert eye for irregularity of presentation and for error. Randall Jones and George Tate prepared the text for the Cornell computer to produce a concordance as basis for our glossary.

We also wish to thank those members of medieval societies at Dublin, Leeds, Liverpool, London (Ontario), London, Rochester (New York), St Anne's College (Oxford), Toronto, and Yale who heard our tentative conclusions as the work proceeded and who commented on some of the problems.

The librarians in our own universities have been unfailingly generous of their time, as well as those at Yale University and at the University of Lund, Sweden. We name one for all, the pleasant and acute Mrs Spicer of Cornell University who faced our continuous requests with equanimity.

Our typists, Joan Welford, Catherine Rees, and Coraleen Rooney, have assured us that they were interested in preparing the copy, but certainly they have lessened our work by their remarkable accuracy. Scholarly foundations have both supported the research and subvented the publication of this book. Some of the work for this book was done during the academic year of 1970–1 when T.D. Hill was a faculty fellow at the Society for the Humanities at Cornell University. And T.D. Hill continued to work on this project in 1973–4 when he was supported by a fellowship from the American Council of Learned Societies. The Society for the Humanities at Cornell again expedited this work by awarding J.E. Cross a senior fellowship in the spring semester of 1975. We are also grateful for the support we have received from the McMaster Old English Studies and Texts series and the scholars who direct that series, Laura Braswell, Maureen Halsall, and Alvin Lee. Finally, but mostly, we are indebted to our respective wives, Joyce and Carol, who have criticized and consoled as needed. Their calmness and cheerfulness have been our impetus.

We hope that this book will not disappoint the expectations of our friends.

J.E.C. / T.D.H.

Liverpool / Cornell 1976

PART ONE

Introduction
Texts

The Old English texts

The Old English *Adrian and Ritheus* and the *Prose Solomon and Saturn* are two examples of a widely spread genre in a number of languages.[1] These examples have been (and may still be) called dialogues,[2] but like other generic titles this has had a wide embrace, and our type of literature here has little similarity with the developed discussion or debate between two speakers either of antiquity or of more modern times.[3] The Old English texts and their closest relations are no more than lists of brief questions and answers in which, except in short series, the successive items are unconnected in subject-matter, and thus such individual lists lack a distinguishable logical sequence. It seems likely that many of the extant lists which are used as illustration in this edition as well as the Old English lists were mixed in origin, augmented, or diminished at the whim or slip of an individual transmitter.

The Old English lists are typically miscellaneous in topic although, like some other lists, they are formulaic in presentation: 'Tell me ... I tell you.' The majority of questions, however, are based on scripture or writings arising from scripture. Some demand direct knowledge of scriptural fact, even of the letter of scripture, some of apocryphal or rabbinic lore, and some of medievally 'scientific' information although these are sometimes dependent on the Hexaemeral traditions. Others draw on ancient medical observation or opinion and yet others on proverbial wisdom, whether scripturally based or not. Most of the questions depend on factual knowledge but a number are catch-questions with a riddling quality.

The appeal of such questions is universal – in their teaching and testing of knowledge and sometimes of wit – but their content reveals aspects of the medieval imagination which may illuminate obscurities in the major literature and certainly accustoms a modern reader to medieval attitudes.

They deal with facts which illustrate the limits of history and of the known world, mainly from books. Who first talked with a dog (ss 34)? Where does the sun shine at night (AR 6)? Which man first thought of tilling with a plough (ss 35)? How did Adam get his name (ss 6, 7)? Such questions, which are common to a number of dialogues, reflect a concern to present and ponder the facts of history or of the universe. This concern with such matters is something which the medieval Latin and vernacular dialogues share with such popular modern books as the *Guinness Book of Records* or the English *Pears Cyclopedia* (a repository of curious knowledge).

Despite the variety of topic the dialogues illustrate dominant attitudes of mind, most notably an accuracy and, indeed, an extreme literalism in knowledge of the Bible. This attitude, on occasions, produces bizarre results to those of us who no longer are tested by catch-questions depending upon accurate knowledge of the Bible, although some may remember such questions even now. One of us indeed recalls the question, 'In the Bible, who first rode a motor-bike?' The answer depends upon a scrupulously literal reading of scripture and an obvious play on the word 'Triumph.' An example, from one of the Latin dialogues, is: 'Who first said: The Lord be with you?'; 'Boos (Booz), the son of Salmon, when he sent his labourers into the harvest' (Suchier AE₁b 92, 18). Obviously the Bible is not a record of all human discourse and there is no indication in the Book of Ruth that the labourers saw anything unusual in the greeting from Booz. But Ruth 2:4 is apparently the first text in the Bible where the phrase occurs and the questioner demands that detailed knowledge. Much more interesting to medievalists, however, are the variations of answer to the questions about the first ploughman in ss 35 and in some Latin dialogues. In the Vulgate Cain is described as a farmer (Genesis 4:2) and one might assume that his would be the name in the answer. But sometimes the answer is Noe, or Noe's son Ham. The reason for the exclusion of Cain is that, although in the Septuagint/Old Latin versions of Genesis, he was the one who 'operabatur terram'; he was simply a farmer ('agricola') in the Vulgate. Noe was the man who first began to work the earth in the Vulgate ('coepitque Noe vir agricola exercere terram'; Genesis 9:20). The name of his son Ham may have been thoughtlessly entered because he shared an alternative naming, Cham, with Cain. If one's Bible was Septuagint/Old Latin clearly the answer was Cain (Cham), if the Vulgate the answer was Noe. The variants, however, serve to remind medievalists that other versions of scripture than the Vulgate were available.

Deference to the authority of a received text is not limited to scripture. A series of questions in both Old English texts (ss 51, 52; AR 33–6), and in some Latin lists, ask for the 'number' of fish, birds, and serpents in the world, and the answers, as a medievalist would expect, are probably based, not on natural observation, but on a count of names from such as Isidore's *Etymologies*. A number of other answers are explained by reference to known books of the medieval world.

The questioners also assume knowledge of a cohesive body of literature which arose to explain the statements or to fill the silences of scripture. Some questions and answers exhibit a casual acceptance of the 'spiritual' understanding of the Bible in terms of the hermeneutics of the patristic and early medieval church. When ss 28 notes that the lily is the best of plants because it signifies Christ, part, at least, of the reason for this statement is the allegorical equation of the lily and Christ in the traditional exegesis of scriptural texts. The comments on the two feet (AR 26) and the four wings (AR 27) of the soul derive from the moralistic traditions of Christian teachers, and an 'etymology' of a word 'caelum' is the reason why 'heaven' is called 'heaven' (ss 3).

But the lists show more interest in the traditions originating in rabbinic and/or Apocryphal lore which speculate or dogmatize on matters about which both the Bible and many more orthodox Christians are silent. How exactly was the body of Adam formed (ss 8, 9)? Where did the fallen angels go (ss 32)? How tall was Adam (ss 11)? etc. A distinguished writer, describing the intellectual attitude of Gregory the Great (who had an excellent sense of his audience), remarks that 'with an unperturbed assurance, in no way motivated by pride, he plunged into all sorts of obscure questions.'[4] This statement may characterize the attitude of our question-masters as well. However seriously some of the questions were taken they do supply solutions for a range of apparent problems which the more scrupulous (or less curious) authorities did not discuss. In the lists also, the orthodox truisms are juxtaposed with heterodox or unorthodox statements, with no attempt to distinguish between them. If we are right in our speculative explanation of the answer that Christ was born from the Virgin Mary's right breast (AR 41) it may be that this reflects heretical (docetic) statements about the immateriality of Christ's body. But the answer is set between two other questions and answers which have a firm Biblical basis, and there is nothing in our text to indicate that it is any more or less authoritative than any other in the series.

It was this aspect of popular medieval religious culture that offended such men as Ælfric who were seriously concerned with the religious life of the laity. Yet his protest about the dissemination of false teaching[5] apparently had little effect, certainly not on the popularity of the dialogues. The question on the manner of Christ's birth is the only one which may be heterodox in its assumptions, but a number of questions can only be answered from knowledge of apocryphal books and unorthodox sources. The question-masters were not concerned with Ælfric's problem.

A modern reader might use the evidence of some of the answers to illustrate the naiveté and ignorance of the authors, particularly on matters of the physical world, but they are, of course, medieval people who simply transmitted (sometimes garbled) knowledge from the ancient authorities. Alternatively, however, some questions and answers exhibit a subtlety of mind about words, their meanings and their application to the facts of human behaviour in moral aphorism. Some of us may still care to ponder that word is best and worst (ss 37, AR 43); that a man's will is dearest to him in life but most hateful after death (AR 44); that the sweet word multiplies friends and appeases enemies (AR 45); that judgment (or life) pleases some and displeases others (ss 49); and so on. Such subtlety with moralistic application reminds us that the title of one traditional series of Latin questions was *Joca monachorum*.[6] These, to some composers were the jests (or puzzles) of monks, the academics of their day, whose subject was morality but whose delight was often in the written word and meaning. Many of the questions and answers instruct but in an entertaining way, and even an aphorism becomes less sententious when framed as a puzzling question. It may also become more memorable as a solved puzzle. Apart from plays on words and their meaning there is simple delight in conundrums. Who was not born and (yet) was buried in his mother's womb (ss 15, AR 28)? What son avenged his father in his mother's womb (AR 12)? All such questions as these, which are intended to entertain as well as teach, indicate that their composers were freed from constraint of serious purpose and that such lists may illuminate aspects of the medieval literary imagination which the more formal context of serious literature only intermittently exemplifies.

The lists, in their variety, present in simple language the kind of knowledge which should be recalled by the alert reader of medieval literature. If the authors of our dialogues drew on extra-scriptural information in their comments on creation so too did the author of the Old English *Genesis B* poem.[7] If they assumed knowledge of typology so also did the *Exodus* poet.[8] Like the composer of *Genesis A* and Old English homilists they knew what an 'etymology' was,[9] and like the homilists they made moral or tropological interpretations. The gnomic or aphoristic injunctions of the dialogues correspond very well with the interjections of the *Beowulf* poet, and similar knowledge of apocryphal story is reflected in the dialogues and the Old English *Christ and Satan* (see especially the comment on Adam's baptism, ss 15).

Seemingly, too, some curious answers in the dialogues can help to explain the creative impetus for illustrations in medieval manuscripts. The scholars who have considered the picture of Cain killing Abel in the British Library manuscript Claudius B iv have cited and debated 'Cain's jawbone' in ss 36.[10] Recently Barbara Raw has recalled ss 1, on God on the wings of the winds at creation, when referring to the Utrecht Psalter and to the Bodleian Library manuscript Junius 11 ('The Cædmon manuscript').[11]

The lists are a delight to antiquarians, those who are curious about the past merely because it is past, but they can, we hope, serve as an entertaining introduction for students to the kind of statements and attitudes which inform much medieval literature.

RELATIONSHIPS AND GENRE

There were, in antiquity, antecedents for the form of question-and-answer series, notably, as L.W. Daly has illustrated,[12] exemplified in 'secular' lists on technical subjects such as medicine, music, and rhetoric, as well as in 'religious' series, found as early as the second century and continuing to the exegetical and dogmatic quaestiones on scriptural texts and moralistic problems. But question-and-answer lists, whether for factual teaching or for amusement, may obviously be created when needed and it is impossible to demonstrate a continuing tradition from antiquity for the complete series of the Old English pieces.

At present there is no single source for either of the Old English lists, but there are clear relationships between these and extant Latin lists which are presented and described in a lengthy study by W. Suchier.[13] He considers what he distinguishes as two groups of lists, one of which he names *Joca monachorum* (JM) from a title in a ninth-century ms,[14] the other as *Adrian and Epictetus* (AE) from the names of the protagonists. It is clear, as Suchier says (p 92), that the Old English lists belong 'to the circle' of the JM group. Of the fifty-nine questions in ss, twenty-four are found in extant JM lists; of the forty-eight questions in AR, twenty are paralleled, although eight of these twenty correspond to questions in ss. If the tract cited as *Collectanea Bedae*, which is extant only in the early printed versions of Bede's works (first in 1563), is as early as the eighth century as a number of scholars agree,[15] nine more questions may be added to the parallels between ss / AR, and JM, since parts of the pseudo-Bede tract certainly have firm contact with extant JM texts, and Suchier[16] rightly regards the comparable sections of the tract as a representative of the JM group.

Some questions in the JM lists, all of which are in Latin, are paralleled in lists in Greek,[17] which are described by Daly,[18] so it could well be that the JM Latin lists owe their origin to Greek series, although immediate contact between any one Latin list and any Greek list is impossible to demonstrate.

In their turn the JM Latin lists are thought by Suchier to influence certain questions in the AE lists,[19] and clearly the vernacular lists printed by Suchier *L'Enfant sage*,[20] which are of a later date than the Old English lists, also take over some questions.

Our commentary notes parallels where they occur from any one of these groups of lists, even if of later date, since a later question may be based on an earlier but lost question in view of the contacts between the groups.

But there are some questions in ss and particularly in AR which, at present, have no correspondences in any other of the kinds of lists, JM, AE, and *L'Enfant sage*. We think it helpful to speculate about these possible 'additions,' partly to suggest that the Old English lists or exemplars were individually or collectively augmented, but also to indicate certain cultural contacts.

Obviously, not all questions without analogue are necessarily unique Old English additions. Questions on Adam, without correspondence at present, on his age at creation and his height (ss 10 and 11) are of a common kind of question and are probably not additions peculiarly by the Anglo-Saxon. Questions also about the sun, its redness at morning and evening (ss 55, 56, AR 7, 8), and perhaps even its place of rising and setting (ss 26, 27, AR 29, 30) and its composition of burning stone (AR 10), may well have had parallels since there were questions about the sun, some of enigmatic nature,[21] in the extant lists. AR 18 on the first doctor is also of a common kind of question.

Yet, at the end of AR, there is a run of four questions: two moralistic (AR 45, 46), on the sweet word and the false friend, taken without real adaptation directly from Ecclesiasticus, one (AR 47) on the sick man, which in its complexity appears to have derived at least ultimately from Augustine's *Confessions*, and one (AR 48) on symptoms of approaching death which can only have originated in Isidore's *Etymologies*. All of these are without extant parallel and not of a kind found in JM and AE lists. They look like additions by the Anglo-Saxon or direct predecessor from moralistic scriptural or patristic reading.

So too appear to be AR 26 and 27 on the two feet and the four wings of the soul since both belong to the moralistic tradition and the only near parallel to the latter question (AR 27) is in a Hiberno-Latin catechism, culled mostly from patristic writers, called *Prebiarum de multorium exemplaribus*, which is thought to be a 'handbook useful to the itinerant preacher, the teacher, or even to the spiritual father charged with the obligation of giving spiritual conferences or instructions.'[22] There are some questions in this eighth-century Latin list which do not fit the general description just given from its editor R.E. McNally, and two questions in it are paralleled in JM lists.[23] As we have suggested, intermixture either way can be expected in such lists. But this contact (in AR 27) does indicate which direction to take in our admitted speculation about cultural contacts. There are three other similarities with AR.[24] The *Prebiarum* has a corrupt form of AR 38 on the three (four) mute things, which is differently corrupted in AR 38 and is paralleled elsewhere only in *Collectanea Bedae*. It alone has an extended form of the abbreviated AR 44 on 'will' being dearest and most hateful, which has a similar but different form in a late text of Suchier's *L'Enfant sage*. It also has the same error as AR 12 which obscures the point about the peculiar nature of the viper by using the general term 'serpent.'

We are not speaking here about immediate contact or direct source but the similarities, though few, are suggestive in two ways, especially since we may surely assume that the *Prebiarum* is only one representative of its kind. A simple question-and-answer technique for religious instruction was particularly favoured by the Irish teachers[25] and McNally and others have published a number of texts.[26] Obviously the technique, as noted above from the discussion by Daly, had antecedents among non-Irish teachers, although we should now record that the *De veteri et novo testamento quaestiones* which Daly includes[27] as by Isidore is now regarded as spurious and as an anonymous Hiberno-Latin text.[28] This text is the one of those mentioned by Daly which is the most similar in form to some JM lists and to SS and AR in recording brief answers to brief questions and in using the 'Dic mihi' form of presentation. It would be easy for abstractions to be made from such Hiberno-Latin catechisms to augment any question-and-answer list.

Another hint from the stated similarities with the *Prebiarum* is that the Anglo-Saxons or their predecessors looked generally to Irish texts or traditions. Such a suspicion is less strange now than it might have been many years ago before the identification and indeed publication of Hiberno-Latin texts and before detailed links between specific Irish and English texts had been demonstrated. General traffic of people to places has been known from Bede, Aldhelm, and others but knowledge of reading contacts depends on continuing source-study and, indeed, still awaits the future publication of identified Hiberno-Latin manuscripts.[29]

In following this hint we turn first to the tract called *Collectanea Bedae* which, as stated, has contact with JM lists but also contains identifiably Hiberno-Latin material and is now taken to be a Hiberno-Latin collection by most scholars.[30] We immediately recall AR 38 above which is similar only to a question in the *Prebiarum* and the *Collectanea* and add that three questions in SS (33, 39, 41) together with one addition to questions extant in JM lists (within SS 15) are found early elsewhere only in the *Collectanea*. The same applies to two questions in AR (23, 39) although one of these (AR 39) corresponds to an SS question (SS 39).

As we indicate in the commentary, a number of other questions also appear to get information from Irish texts or traditions. The names of the wives of Noah and his sons (SS 19, 20, 21) derive, it appears, from two separate groupings of names, both of which are found in Irish vernacular or Hiberno-Latin texts, although one group disseminates to the scribe of the Old English poem *Genesis A* and the other to the later Peter Comestor. The reasons for stones being unfruitful (SS 36) and for the raven being black (AR 21) are paralleled in Irish vernacular texts and may point to earlier traditions. And the places where the apostate angels fell (SS 32), which seems to be based on a commentary to Apocalypse 12:4, is linked, at present, with an Irish gloss on the text. Some of these individual suggestions may eventually turn out to be indistinctive but the number of present contacts suggests some augmentation of the JM type of lists under the influence of texts or traditions which appear to be of Irish origin.

Our Old English texts were written at the end of the period so it is also reasonable to speculate on 'additions' to the lists from earlier Anglo-Saxon texts. The most distinctive are the addition to SS 12, on Adam in hell, and AR 20, on the supernatural homes of Enoch and Elias. The question about the length of Adam's life on earth is common in JM lists but brief in answer: nine hundred and thirty (years); and it is based on Genesis 5:5. But the unnecessary extension by the SS writer on Adam in hell corresponds verbatim, apart from one word, with a thirty-eight word description in the exemplar of Vercelli Homily XIX, a piece which is extant in four Old English manuscripts. Further, this extension includes a probable error on the time Adam spent in hell (5228 years) which is found elsewhere in Old English texts and which is discussed in the commentary to SS 17. In the case of AR 20 we suggest in the commentary that the originator of the information saw an Old English gloss on Aldhelm's poem *De virginitate*.

There are other questions or answers, particularly in SS, which have no correspondence in earlier JM lists and, in ss, are unlike the brief answers in such lists, for example, the irrelevant extension to a question on Mary which is a record of ages of the world (ss 17) and the rambling answer of ss 59. We consider some of these below in the discussion on the extent of *Adrian and Ritheus* and suggest that these are peculiar to the habit of the ss scribe or exemplar[31] and different from the habit of the AR scribe or exemplar.

It appears that both ss and AR (or exemplars) individually and collectively have augmented basic JM lists and both appear to have had contact with Irish texts and traditions as well as with Old English vernacular texts.

One final set of correspondences needs consideration, that between ss and AR and between these and some other vernacular texts. Seventeen questions in ss and AR correspond in content but it is notable that each one differs in Old English phrasing, slightly or largely, from its parallel. These differences of word in each case indicate, at least, no mindless copying of one by the other in either direction and suggest that there was no direct contact between the manuscript lists and no common immediate exemplar. Of these seventeen questions eight have parallels in JM lists, one (ss 47, AR 40) in Hiberno-Latin catechisms, which in its form could easily have entered the JM type of lists at some stage, and one (ss 42, AR 25) at present extant elsewhere only in the late *Alfræði Íslenzk*.[32] *Alfræði Íslenzk*, however, has contact with the JM type of lists and also has eighteen questions corresponding with ss and eleven corresponding with AR, although six of these are also in ss. Among these eighteen questions there are only two, ss 42, AR 25 above and ss 3 on the name 'caelum' ('heofon,' heaven) which have no extant Latin parallel. The majority of questions and statements in *Alfræði Íslenzk* have parallels in extant Latin lists or texts and this indicates the probability that ss 42, AR 25 as well as ss 3 were translated from lost Latin questions into Icelandic and Old English. Of course, ss 3 is based on the etymology of a Latin word.

Five questions, common to ss and AR, remain; two (ss 26, 27, AR 29, 30) on the place of sunrise and sunset, two (ss 55, 56, AR 7, 8) on the reasons why the sun is red in morning and evening, and one (AR 1 and 2, ss 16) on Adam's stay in Paradise. The last has no exact parallels in earlier Latin lists but the problem was presented. Yet all these five questions, apart from one, probably by simple omission,[33] are found in the Middle English *Questiones bytwene the Maister of Oxenford and his clerke*.[34]

These Middle English *Questiones* in the Harley manuscript have a remarkable similarity with ss alone and Förster is probably right in suggesting that the piece was 'translated from the same Latin original as the

Old English *Solomon and Saturn.*[35] Certainly it was not a simple 'modern-ization' of the Old English texts, but common errors in comparison with extant Latin parallels, and different errors many of which could have derived either from ss or a Latin text, do suggest that the Middle English *Questiones* derived from a very near relative to ss. But some differences suggest that the Middle English composer did not actually draw on ss.[36]

If this relationship is accurately surmised, a Latin text or texts did exist which contained those remaining questions common to ss and AR, yet the differing answers in AR 7 from ss 56 and in AR 1 and 2 from ss 16 indicate that the two texts did not draw on an immediate common source for these questions and answers.

Both lists, in effect, were composed independently of each other, al-though drawing on some common sources, no doubt at different removes. This difference is emphasised by the different names of the protagonists for the two Old English lists. It is most certain that the Adrian of AR is the Adrian (Hadrian) of the altercations or disputations between Adrian and Epictetus, or in fuller title, Hadrianus Augustus and Epictetus Philosophus, in the works printed in Daly-Suchier.[37] Kemble commented that 'the character of the Emperor Hadrian as sophist or philosopher pointed him out as a fitting interlocutor.'[38] The name Ritheus in the Old English text is more difficult to link with other protagonists in known dialogues but Suchier[39] speculates that it is a scribal corruption of Epictus; if so, fairly clearly at a number of removes from the original name. Kemble (208) suggested Pittheus, a Greek enigmatist. One might offer Ripheus, 'iustissimus ... et servantissimus aequi' (*Æneid* II 426–7), whom Dante places in heaven (*Paradiso* XX 67–72) as one of the two unbaptized pagans whom he admits to salvation. But it seems probable that the names in the Old English text came as a pair of interlocutors and the most likely couple of originals are Adrian and Epictetus.

The pair heading the other Old English series are almost certainly the same as the interlocutors in the other Old English dialogues between Solomon and Saturn[40] presented in two poems divided by a prose section. Whether the names in our prose list came by derivation from the poetical series or from a common ancestor is a matter for conjecture alone, but, as Menner says (26), the Old English pieces are the only ones in which Solomon's opponent is Saturn, and there appears to be a connection of title. This, however, is the only contact since the poetical series with prose insertions are concerned with altercations between Christian and pagan, whereas our prose text has a different intention, as our description has shown. Solomon was an obvious representative of Christian wisdom in the poetical dialogues. Scripture records his skill in debate when the Queen of Sheba came to test him with hard questions (3 Kings 10, Vulgate), and, after his answers, saw the wisdom of the king. As Menner illustrates (21–6), his reputation for wise subtlety in argument even against demons spread widely in varied literature. Saturn, as Kemble (113–31) argues, could be the prime pagan opponent since he was regarded as a pagan god.[41]

But for both our prose dialogues ss and AR, the names as caption are merely names abstracted from other dialogues. None of the extant Latin lists of the *Joca monachorum* type (with which our series have a definite relationship) have named protagonists and they conduct question and answer simply by the 'dic mihi' formula or through 'interrogavit-respondit.'

Manuscripts and Transcripts

The text is preserved in the British Library manuscript Cotton Vitellius A
xv, fols 86v–93v. The manuscript has been fully described by N.R. Ker[1] art
215, 279–81. It is now bound with the Beowulf manuscript (Ker art 216).
Our manuscript contains:

1 fols 4–59v, 'a free rendering of the Soliloquia of St Augustine, attributed
  in a colophon to King Alfred' (Ker, 279), printed by W. Endter[2] and,
  most recently, by Thomas A. Carnicelli,[3]
2 fols 60–86v, a translation of the Gospel of Nicodemus with a brief section
  of the beginning missing, printed by W.H. Hulme,[4]
3 fols 86v–93v, the prose Solomon and Saturn,
4 fol 93v, the first few lines of a homily on St Quintin, printed by M.
  Förster.[5]

N.R. Ker (280) regards the manuscript as having been copied by one scribe,
whose hand is dated as mid-twelfth century, a dating which is approximately supported by certain features of language and/or orthography. The
manuscript for our text has deteriorated at the folio edges and is badly
discoloured, as indicated in the textual notes. But the hand, where it is
legible, is clear, and corrections appear to have been made by the same
hand. The manuscript folios are now inlaid in frames of heavy paper.
According to M. Förster[6] and E.V.K. Dobbie[7] this was probably done
between 1860 and 1870.

Transcript
G. Hickes *Linguarum Vett. Septentrionalium Thesaurus Grammatico-
Criticus et Archaeologicus* Oxoniae: e teatro Sheldoniano, 1705, 2 vols,

Lib II (by Humfrey Wanley) 218. (Incipit: introduction and ss 1; and desinit: last lines of ss 59). Cited as Wanley.

ADRIAN AND RITHEUS (AR)

The text is contained in the British Library manuscript Cotton Julius A ii, fols 137v–140. The manuscript, a fragment of only nine folios bound with a larger manuscript under the same title (Ker art 158), has been fully described by N.R. Ker art 159, 202. It contains:

1 fols 136–7, a metrical prayer now printed by E.V.K. Dobbie,[8]
2 fols 137v–40, Adrian and Ritheus,
3 fol 140v, miscellaneous notes which are discussed below,
4 fols 141–4v, 'a free translation of some of the Distichs of Cato, followed by apophthegms independent of the Distichs' (Ker 202). This has now been edited, with textual notes, most recently by R.S. Cox,[9] although our ms text was printed by Kemble.[10]

N.R. Ker dates the scribal hand as mid-twelfth century, but R.S. Cox (31) thinks that the hand 'seems conservative for such a late date and perhaps belongs instead to the end of the eleventh century.' Features of the language and/or orthography are of that period known loosely as 'transitional' whose present limits would cover both these dates. Ker notes that the manuscript was damaged by the fire of 1731 in the Cotton Library. The folios for our text have deteriorated at the edges and there is some warping and splitting, particularly at the top of the folio, which affects legibility as indicated in the textual notes. But the hand, where legible, is clear. There are no orthographic corrections to the AR text.

Transcripts

1 Ms Junius 45, Bodleian Library, noted by Ker, 202, and described by F. Madan etc[11] as being 'written in the seventeenth century by Francis Junius.' The transcript, of six quarto pages, is immediately followed by a transcript of item 3 of ms Cotton Julius A ii, but this is marked off with a heading 'Appendix.' The six pages of AR are cancelled with a deletion-line running diagonally down the page, and the ending of item 3 (on the seventh page) is additionally cancelled by a number of perpendicular and some horizontal deletion-lines criss-crossing on the page.
2 Ms Junius 61, Bodleian Library. The late C.L. Wrenn drew our attention to this transcript which is described by F. Madan etc,[12] but not fully. *The Summary Catalogue* notes that it was 'written in the mid-seventeenth century by Francis Junius.' The transcript of six pages, is clearly written,

and, again, is immediately followed, on the sixth page, by item 3 of ms Cotton Julius A ii, again marked off as 'Appendix.' While the transcript of AR stands, item 3, on the sixth and seventh pages, is thoroughly cancelled by horizontal deletion-lines through each line.
3 Wanley Lib II 183. (Incipit: introduction and AR 1; and desinit: AR 48).

The extent of Adrian and Ritheus

Max Förster[13] printed item 3 of ms Cotton Julius A ii (433–4), which contains notes, as direct statements, on the two thieves hanged at the Crucifixion, on the measurements of Noah's Ark, St Peter's Church, Solomon's Temple, the world ('Istorius sæde'), and on the number of a man's bones and veins (sinews) and days in the year, this last being similar to ss 59 and being cited in our commentary. Förster suggested (434) that these jottings should be taken as part of the AR text, especially since they are similar to the extension, in direct statement, of the last answer in ss (59). But both the habit of the AR writer or copyist in contrast with the ss composer or copyist and the presentation of the material in ms Cotton Julius A ii appear to oppose this suggestion. The AR text holds rigidly to a relevant answer to each of its forty-eight questions, unlike the text of ss which verbosely extends its answers by direct statements at numbers 5, 13, 17, as well as at number 59. There is also a blank space after the last answer of AR on fol 140, of approximately two lines of text, by which the copyist clearly intended to mark off the ending of AR. The notes on the following folio begin with a large capital for the first word. If Förster had considered A. Napier's[14] printing of such miscellaneous notes, he might have concluded that such unconnected additions are not unparalleled in Anglo-Saxon manuscripts. In our limitation of the AR text to the forty-eight questions we are fortunate to agree with Franciscus Junius, who marked off the notes as 'Appendix' in mss Junius 45 and 61, and with Humfrey Wanley and N.R. Ker, who itemized the AR text and the miscellaneous notes separately.

EDITIONS AND EDITORIAL COMMENTARY

All the editions recorded below contain errors of transcription and/or proof-reading errors. Some contain debatable editorial emendations, and also 'normalizations' which we have avoided. We do not, however, call particular attention to differences or errors in these earlier editions, since they presented these texts to students, and we all may err. But on occasions some earlier readings, especially of Thorpe 34 for ss, and Wright and

Kemble for AR, are noted, as these editors saw the respective mss at an earlier time.

Solomon and Saturn (SS)

1 *Analecta Anglo-Saxonica* 95–100, ed Benjamin Thorpe. London, John and Arthur Arch, Cornhill, 1834. (Mainly a diplomatic text, noted as Thorpe 34)

2 *Analecta Anglo-Saxonica* 110–15, ed Benjamin Thorpe. London, Smith, Elder and Co, Cornhill, 1846. (This includes editorial changes, noted, where appropriate, as Thorpe 46)

3 *Analecta Anglo-Saxonica* 110–15, ed Benjamin Thorpe. London, John Russell Smith, Soho Square, 1868. (This contains some proofreading errors in comparison with Thorpe 46)

4 *The Dialogue of Salomon and Saturnus, with an historical introduction*[15] 178–92, by John M. Kemble. London, printed for the Ælfric Society, 1848. (Kemble, 178 states that SS 'was printed by Thorpe ... and is only repeated here by me for the sake of rendering my work complete.' Evidence presented in the textual notes indicates that Kemble did not consult the manuscript.)

5 F.W. Ebeling *Angelsächsisches Lesebuch* 40–5; Leipzig, J.A. Romberg 1847. (Based on Thorpe 34.)

6 Louis F. Klipstein *Analecta Anglo-Saxonica* I 187–94; New York, George P. Putnam 1849. (Based directly or indirectly on a Thorpe edition.)

7 L. Ettmuller *Engla and Seaxna Scopas and Boceras* 42–3, *Bibliothek der Gesammten Deutschen National-Literatur* bd 28; Quedlinburgh et Lipsiae, Godofredus Bassius; London, Williams and Norgate 1850. (Contains SS 6, 7, 8, 9, 26, 27, 32, 41, 50, 55, 56; based on Thorpe 34. We note one shrewd reconstruction of the ms reading: 'sefa and' for Thorpe's nonsensical reading: 'se fat and'; see textual note to SS 9.)

Adrian and Ritheus (AR)

1 T. Wright 'Adrian and Ritheus' *Altdeutsche Blätter* von M. Haupt und H. Hoffmann II 189–93; Leipzig, F.A. Brockhaus 1840. (A diplomatic text.)

2 J.M. Kemble, 198–206.

3 L. Ettmuller, 39–42. (Based on Wright.)

Editorial commentary

M. Förster 'Zu Adrian und Ritheus' *Englische Studien* 23 (1897), 432–3. (Corrections to Kemble's edition.)

EDITORIAL PROCEDURE

We have attempted to produce a readable and accurate text, but one which is as nearly diplomatic as possible in view of the comparative lack of knowledge about permissible scribal variations in the eleventh/twelfth century. But emendations are made where an error is certain or very probable, or an omission obvious and reasonable speculation permissible. The punctuation takes note of ms pointing where it can coincide with a modern system, abbreviations are expanded and marked by italics, but capitalization is left as in the mss.

LANGUAGE

The language of the texts is the language of their respective scribes, possibly modified on occasions by the language of their respective exemplars. Detailed conclusions about the language would depend on a thorough study of all the pieces in each manuscript, considered against their exemplars and/or parallel texts where these are available. We have decided not to do this for the few folios of manuscript for each of our texts. But in order to present an edited text we have considered editions of other pieces in each manuscript (cited above under 'Manuscripts and Transcripts') and also general linguistic studies of manuscripts of the same period as ours, as well as editorial and linguistic comments on individual texts of the period. These latter are cited in the textual notes where necessary. The glossary, which is inclusive and contains cross-references to variant forms, is intended to aid any future study of the language of the manuscripts.

Notes

1 Individual questions connected with the genre are found elsewhere in OE texts. J.B. Trahern 'The *Ioca Monachorum* and the Old English *Pharaoh' English Language Notes* 7 (1970), 165–8, argues that the brief poem in the *Exeter Book* is based on such a question and answer. One of the scribal snippets printed by A. Napier 'Altenglische Kleinigkeiten' *Anglia* XI (1889), no 1, 1, from ms Cotton Tiberius A iii, is presented as a question on Adam, and other questions from Anglo-Latin writings are presented where relevant in our commentary to the OE SS and AR. Suchier's monographs (cited in notes 13 and 20 below) print many lists in Latin and the vernacular languages of Europe.

2 Elizabeth Merrill *The Dialogue in English Literature* Yale Studies in English XLII (New York, Henry Holt and Co 1911), 20–1, noted and briefly described the two OE lists.

3 In *Altercatio Hadriani Augusti et Epicteti Philosophi* by L.W. Daly and W. Suchier, Illinois Studies in Language and Literature XXIV, 1–2 (Urbana, University of Illinois Press 1939), chapters 2 and 3, 20–84, Daly discusses at length antecedents and variants of the 'question-and-answer dialogue,' and illustrates differences from the developed dialogue.

4 E.J. Montano *The Sin of Angels: Some aspects of the teaching of St Thomas* Catholic University of America Studies in Sacred Theology, second series 89 (Washington, Catholic University of America Press 1955), 40.

5 See eg P. Clemoes 'Ælfric' in *Continuations and Beginnings* ed E.G. Stanley (London, Thomas Nelson 1966), 184.

6 For fuller reference see below under 'Relationships and Genre.'

7 See, for example, the discussion by J.M. Evans 'Genesis B and its background' *Review of English Studies* ns 14 (1963), 1–16 and 113–23.

8 See, for example, J.E. Cross and S.I. Tucker 'Allegorical tradition and the Old English *Exodus*' *Neophilologus* 44 (1960), 122–7.

9 See especially the paper by F. Robinson 'The significance of names in Old English literature' *Anglia* 86 (1968), 14–58; and others by him in *Neuphilologische Mitteilungen* 69 (1968), 161–71; *Names* 21 (1973), 133–6.

10 In *The Old English Illustrated Hexateuch, British Museum Cotton Claudius B iv* ed C.R. Dodwell and P. Clemoes *Early English Manuscripts in Facsimile* 18 (Copenhagen, Rosenkilde and Bagger 1974), 19.

11 Barbara Raw 'The probable derivation of most of the illustrations in Junius 11 from an illustrated Old Saxon *Genesis*' *Anglo-Saxon England* 5 (Cambridge 1976), 143.

12 Daly-Suchier 25–44.

13 W. Suchier *Das Mittellateinische Gespräch Adrian und Epictitus, nebst verwandten Texten (Joca Monachorum)* (Tübingen, Max Niemeyer Verlag 1955).

14 Ms Schlettstadt Stadtbibliothek 1073 printed and discussed by E. Wölfflin-Troll in *Monatsberichte der Königlich preussischen Akademie der Wissenschaften zu Berlin* (1873), 106–15. Suchier 90 lists this text as JM E and notes that is now called ms no 2.

15 The full title of the text is *Excerptiones patrum, collectanea, flores ex diversis, quaestiones et parabolae*, printed in Migne PL 94 col 539 seq. Suchier 137–8 abstracts some questions and answers in this tract from the 1563 printing of Bede's works and calls the series JM R. No doubt confused by the printings of statements between series of questions, he omits to print some questions within Migne's text which correspond to extant JM questions. We therefore cite from Migne's text in the commentary. For the dating of the text see the comment and references in E. Dekkers and A. Gaar *Clavis patrum latinorum, sacris erudiri* III (editio altera 1961) no 1129, pp 250–1. B. Bischoff 'Wendepunkte in der Geschichte der Lateinischen Exegese im Frühmittelalter' *Sacris Erudiri* VI (1954), 222 regards the text as Hiberno-Latin, and so do other scholars.

16 Suchier 137–8.

17 Suchier 93.

18 Daly-Suchier 33–6.

19 Daly-Suchier 37.

20 W. Suchier *L'Enfant sage (Das Gespräch des Kaisers Hadrian mit dem Klagen Kinde Epitus)* Gesellschaft für romanische Literatur 24, (Dresden, Max Niemeyer Verlag 1910).

21 See the commentary on AR 9.

22 The text is edited in *Scriptores Hiberniae Minores, Pars I* by R.E. McNally, CCSL 108B (Turnhout, Brepols 1973), 161–71. The description is that of McNally 155, where the dating is given.

23 Questions 35 and 36, McNally 164.

24 See the commentary on AR 38, 44, and 12.

25 McNally 155.

26 See McNally passim and his references.

27 Daly-Suchier 31.

28 Now most recently edited by McNally in *Scriptores hiberniae minores, pars* I 197–205 and discussed 189–95.

29 A number of Hiberno-Latin texts noted by Bischoff in 1954 (see note 15) are still unpublished.

30 See note 15. The only dissentient suggests that it may be of Anglo-Saxon origin.

31 Some of these questions appear in the later ME *Questiones by-twene the Maister of Oxenford and his clerke* whose relationship to SS is considered below. The discussion there does not preclude some individuality in the SS exemplar or close predecessor.

32 Printed in *Alfræði Íslenzk: Islandsk Encyclopaedisk Litteratur* ed Kr. Kålund and N. Beckman, 3 vols *Samfund til Udgivelse af Gammel Nordisk Litteratur* (København: S.L. Møllers Bogtrykkeri 1908–18) III, 36–44.

33 SS 26, AR 7. This is the city of sunrise. One would assume that the questions in the ME which have a close relationship with SS, as discussed below, would have presented the pair as in SS and AR.

34 Two mss versions are extant, one from the Harley ms 1304 printed by C. Horstmann *Englische Studien* VIII (1885), 284–7, the other from the Lansdowne ms 762 printed by J.M. Kemble *The Dialogue of Salomon and Saturnus* (London, R. and J.E. Taylor 1848), 216–20.

35 'Two Notes on Old English Dialogue Literature' *An English Miscellany, presented to Dr Furnivall* (Oxford, The Clarendon Press 1901), 87, note 8. Förster's note appears to suggest that the two mss of the ME text derived independently from 'the original of SS,' but it is more likely that Lansdowne was copied from Harley or its predecessor, with omissions.

36 The case of SS 3, which is paralleled as a question in *Alfræði Íslenzk*, is a hint. The answer in SS 3 states that 'heaven' is called 'heaven' 'because it conceals everything that is *above* it,' but the ME varies in saying: 'all þat is vnder hym' and in this variation agrees with *Alfræði Íslenzk*, 'undir sig.' The agreement of the ME and the Icelandic suggests that both saw a different version of the answer than that in SS.

37 See notes 3 and 13 for the titles.

38 Kemble 206.

39 Suchier 75.

40 Printed by Kemble 134–76 and by R.J. Menner *The Poetical Dialogues of Solomon and Saturn* (New York, Modern Language Association; London, OUP 1941), 80–104.

41 Menner 31–5 discusses the relationship of Saturn with the other name for Solomon's opponent, Marcolf, in other examples of the disputation.

MANUSCRIPTS AND TRANSCRIPTS

1 N.R. Ker *Catalogue of Manuscripts containing Anglo-Saxon* (Oxford, The Clarendon Press 1957).

2 *König Alfreds des Grossen Bearbeitung der Soliloquien des Augustinus* hrsg W. Endter *Bibliothek der Angelsächsischen Prosa* XI (Hamburg, Henri Grand 1922).

3 *King Alfred's version of St Augustine's Soliloquies* ed Thomas A. Carnicelli (Cambridge, Mass, Harvard University Press; London, OUP 1969).

4 W.H. Hulme 'The Old English version of the Gospel of Nicodemus' *PMLA* 13, ns 6 (1898), 473–515.

5 M. Förster 'Zur altenglischen Quintinus-Legende' *Archiv für das studium der neueren sprachen und literaturen* bd 106 (1901), 258–9.

6 M. Förster *Die Beowulf-Handschrift* p 11, *Berichte über die Verhandlungen der Sächsischen Akademie der Wissenschaften zu Leipzig* Philol-Hist. Klasse, bd 71.4 (Leipzig, B.G. Teubner 1919).

7 *Beowulf and Judith* ed E.V.K. Dobbie *The Anglo-Saxon Poetic Records* (*ASPR*) IV (New York, Columbia University Press; London, Routledge and Kegan Paul 1953), ix.

8 *The Anglo-Saxon Minor Poems* ed E.V.K. Dobbie *ASPR* VI, (1942), 94–6.

9 R.S. Cox 'The Old English Dicts of Cato' *Anglia* 90 (1972), 1–29.

10 J.M. Kemble *The Dialogue of Salomon and Saturnus* (see Editions, p 17) 258–68 as 'Anglo-Saxon Apothegms.'

11 *A Summary Catalogue of Western Manuscripts in the Bodleian Library at Oxford* F. Madan, H.H.E. Craster, and N. Denholm-Young (Oxford, The Clarendon Press 1937) II, pt ii, 974 (no 5157).

12 Ibid, 977 (no 5172).

13 M. Förster 'Zu Adrian und Ritheus' *Englische Studien* 23 (1897), 433–4. Cited as Förster.

14 A. Napier 'Altenglischen Kleinigkeiten' *Anglia* XI (1889), 1–10. Förster thought (433) that the miscellaneous notes (item 3) had not been printed before.

15 Henning Larsen 'Kemble's Salomon and Saturn' *Modern Philology* 26
(1928–9), 445–50, considers the 'earlier' edition dated in the *Dictionary of
National Biography* xxx, 369 ff as '1845(?),' but demonstrates that 'it is rather a
bound page proof of a proposed edition' (445). He also notes that 'the Old
English text of Salomon and Saturn (both prose and poetry) ... appears only in
the edition of 1848' (446).

The *Prose Solomon and Saturn*

Cotton Vitellius A xv fols 86v–93v

Her kið hu saturnus *and* Saloman fettode ymbe heora wisdom.   86v
þa cwæt saturnus to salomane.

1 [S]age¹ me hwer god sete þa he geworhte heo|[fo]nas²   87r
   and eorðan.
   Ic þe secge, he sætt ofer [winda]³ feðerum.

2 Sage me hwilc word ærust forðeode of godes muðe.
   Ic þe secge: fiat lux *et* facta *est*⁴ lux.

3 Saga me for hwilcum ðingu*m* heofon sy gehaten heofon.
   Ic ðe secge, for þon he behelað eall *þæt* hym beufan byð.

4 Saga me hwæt ys god.
   Ic þe secge, *þæt* ys god þe ealle ðing on hys gewealdum
   hafað.

5 Saga me on hu fala dagum god geworhte ealle gesceafta.
   Ic þe secge, on vi dægum god gesceop ealle gesceafta.
   On þam ærosta*n* dæge he gesceop leoht. On þam æfteran dæge he
   gesceop þa gesceapu ðe þisne heofon healdað. On þam þriddan dæge he

---

1 The initial capital of '[S]age' is completely faded; Thorpe 34: Sage.
2 The top left-hand corner of fol 87r has crumbled. The first legible letters are 'nas';
   Wanley, Thorpe 34: heofonas.
3 The top right-hand corner of fol 87r is badly discoloured. 'Ofer' (Thorpe 34) is still just
   legible, but there is room for another word so 'winda' (Kemble), an obvious suggestion in
   view of the answer to the same question at AR 4: 'Ofer winda fiðerum,' and Latin
   parallels. Wanley apparently read 'winda.'
4 Thorpe, Kemble missed the abbreviation ∼ for 'est' at the end of fol 87r, l 3.

gesceop sæ *and* eorðan. On þam feorðan dæge he gesceop heofonæs tunglon, *and* on ðam v dæge he gesceop fixas *and* fugelas, *and* on ðam vi dæge he gesceop deor *and* nytenu, *and* Adam ðone ærostan man.

6 Saga me hwanon wæs adames nama gesceapen.
| Ic þe secge, [fr]am⁵ iiii steorrum.   87v

7 Saga me h[wæt]⁶ [h]atton⁷ þage.⁸
Ic þe secge, Arthox, Dux, Arotholem, Minsymbrie.

8 Saga me *þæt* andworc þe adam wæs of geworht, se ærustan man.
Ic ðe secge, of viii punda gewihte.

9 Saga me hwæt hatton þage.⁸
Ic ðe secge, *þæt* æroste wæs foldan pund of ðam him wæs flesc geworht. Oðer wæs fyres pund; þanon hym wæs *þæt* blod read *and* hat. Ðridde wæs windes pund; þanon hym wæs seo æðung geseald; feorðe wæs wolcnes pund; þanon hym wæs his modes unstaðelfæstnes geseald. Fifte wæs gyfe pund; þanon hym wæs geseald sefa *and*⁹ geðang. Syxste wæs blosmena pund; þanon hym wæs eagena myssenlicnys geseald. Seofoðo wæs deawes pund; ðanon him becom swat. Eahtoðe wæs sealtes pund; þanon hi*m* wæron þa tearas sealte.

10 Saga me on hwilce|re ylde wæs adam ða he geseapen¹⁰ wæs.   88r
Ic þe secge, he wæs on xxx wintra yldo.

5 The upper parts of 'f' and 'r' are excised by a cut at the top of fol 87v; Thorpe 34: fram.
6 The top right-hand corner of fol 87v is lost, excising a short word beginning with a legible 'h.' Thorpe 34 reads: hwæ, but 46 edits: hwæt.
7 A cut excises the ascender of 'h' in '[h]atton' at the beginning of fol 87v, l 2.
8 ms: þage. M. Förster, *Anglia Beiblatt* 53 (1942) 86–7, commented on this example as an alternative form of 'þæge,' plural demonstrative. On 'þæge' see A. Campbell *An Old English Grammar* (Oxford, The Clarendon Press 1959) §713.
9 ms: sefa 7; Thorpe 34: se fat; Kemble: se fæt; and so recorded as a unique noun, sv 'fætt,' in Bosworth-Toller Supplement. The error was first suspected and emended by Ettmuller 42 (see Editions), then noted independently by M. Förster *Archiv für Religionswissenschaft* xi (1907–8), 494, footnote 2, and considered again by A.J. Wyatt *Modern Language Review* xi (1916), 215. It was corrected by Toller in Supplement 'Additions and Corrections.'
10 ms: geseapen. This is an attested scribal variant for 'gesceapen' in 'transitional English' mss and in this ms. On 's' for 'sc' generally see W. Schlemilch *Beiträge zur Sprache und Orthographie spätaltengl. Sprachdenkmäler der Übergangzeit (1000–1150)* in *Studien zur Englischen Philologie* hrsg L. Morsbach (Halle, Max Niemeyer 1914), 52. On 's' for 'sc' in this ms see textual note 62 and W. Hulme's printing of the OE Gospel of Nicodemus in *PMLA* 13, ns 6 (1898), from this ms, eg p 473, l 26: seoldest; p 489, l 14: seolon; p 497, l 24: seoldon; p 515, ll 20 and 24: seoldon.

11 Saga me hu lang wæs adam on længe geseapen.[10]
Ic ðe secge, he wæs vi *and* cx ynca lang.

12 Saga me hu fela wintra leofode adam on þissere worulde.
Ic þe secge, he leofode ix hund wintra *and* xxx wintra on geswince *and*
on yrmðe, *and* syððan to helle ferde *and* þar grimme[11] witu ðolode v
þusend wintra *and* twa hund wintra *and* viii and xx wintra.

13 Saga me hu fela wintra hæfede adam ær he bearn strinde.
Ic þe secge, an hund wintra *and* xxx wintra ær he bearn strinde; *and* þa
gestrinde he bearn on hys cnihthade se hatte Seth; *and* he þa leofode[12]
ealles nygon hundred wintra *and* xxx wintra on þissere worulde. Ða
lyfde Seth hys sunu an hund wintra *and* v wintra ær he bearn gestrinde;
and þa gestrinde he | bæarn on hys cnihthade se hætte enos,   88v
and ða lyfde he hym sylf[13] ealles nygon hund wintra *and* xii wintra.
Ða[14] hæfede enos an hund wintra þa gestrinde he chanan *and* þa lyfde
he enos ealles nygon hund wintra *and* v wintra; *and* Ða hæfede chanan
lxx wintra þa gestrinde he malaleh, *and* canan lyfde þa ealles nygon
hund wintra *and* x wintra. Ða hæfede malaleh v *and* lx wintra ða
gestrinde he iared, *and* malaleh he lyfde ealles nygon hund wintra *and*
v wintra. Ða hæfede iared ii *and* lx wintra *and* an hund wintra þa
gestrinde he enoh, *and* Iared hys fæder lyfde ealles eahta hund wintra
and ii *and* lx wintra. Ða hæfede enoh v *and* lx wintra þa gestrinde he
matusalem, *and* enoh lyfde ealles ccc wintra *and* v *and* lx wintra. Ða
genam hine god myd sawle *and* myd lychaman up in þone heofon. Ða
| hæfede mathusalem vii *and* lxxx wintra *and* an hund   89r
wintra þa gestrinde he[15] lamec, *and* matusalem hys feder lyfde ealles
nygon hunð wintra *and* ix *and* lx wintra. Ða hæfede lamec an hund
wintra *and* lxxxii wintra þa gestrinde he Noe, *and* lamec lyfde ealles vii

11 ms: grīme. Thorpe 34, Kemble: grimme. Although the abbreviation mark is unusually
placed (but compare 'þrī' for þri*m*' in ss 41), the extension of the early editors is
acceptable in view of the same statement about Adam in the same words (except ss
'ferde' for 'for') in the unpublished Vercelli homily xix (and variants), fol 107r (cf ms
Hatton 115, fol 155, printed by N.R. Ker, *Catalogue*, 402). The edited Vercelli version
runs: 'Nigon hund wintra *ond* þritig wintra Adam lifde on þysse worulde on geswince *ond*
on yrmþe, *ond* syððan to helle for *ond* þær grimme witu þolode fifþusend wintra [*ond* twa
hund wintra – from variant mss] *ond* eahta *ond* xx wintra.' See also the commentary to ss
12.
12 The first 'e' is inserted above the 'o.'
13 ms: syltf; Thorpe 34: syl..; 46: sylf.
14 'wæs' after 'Ða' is partially erased but legible.
15 'malec' after 'he' is partially erased but legible.

hund wintra *and* lxxvii wintra. Da hæfede noe Ð wintra ða gestrinde he bearn Sem, cham, Iafet, *and* Noe lyfde ealles in ðissere worulde dcccc wintra *and* l wintra.

14 Saga me hu fæla þeoda awocon of hys iii bearnu*m*.
Ic þe secge, lxxii þeoda sindon; *and* of seme hys yldestan suna awocon xxx *and* of cham xxx *and* of Iafeðe xii.

15 Saga me hwæt wæs se ðe acenned[16] næs *and* æft bebyrged was on hys moder innoðe, *and* æfter þam deaðe gefullod wæs.
Ic þe secge, *þæt* was adam.

16 Saga me hu lange lyfde adam on neorxenawange.
Ic þe sæcge, ... *and* on þam ...[17] | [h]e abyrgd[e][18] þa   89v
farbodenan fictrewæs blæda, *and* þæt on frigdæg *and* þurh *þæt* he was on helle v ðusend wintra *and* iic wintra *and* viii *and* xx wintra.

17 Saga me of sa*nct*a maria ylde.
Ic þe secge, heo wæs iii *and* syxtig geara eald þa heo belyfon wæs, *and* heo wæs xiiii wintra þa heo crist cende *and* heo wæs myd him xxxiii geara on myddaneardde, *and* heo was xvi ger æft*er* hym on worulde; *and* fram adame *and* of fri[m]ðe[19] myddaneardes was on getal gerimes o[ð][20] ðone micclan Noes flod ii ðusend wintra *and* iic wintra *and* ii *and* lx wintra, *and* fra*m* ðam flode þa wæs o[ð][21] abrahames gebyrtide ixc wintra *and* ii *and* xl wintra, *and* fram abrahame was þa forð oð moises tid, *and* israela oferfar ut of egyptum vc wintra *and* viii wintra, *and* fram frimðe myddaneardes o[ð][22] cristes ðrowunge wæron vi ðusend wi[n] | tra[23] *and* c wintra *and* viii *and* l wintra.   90r

16 'wæs se ðe acenned' is written over erasure.
17 Neat erasures cause blank spaces after 'sæcge' and 'þam.' Thorpe 34 does not speculate, nor shall we, but Kemble suggests 'þrittine wintra' after 'sæcge' which is too large for the ms space, and 'feowerteoðan' after 'þam' which could just fit if the final nasal were omitted in abbreviation. Kemble's figures are based on the answer to AR I.
18 Cuts in the top of fol 89v excise the ascender of 'h' in '[h]e' and the top of the loop of 'e' in 'abyrgd[e].'
19 ms: friðe.
20 ms: of; probably by vertical slip from 'of' before 'fri[m]ðe' in the line above. Thorpe 34, Kemble: oð.
21 ms: of; Thorpe 34: of; Kemble: oð.
22 ms: on; Thorpe 34, Kemble: oð.
23 The last stroke of 'n' in 'wi[n]tra' is very faint at the end of the last line of the folio; Thorpe 34, Kemble: wintra.

18 Saga me hu lange worhte men Noes earce.
Ic þe secge, lxxx wintra, of ðam treowcinne þe ys genemned Sem.

19 Saga me hwæt hatte noes wyf.
Ic þe secge, heo hætte dalila.

20 *And* hwæt hatte chames wif.
Iaitarecta heo hatte.

21 *And* hwæt hatte Iafeðes wyf.
Ic þe secge, Catafluuia heo hatte; *and* oðrum naman hyg sindon genemnede, olla *and* ollina *and* ollibania,[24] swa hyg ðreo hatton.

22 Saga me hu lange was noes flod ofer eorðan.
Ic þe secge, xl daga *and* nihta.

23 Saga me hu lang was noes earc on lenge.
Ic þe secge, heo was ccc fæðema lang *and* l fæðema wid *and* xxx fæðema heah.

24 Saga me hwæt sunu hæfede adam.
Ic þe secge, xxx sunena *and* xxx dohtra.

25 Saga me hwilc man atimbrode ærust cæastræ.
Ic ðe secge, Enos[25] hatte | *and* was niniuem seo burh, *and*   90v
wæron þarin gemanna hundtwel[f]tig[26] ðusenda *and* ...[27] xx þusenda, *and* hierusalem seo burh heo wæs ærost ofer[28] þam noes flode getymbrod.

26 *And* hwæt hætte seo burh þær sunne up on morgen gæð.
Ic þe secge, Iaiaca hatte seo buruh.

27 Saga me hwar gæð seo sunne on æfen to sætle.
Ic þe secge, Garita hatte seo burh.

28 Saga me hwilc wyrt ys betst *and* selust.[29]
Ic þe secge, lilige hatte seo wyrt for þon þe heo getacnað crist.

24 Thorpe 34, Kemble: Ollibana, incorrectly.
25 Thorpe 34, Kemble: Knos, incorrectly.
26 ms: tweltig.
27 No gap in ms. See illustrative note to ss 25.
28 ms: ofer, written over erasure. Thorpe 34, Kemble: æfter, but see Bosworth-Toller Dictionary and Supplement sv 'ofer' I.8, prep. with dat., (after.)
29 ms: selust, with erasure of a single letter after 'l' in each of the five cases.

29 Saga me hwilc fugel ys selust.[29]
Ic ðe secge, Culfre ys selust;[29] heo getacnað þone halegan gast.

30 Saga me hwanon cymð[30] ligetu.
Ic secge, heo kimð fram winde *and* fram watere.

31 Saga me hwilc water ys selust.[29]
Ic þe secge, Iordanem seo ea ys selust[29] for þon ðe crist was on
hyre gefullod.

32 Saga me hwader gewiton þa engelas þe gode wyðsocon on heofona rice.
Ic þe secge, | [h]yg[31] todældon on þri dælas; anne dæl he asette   91r
on þæs lyftes gedrif; Oðerne dæl on þæs wateres gedryf; þriddan dæl on
helle neowelnysse.

33 Saga me hu fela ys woruld watra.
Ic þe secge, twa syndon sealte sæ *and* twa fersce.

34 Saga me hwilc man erost wære wyð hund sprecende.
Ic þe secge, s*anctu*s petrus.

35 Saga me hwilc man aðohte ærust myd sul[32] to æriende.[33]
Ic þe secge, þ*æt* wæs cham, noes sunu.

36 Saga me for hwam stanas ne synt berende.
Ic þe secge, for ðon þe abeles blod gefeoll ofer stan þa hyne cham hys
broðer ofsloh myd annes [esole]s[34] cyngbane.

37 Saga me hwæt ys betst[35] *and* wyrst betwinan mannon.
Ic þe secge, word ys betst *and* wyrst betwix mannon.

---

30 ms: cymð. The word is divided over two lines as 'cym' / 'mð,' with partial erasure of
the first 'm.'
31 The ascender of 'h' in '[h]yg' is excised with the loss of the top left-hand corner of fol 91r.
32 ms: sul, with erasure of a single letter after 'l.'
33 ms: æriende; Thorpe 34: æriende; Kemble: erianne. The inflected infinitive '-enne'
appears commonly as '-ende,' particularly in 'transitional English' manuscripts. For
comment and examples see *The Salisbury Psalter* ed C. and K. Sisam, *EETS* no 242
(1959), 34, §74.
34 Thorpe 34 reads: esoles, for an erased word after 'annes'. The visible top of a first 'e' and
of an 'l,' together with a clear 's' in appropriate positions support his suggestion, as does
an incomplete sense without the erased word. We accept the suggestion as an emenda-
tion not as a reading (as in Thorpe 34, Kemble).
35 ms: best, with an extra 't' above the 'e'.

38 Saga me hwæt ys cuðost mannon on eorðan to witanne.
Ic þe secge, þæt nys nænygum men nanwyht swa cuð swa he sceal deað
þrowian.

39 Saga me | hwæt syndon þa iii ðing þe nan man buton lufian[36] ne   91v
mæg.
Ic þe secge, on ys fyr, oðer ys wæter, ðridde ys ysen.

40 Saga me hwilc treow ys ealra treowa betst.
Ic þe secge, þæt ys wintreow.

41 Saga me hwar resteð þas mannes sawul þone se lychaman[37] slepð.
Ic þe secge, on þrim stowum heo byð; on þam bragene, oððe on þere
heortan, oððe on þam blode.

42 Saga me for hwan wæs seo sæ sealt geworden.
Ic þe secge, of ðam x wordon ðe moises gesomnode in þære ealdan æ,
godes bebode, *and* he awearp þa x word in ða sæ, *and* hys tearas aget in
ða sæ; for þon wearð seo sealt.

43 Saga me hwæt wæron þa word.
Ic þe secge, þæt forme word wæs, Non habeos deos alienos, þæt ys, Ne
lufa[38] þu oðerne god ofer me; þæt oðer word wæs, Non adsumes nomen
domini in uanum; Ne cig | [þ]u[39] godes naman on ydel; þæt   92r
ðridd[e word wæs],[40] healdað þone haligan restendæg; þæt [feorðe
word][40] wæs, Ara þinon fæder *and* þinre meder; [þæt fifte][40] word wæs,

---

36 ms: lufian; Thorpe 34: lufian; Kemble: lifian. OE 'lufian' in this ms is a spelling for 'lyfian'
(to live). On the spelling generally see Schlemilch 47, Sisam, 24, §49 and 24, footnote 2,
and for examples in our ms see Carnicelli, 22.

37 ms: lychaman; Thorpe 34: lychama; Kemble: lichama, for the nominative singular.
There is confusion about final 'n' in this ms so we read as manuscript, although this may
be a careless spelling. On such spellings see Sisam 21, §42.

38 ms: ne lufa is written over an erasure.

39 Damage at the top left-hand corner of fol 92r excises all but part of the forward loop of 'þ'
in '[þ]u.'

40 There is excision of words at the end of the first four lines of fol 92r caused by the loss of
the top right-hand corner of the folio. Thorpe 34 prints only what he reads, but Kemble
emends and we comment line by line.
Line 1, Thorpe: þrid ...; Kemble: þrid[de word wæs]; but ms: ðridd ...; and we suggest:
ðridd[e word wæs].
Line 2, Thorpe: þæt ...; Kemble: Ðæt [feorðe word]; but ms: þæt ...; and we suggest: þæt
[feorðe word].
Line 3, Thorpe: meder ...; Kemble: meder [Ðæt v]; and we suggest: meder [þæt fifte].

Non occides, Ne sleh þu man u[nscil]dine;[40] *þæt* vi word wæs, Non
mechaberis, on unriht ne hæm[41] þu; *þæt* vii word wæs, Ne stala þu; *þæt*
viii word wæs, Ne sæge lease gewitnysse; *þæt* ix word wæs, Non
concupiscens[42] rem *et* om*n*ia[43] proximi tui, Ne gewilna ðu oðres mannes æhta myd unrihte; *þæt* x word wæs, Non concupiscens uxorem
proximi tui, Ne gewilna ðu oðres mannes wyfes on unriht.

44 Saga me hwær ys moyses byrgen ðæs kininges.
    Ic þe secge, heo ys be þam huse þe fegor hatte *and* nan man nys þe hyg
    wite ær þa*m* miclan dome.

45 Saga me for hwilcum þingu*m* þeos eorðe awyrgeð wære, oððe æft
    gebletsod.
    Ic þe secge, þurh adam heo wæs awirgeð *and* þurh abeles blod *and* æft
    heo wæs gebletsod þurh noe *and* | [þurh abrah]am[44] *and* þur[h]   92v
    [fulluhte].[44]

'*þæt*' is normally abbreviated in this passage and the space remaining would allow the
ordinal to be written in full.
Line 4, Thorpe: Ne sleh þu man ...; Kemble: ne sleh ðu man ...; and we suggest: Ne sleh
þu man u[nscil]dine. A diagonal break and loss of the edge of the ms yet leaves a legible
'u' as the first letter of a new word (after 'man'), followed by the lower part of a minim on
the line which could be 'n,' followed by a little of a descender below the line which could
be 's.' There is room for three more letters to an imaginary line drawn up from 'unrihte,'
fol 92r, l 9, or from 'þeos,' fol 92r, l 15. 'dine' is clear at the beginning of line 5.
'Unscildine,' adj. accus. masc. sing., 'innocent,' is an addition to the scriptural commandment: 'Non occides,' but acceptable to such as Ælfric who explains the Biblical
text: '*þæt* is seo mæste sinn *þæt* man mann ofslea unscyldigne,' echoing the Latin of the
Boulogne-sur-Mer ms: 'Maximum peccatum est occidere innocentem' in B. Fehr *Die
Hirtenbriefe Ælfrics* (Hamburg 1914), 198.
41 ms: hæmð þu; so Thorpe 34; Kemble: hæm ðu.
42 Thorpe 34 omits 'rem ... concupiscens,' obviously having let his eye fall from 'concupis-
    cens' to its repetition in the tenth commandment. Kemble accepts this omission and thus
    indicates that he did not look at the manuscript.
43 *et* om*n*ia is inserted above the line.
44 The top of fol 92v is damaged horizontally, and also diagonally across the left-hand
    corner. Thorpe 34: '... and þurh fulluhte Saga me hw ...'; so Kemble with emendation
    'hw[a]'. We suggest: '[þurh abrah]am *and* þur[h] [fulluhte]. [S]aga me[hwa].' The ascen-
    der of 'h' in 'þurh' before 'fulluhte' and the upper part of 's' in 'Saga' are now lost; so too
    are all the upper parts of the letters of 'fulluhte,' but the remaining lower parts confirm
    Thorpe's reading or suggestion. The ascender of 'h' and forward loop of *wynn*, 'w,' in
    [*hwa*] are also lost through what appears to be a cut. Ms however clearly has 'am' before
    the abbreviation of 'and' preceding the visible 'þur[h].' In support of the emendation
    '[þurh abrah]am,' see parallels to this question and answer in the commentary to ss 45.

46 [S]aga me [hwa][44] [wi]ngeard[45] erost plantode.
Ic þe secge, þæt [wæs Noe se][46] heahfæder.

47 Saga me hwa nemde [ærost][47] godes naman.
Ic þe secge, se deoful nemde ærost godes naman.

48 Saga me hwæt ys hefogost to berende[48] on eorðan.
Ic þe secge, mannes synna *and* hys hlafordes yrre.

49 Saga me hwæt ys þæt oðrum licyge *and* oðrum myslycige.
Ic þe secge, þæt is dom.

50 Saga me hwæt syndon þa iiii ðing ðe næfre fulle næron, ne næfre ne
beoð.
Ic þe secge, an ys eorðe,[49] oðer ys fir, ðridde ys hell, feorðe ys se
gytsyenda man worulde welena.

51 Saga me hu fela ys fleogendra fugelcynn[a].[50]
Ic þe secge, iiii.l.

52 Saga me hu fela ys fisccynna on wætere.
Ic ðe secge, vi *and* [x]xx.[51]

53 Saga me hwilc man ærost mynster getimbrode.
Ic þe secge, Elias *and* Eliseus þa witega[52] and, æfter fulluhte, paulus
and antonius þa ærostan ancran.

54 Saga me hwæt syndon þa streamas *and* þa | [e]an[53] ðe [on][54]   93r
neorxenawange flowað.[55]

---

45 ms: ngeard; Thorpe 34: wingeard.
46 Thorpe 34: þæt ... se heahfæder; Kemble: ðæt [wæs Noe] se heahfæder. We suggest: þæt
[wæs Noe se] heahfæder, since 'se' is not now visible.
47 Thorpe 34; Kemble: ærost; but only the lower parts of 'st' are now visible.
48 ms: berende; Thorpe 34: berenne. Ms 'berende' is a permissible form of the inflected
infinitive. See note 33.
49 ms: eoðe, with 'r' inserted above 'o.'
50 ms: fugelcynn; Thorpe 34: fugelcynn; 46: fugelcynna; Kemble: fugelcynna. Syntax
demands the genitive plural case.
51 Thorpe 34, Kemble: xx. The sequence of letters is obscured by a smudge but 'xx' is
legible, together with the upper part of a preceding 'x.'
52 ms: witega; Thorpe 34, Kemble: witegan; as nominative plural. Read as ms. See note 37.
53 Thorpe 34: ...an, the first letters of fol 93r, l 1; Kemble: [burn]an; but there is room for
only one letter preceding the legible 'an.' Miss Valerie Hill suggested: '[e]an,' a recorded
form of the nom. plur. of 'ea' (river).
54 Thorpe, Kemble: on. The upper parts of 'on' are not now visible.
55 ms: flowað; Thorpe 34: flotað. Kemble's adaptation, 'fleotað' causes an incorrect entry
in Bosworth-Toller Supplement sv 'fleotan' II (to flow). This is now deleted, at our

Ic þe secge, heora syndon iiii. Seo æroste hatte fison, seo oðer hatte geon, *and* seo iii hatte Tygres, seo feorðe Eufraten, þæt ys meolc *and* hunig *and* æle *and* win.

55 Saga me for hwan byð seo sunne read on æfen.
Ic þe secge, for ðon heo locað on helle.

56 Saga me hwi scyneð heo swa reade on morgene.
Ic þe secge, for ðon [hy]re[56] t[wy]nað[57] hwæðer heo mæg þe ne mæg þisne myddaneard eondscynan swa hyre beboden ys.

57 Saga me þas iiii wætera þe þas eorðan fedað.
Ic þe secge, þæt ys snaw *and* wæter *and* hagol *and* deaw.

58 Saga me hwa ærost bocstafas sette.
Ic þe secge, Mercurius se gygand.

59 Saga me hwæt bockinna, *and* hu fela syndon.
Ic þe secge, kanones bec syndon ealra twa *and* hundseofontig; eall swa fela ðeo[da] [s]yndon[58] on gerime *and* eall swa fela leornyngcnihta buton þam xii ap*ostolu*m. Mannes bana syndon on gerime ealra cc *and* xviii. Mannes addre | [þ]a beo[ð][59] ealra ccc *and* v *and* lx. Mannes 93v to[ð]a[60] beoð on eallum hys lyfe ii *and* xxx. On xii mo[n]ðum[61] beoð ii *and* l wucena *and* ccc dagena *and* v *and* lx daga; on xii mo[n]ðum[61] beoð ehta þusend tyda *and* vii hund tyda. On xii mo[n]ðum[61] þu sealt[62] syllan þinon ðeowan men vii hund hlafa *and* xx hlafa buton morgeme[tt]en[63] *and* nonmettum.

suggestion, by A. Campbell, *Enlarged Addenda and Corrigenda* (to Bosworth-Toller Supplement) (Oxford, The Clarendon Press 1972) sv 'flēotan.'

56 Thorpe 34: hyre, but the ascender of 'h' and the letter 'y' are not visible now.

57 Thorpe 34: twynað; 'w' and 'y' are now very faint, but the syntax ('twynian,' impers. with dat.) and the meaning confirm the reading.

58 Thorpe 34: þeo ... syndon; Kemble: þeo[da] sindon; but to us 's' of 'syndon' is also completely illegible.

59 Thorpe 34: ... eallra; Kemble: [sindon] ealra. We read: [þ]a beo[ð] ealra. The top of fol 93v is badly discoloured and warped, with a small split through '[ð]' of 'beo[ð],' but the letters indicated above as visible were all legible against the morning sunlight of 13 November 1970. Kemble's 'sindon' is a guess.

60 Thorpe 34: toþa; Kemble: toða. The lower part of 'ð' in 'to[ð]a' is visible.

61 ms: moðum on the three occasions.

62 ms: sealt, see note 10.

63 ms: morgem...en; Wanley: morgemetten; Thorpe 34: morge-mettum; Kemble: morgemetum. The letters preceding the clear ending 'en' are now obscured by a smudge.

Adrian and Ritheus

Cotton Julius A ii fols 137v–140r

Adrianus cwæð to Ritheus; 137v

1 Saga me hu lange wæs Adam on neorxnawange.
Ic þe secge, he wæs þrittine gear.

2 Saga me on hwilcne dæig he gesingode.
Ic þe secge, on frydæig *and* on þone dæig he was ær gesceapen, *and* on
þam dæge he eft asweolt *and* for þam crist eft þrowede on þam dæge.

3 Saga me on hwæðere Adames sidan nam ure drihten þæt ribb þe he þæt
wif of geworhte.
Ic þe secge, on ðære winstran.

4 Saga me hwær sæt ure drihten þa he geworhte heofonan *and* eorðan
and ealle gesceafta.
Ic þe secge, ofer winda fiðerum.

5 Saga me hwær is seo eorðe þe næfre sunne on ne scean, ne mona, ne
næfre wind on ne bleow, nane tid dæges ne ær ne æfter.
Ic þe secge, seo eorðe is in þære readan sæ ofer þære eode israela folc of
egipta heaftnode.[1]

6 Saga me hwær scyne seo sunne on niht.
Ic þe secge, on þrim stowum; ærest on þæs hwales innoðe þe is cweden
leuiathan *and* on oðre tid heo scynð |on helle *and* þa ðridda tid 138r

---

1 ms: heafnode with insertion of 't' above the line.

heo scynð on þam ealond þæt is gl[i]ð² nemned, *and* þar restað
haligra manna sa[u]la³ oð domesdæig.

7 Saga me for hwam scyne seo sunne swa reade on ærnemorgien.
Ic þe secge, for þam ðe heo kymð up of þære sæ.

8 [S]aga⁴ me for hwam byð seo sunne swa read on æfen.
[I]c⁴ þe secge, for þan þe heo lokað ufan on helle.

9 [S]aga⁴ me hu mycel seo sunne sy.
Ic þe secge, heo ys mare þonne eorðe for þam heo byð on ælcum lande
hat.

10 Saga me hwilc sy seo sunne.
Ic þe secge, Astriges se dry sæde þæt hit wære byrnende stan.

11 Saga me hwæt þæs liuigendan mannes gleng sy.
Ic þe secge, þas deadan swat.

12 [S]aga⁵ me hwilc sunu wræce ærest hi[s]⁶ fæder on hys moder innoðe.
Ic þe secge, þære næddran sunu, for þam ðe seo moder ofsloh ær þane
fæder, *and* þonne ofsleað þa bearn eft þa moder.

13 Saga me hwilc bisceop wære ærest on þare ealdan æ ær cristes tokyme.
Ic þe secge, Melchisedech *and* Aaron.

14 Saga me hwilc bisceop wære on þære niwan æ.
Ic þe secge, petrus *and* iacobus.

15 [S]aga⁷ me hwilc man witegode ærest.
|Ic þe secge, Samuel.   138v

16 Saga me hwa wrat bocstafas ærest.
Ic þe secge, Mercurius se gigant.

---

2 ms Junius 45: gliðð; Junius 61: Gliðð; Wright, Kemble: Gliðð; uncorrected by Förster, but ms
   now discoloured, warped, and split, obscuring the third letter of 'gl[i]ð.'
3 Junius 45, 61: saula; Wright: saula; Kemble: sawla; uncorrected by Förster, but 'u' on a
   split is not clearly visible now in 'sa[u]la.'
4 ms crumbling at the inner margin excises the initial letters of the three words so
   numbered. Förster noted this in correcting Kemble.
5 ms hole excises the initial letter, as noted by Förster.
6 ms: hif.
7 ms hole excises the initial letter, as noted by Förster.

17 Saga me hwa sette ærest wineardas of þe hwa dranc ærest wi[n].[8]
Ic þe secge, Noe.

18 Sæga me hwa wære ærest læce.
Ic þe secge, Aslerius se wæs cwæden.

19 Sæga me hwæt sint þa twegen men on neorxnawang *and* þas gelomlice
wepað *and* beoð unrote.
Ic þe secge, enoc *and* helias; hi wepað for þam ðe hi sceole cuma on
ðisne middangeard *and* beon deade þeah hy ær þone[9] deað longe yldon.

20 Saga me hwær wuniað hy.
Ic þe secge, Malifica *and* Intimphonis; *þæt* is on simfelda[10] *and* on
sceanfelda.

21 Saga me for hwam si se hreuen swa sweart þe ær wæs hwit.
Ic þe secge, for þy þe he eft ne gehwirfde to noe in to þære arke þe he ær
of gesend was.

22 [S]aga[11] me for hwam se hrefen þurh gehyrsumnisse geþingode *þæt* he
ær þurh ofermodignisse agilte.
Ic þe secge, þa he fedde heliam þa he in eode[12] to þam westenne[13] *and*
him þenode.

---

8 Junius 45, 61, Wright, Kemble: win, (agreed by Förster); but 'n' of 'wi[n]' is now
illegible.

9 ms Junius 45: þoñ; Kemble, Junius 61: ðonne; Förster: þonne. We prefer to extend the
abbreviation to 'þone,' definite article, accus. masc. sing., qualifying 'deað.' The mas-
culine noun 'deað' is commonly preceded by the definite article, certainly in AR 28 ('æfter
þam deaðe'). On the two occasions when our scribe writes 'þone, þane' in full, AR 2 ('on
þone dæig'), AR 12 ('þane fæder'), it has a single 'n,' although n/nn variations are
common, particularly in 'transitional English' manuscripts. The abbreviation 'þoñ'
appears to be for 'þone' in the text printed by N.R. Ker in *English and Medieval Studies*
... *to J.R.R. Tolkien* ed N. Davis and C.L. Wrenn (London 1962), 82, l 37, and see
comment 79. Such an abbreviation 'þoñ' for 'þone' appears probable in AR 23, 'ut þurh
þone muð.'

10 Wright: scinfelda; Kemble (agreed by Förster); sunfelda; but the joining of the three
minims is at the top for 'm,' nor is there joining of the first two minims at the bottom for
'u.' Ms is clear at this place: simfelda. Junius 45, 61: simfelda. See the commentary to AR
20.

11 ms hole excises initial letter, as noted by Förster.

12 ms: þa// in eode// he, with transposition marks above the line after 'þa' and 'eode,' as
noted by Förster.

13 ms: westerne. Probably an error for 'westenne' in this ms. See Bosworth-Toller Dictionary sv 'westenn.'

23 Saga me hwær byð mannes mod.

| Ic þe secge, on þam heafde *and* gæð ut þurh þone[14] muð.   139r

24 Saga me hwilce wihta beoð oðre tid wifkinnes *and* oþre tid wæpnedkin-
nes.

Ic þe secge, Belda se fisc on sæ *and* Viperus seo næddre *and* Coruus se
fugel, þæt is se hrefen.

25 [S]aga[15] me for hwam seo sæ si sealt.

Ic þe secge, for þam þe moyses wearp on sæ þa tin word ðære æaldan æ,
þa ða he worhte þa breda for þam þe israela folc wurðedon deofolgild.

26 Saga me hwæt sindon þa twegen fet þa þeo sawul habban sceal.

Ic þe secge, godes lufu *and* manna *and* gif heo ðæra naðer nafað þanne
byð heo healt.

27 Saga me on hu manegum fiðerum sceal seo sawul fleogan gif heo sceal
to heofonum fleogan.

Ic þe secge, feower, Glæwnisse, geþwærnisse, strengþe, *and* rihwisnisse.[16]

28 Saga me hwilc man wære dead *and* nære acenned *and* æfter þam deaðe
wære eft bebyried in his moder innoðe.

Ic þe secge, þæt wæs Adam se æresta man, for þam eorðe wæs his
moder *and* he wæs bibiriged eft in þære eorðan.

29 Saga me þære burge naman þær sunne upgæð.

Ic þe secge, Iaiaca heo hatte.

30 Saga me hwæt hatte þæt þær heo on sætl gæð.

| Ic þe secge, Iainta[17] hit hatte.   139v

31 Saga me hwilc word wæs ærest.

Ic þe secge, drihten cwæð, gewurðe leoht.

---

14 ms: þoñ; Kemble: ðone; Wright: þonn; Förster: þon*n*e, but we read: þon*e*; see note 9.

15 ms crumbling excises initial letter, as noted by Förster.

16 ms: rih wisnisse, the word being divided as indicated here and the final syllables being
written on the line above 'rih.' Junius 45, 61, Wright, Kemble: rihtwisnisse; Förster
curiously: rih-þwisnisse. We read as ms (for 'rihtwisnisse') in view of the common loss of
't' as a middle consonant of a group of three in manuscripts of this period, eg Hulme
PMLA 13, ns 6 (1898) (Cotton Vitellius Axv, first part), 499, ll 9, 24, mildheornisse, 497, l
18, beorhnisse, 505, l 29, byornisse. See also examples in Sisam, 32, §70.iv.

17 Kemble: Janita, uncorrected by Förster; Junius 45: Iainta; 61: Jainta; Wright: Jainta.

32 Saga me hwæt is hefegost mannum on eorðan.
  Ic þe secge, hlafordes yrre.

33 [S]aga[18] me hu fela si fleogendra fugela kynna.
  Ic þe secge, twa *and* fiftig.

34 Saga me hwæt nædderkinna si on eorðan.
  Ic þe secge, feower *and* þrittig.

35 Saga me hwæt fisckinna si on wætere.
  Ic þe secge, six *and* þrittig.

36 [S]aga[19] me hwa gesceope ealra fisca nama.
  Ic þe secge, Adam se æresta mann.

37 Saga me hu fela wæs þære kempena þe cristes hregel dældon.
  Ic þe secge, seofon heora wæron.

38 Saga me feower stafas dumbe.
  Ic þe secge, an is mod, oðer geþanc, þridde is stef,[20] feorðe is ægesa.

39 Saga me hwæt sint þa þreo ðinc ðe nan mann butan ne mæig beon.
  Ic þe secge, þæt is wæter *and* fyr *and* isen.

40 Saga me hwa godes naman nemnede ærest.
  Ic þe secge, deofol.

41 |[Saga][21] me hu wæs[22] crist acenned of maria his meder.   140r
  [Ic þe][23] secge, ðurc[24] þæt swiðre breost.

42 [Sa]ga[25] me hwa dyde *þæt* sunne stod ane tid dæiges.
  Ic þe secge, Iosue hit gedyde in moyses gefeohte; þeo dun hatte gabaon
  þe heo onstod.

43 Saga me hwæt byð betst[26] *and* wyrst.
  Ic þe secge, mannes word.

18 ms hole excises initial letter, as noted by Förster.
19 ms hole excises initial letter, as noted by Förster.
20 Kemble: swefn, corrected by Förster.
21 ms has crumbled and is badly faded and patched in the top left-hand corner of f 140r.
   'Saga' is not visible, as noted by Förster.
22 Junius 45, 61, Wright, Kemble, Förster: wæs; it is difficult to be certain about 'æ' now.
23 Förster notes only that 'ic' is excised.
24 ms 'ðurc' is clear, as noted by Förster; Junius 45, 61; ðurh.
25 'Sa' of [Sa]ga lost, as noted by Förster.
26 ms 'best' struck out with horizontal line before 'betst.'

44 Saga me hwæt þam men si leofust on his life *and* laðest æfter his deaðe.
Ic þe secge, his willa.

45 [S]aga[27] me hwæt deð þæt swete wurd.
Ic þe secge, hit gemanifealdað mannes freondscype *and* stilleð mannes feond.

46 Saga me hwylc byð se leasa freond.
Ic þe secge, he byð mannes gefera to beode *and* nang to neodþærfe.

47 Saga me hwæt onscunað se seoca man þe ær him[28] gesund lufode.
Ic þe secge, þam seoca[29] men byð mete lað þe him ær was leof *and* his eagum byð leoht lað þe him æror wæs leof.

48 Saga me on hwam mæig man geseon mannes deað.
Ic þe secge, twege manlican beoð on mannes eagum; gif þu þa ne gesihst þonne swilt se man *and* bið gewiten ær þrim dagum.

27 ms hole excises initial letter, not noted by Förster.
28 ms: þe// him// ær, with transposition marks above the line after 'þe' and 'him,' as noted by Förster.
29 See textual note 37 to ss on final 'n.'

PART TWO

Commentary

Abbreviations

The list of abbreviations contains only the works which are cited in abbreviated form in the commentary, except of well-known classical and patristic authors such as Augustine, Pliny, etc, whose works are either in the Patrologia Latina or (and) in the Loeb series, but which readers may wish to consult in their own editions. Works of such authors are cited by title, book, chapter, and paragraph. Entries below are given in alphabetical order of the abbreviated references, but cross-references are listed where appropriate. Brief comments are provided on some entries and in citing the various versions of the Latin and other vernacular dialogues we have noted the provenance and date of relevant mss as given by previous editors. All quotations of OE poetry are from the ASPR by line numbers.

Ælfric *CH*
Ælfric *The Homilies of the Anglo-Saxon Church* (The Catholic Homilies). Ed Benjamin Thorpe. 2 vols. Printed for the Ælfric Society. London, Richard and John E. Taylor 1844–6

Ælfric *Heptateuch*
The Old English Version of the Heptateuch: Ælfric's Treatise on the Old and New Testament and His Preface to Genesis. Ed S.J. Crawford, with the text of two additional manuscripts transcribed by N.R. Ker. EETS OS 160, 1922; rpt London, New York, Toronto, Oxford University Press 1969

Ælfric *Hirtenbriefe* ed Fehr
Die Hirtenbriefe Ælfrics in altenglischer und Lateinischer Fassung. Hrsg von Bernhard Fehr. Bibliothek der Angelsächsischen Prosa. IX Band, 1914; rpt with a supplement to the Introduction by Peter Clemoes. Darmstadt, Wissenschaftliche Büchgesellschaft 1966

Ælfric *Lives of Saints*
Ælfric's Lives of Saints. Ed W.W. Skeat. 2 vols. EETS OS 76, 82, 94, 114, 1881, 1885, 1890, 1900; rpt London, New York, Toronto, Oxford University Press 1966

Alfrœ∂i Íslenzk
Alfrœ∂i Íslenzk: Islandsk Encyklopaedisk Litteratur. Ed Kr. Kålund and N. Beckman. 3 vols. Samfund til Udgivelse af Gammel Nordisk Litteratur. København, S.L. Møllers Bogtrykkeri 1908–18

Apostolic Fathers
The Apostolic Fathers. Ed and trans Kirsopp Lake. 2 vols. Loeb Classical Library. London, New York, William Heinemann, G.P. Putnam's Sons 1919–24

Baesecke *Vocabularius*
Baesecke, Georg *Der Vocabularius Sti. Galli in der Angelsächsischen Mission*. Halle, Max Niemeyer 1933

Bibliotheca Casinensis
Bibliotheca Casinensis seu Codicum manuscriptorum qui in tabulario casinensi asservantur. Cura et studio monachorum ordinis s. Benedicti abbatiae montis Casini. Ex typographia Casinensi 1873 seq

Binchy *Ériu* 19
Binchy, D.A. 'The Old-Irish Table of Penitential Commutations' *Ériu* 19 (1962) 47–72

Birch *Liber Vitae*. See Hyde Register

Blake, N.F. *The Phoenix*
Blake, N.F. ed *The Phoenix* Old and Middle English Texts. Manchester, Manchester University Press 1964

Boswell. See 'Fis Adamnáin'

Bosworth-Toller, Dict
An Anglo-Saxon Dictionary, based on the manuscript collections of ... Joseph Bosworth, edited and enlarged by T. Northcote Toller. Oxford, The Clarendon Press 1898

Budge *Cave*
Budge, E.A.W. *The Book of the Cave of Treasures*. London, The Religious Tract Society 1927

Budge *Coptic Apocrypha*
Budge, E.A.W. *Coptic Apocrypha in the dialect of Upper Egypt*. Oxford, Horace Hart 1913

Calder
Calder, George ed *Auraicept na n'Éces: The Scholar's Primer*. Edinburgh, John Grant 1917

Carney *The Poems of Blathmac*
Carney, James, ed *The Poems of Blathmac Son of Cú Brettan, together with the Irish Gospel of Thomas and A Poem on the Virgin Mary*. Irish Texts Society 47. Dublin, Educational Company of Ireland Ltd 1964

Charles II
Charles, R.H. ed *The Apocrypha and Pseudepigrapha of the Old Testament in English*. vol II, *Pseudepigrapha*. Oxford, The Clarendon Press 1913

Clubb *Christ and Satan*
Clubb, M.D. ed *Christ and Satan: An Old English Poem*. Yale Studies in English LXX. New Haven, London, Yale University Press: Humphrey Milford, Oxford University Press 1925

Colker 'Anecdota Dublinensia'
Colker, Marvin L. 'Anecdota Dublinensia' *Medievalia et Humanistica* 16 (1964) 39–55. [Section two, pp 41–3, contains a brief Latin dialogue edited from a thirteenth century English ms now in Dublin.]

Collectanea Bedae
Collectanea. (Excerptiones patrum, collectanea, flores ex diversis, quaestiones et parabolae.) PL 94, cols 539–60. [For discussion and bibliography on this early Anglo-Saxon or Irish Latin miscellany see the *CPL*, no 1129.]

Cook *Biblical Quotations (1898)*
Cook, Albert S. *Biblical Quotations in Old English Prose Writers*. London, New York, Macmillan 1898. [To be distinguished from the volume with the same title and author published by Scribners in 1903.]

CCSL
Corpus Christianorum. Series Latina. Turnhout, Brepols 1954 seq

CSEL
Corpus Scriptorum Ecclesiasticorum Latinorum. Vienna 1866 seq

CPL
Dekkers, E. and A. Gaar eds *Clavis patrum latinorum*. Editio altera. *Sacris Erudiri, Jaarboek voor Godsdienstwetenschappen* III (1961). Bruges, The Hague, C. Beyaert, M. Nijhoff 1961

Cross *Anglia* 90
Cross, J.E. '*De Ordine Creaturarum Liber* in Old English Prose' *Anglia* 90 (1972) 132–40.

Daly-Suchier
Daly, Lloyd William, and Walther Suchier, eds *Altercatio Hadriani Augusti et Epicteti Philosophi*. Illinois Studies in Language and Literature 24 nos 1–2 (1939). Urbana, University of Illinois Press 1939

Daly-Suchier AHE
Ibid pp 104–7 [fifteenth-century Oxford ms as base for the text; eleven other mss and editions; Daly (p 79) suggests second/third century (AD) archetype.]

Daly-Suchier DAE
Ibid 'Disputatio Adriani Augusti et Epicteti philosophi' pp112–13 [(see also Suchier *L'Enfant sage* II 277–8.) The text is based upon an eleventh/twelfth century ms Angers, Bibliothèque publique, ms 283.]

Daly-Suchier DPA
Ibid 'Disputatio Pippini cum Albino' pp 137–43. [The earliest ms is from the ninth/tenth century; Vienna Staatsbibliothek, nr 808.]

Daly-Suchier G
Ibid 'Text G' pp126–7. [Edited from St Gall Stiftsbibliothek ms 426, ninth century. Brief dialogue related most closely to Daly-Suchier K and DAE.]

Daly-Suchier K
Ibid 'Text K' pp118–21 [Edited from Cologne Dombibliothek ms 15, ninth century. Brief dialogue related most closely to Daly-Suchier G and DAE.]

Daly-Suchier M
Ibid pp130–2. [This is an abridged variant dialogue related most closely to AHE. The text is based on a single sixteenth century ms, Munich Staatsbibliothek ms Lat. 4424.]

Daly-Suchier, Sec
Ibid 'Gespräch des Kaisers Hadrian mit dem Philosophen Secundus' pp152–9. [The earliest ms (Latin) is the twelfth-century manuscript, Paris Bibliothèque de l'Arsenal 943.]

Dottin 'Dá brón flatha nime'
Dottin, G., ed and trans 'Les deux chagrins du royaume du ciel' *Revue celtique* 21 (1900) 349–87. [Edition and translation of the 'Dá brón flatha nime.']

Durham Ritual
Rituale ecclesiae Dunelmensis. The Durham Collector. Ed U. Lindelöf. Surtees Society vol 140. Durham and London, Andrews and Co, Bernard Quaritch 1927

EETS
The Early English Text Society

Eusebius *Chronicon* ed Schoene and Petermann
Schoene, A., H. Petermann eds *Eusebii Chronicorum libri duo.* Dublin, Zurich, Weidmann 1967

Eusebius *Chronicle* ed Fotheringham
Fotheringham, J.K. ed *Eusebii Pamphili chronici canones.* London, Humphrey Milford 1923

Eusebius *Eccles. Hist*
Lawlor, H.J., and J.L.L. Oulton trans *Eusebius … The Ecclesiastical History and the Martyrs of Palestine*, London, New York, Macmillan 1927, 1928 (2 vols), rpt 1954

FAB
The Four Ancient Books of Wales. Ed W.F. Skene. 2 vols. Edinburgh, Edmonston and Douglas 1868

Fehr *Hirtenbriefe*.
See Ælfric *Hirtenbriefe*

'Fis Adamnáin' ed Boswell
Boswell, C.S. ed and trans. 'Fis Adamnáin' in *An Irish Precursor of Dante.* London, D. Nutt 1908, pp 28–47

Fischer
Fischer, Bonifatius et alia edd *Vetus Latina.* Freiburg; Herder 1949 seq

Förster 'Adams Erschaffung und Namengebung'
Förster, M. 'Adams Erschaffung und Namengebung: Ein lateinisches Fragment des s.g. slawischen Henoch' *Archiv fur Religionswissenschaft* XI (1907–8) 477–529

Förster, 'Kleinere mittelenglische Texte'
Förster, M. 'Kleinere mittelenglische Texte' *Anglia* 42 (1918–19) 145–224

Förster 'Gesprächbüchlein'
Förster, Max 'Das älteste mittellateinische Gesprächbüchlein' *Romanische Forschungen* 27 (1910) 342–8. [Edited from Schlettstadt Stadtbibliothek ms 1093, about 700 AD, with variants from Cod.Vat. Lat.Reg. 846, ninth century.]

Förster 'Die Weltzeitalter'
Förster, Max 'Die Weltzeitalter bei den Angelsachsen' *Die Neueren Sprachen. Festgabe Karl Luick*. 6 Beihefte (1925) 183–203

Frank
Frank, Roberta. 'Some uses of Paronomasia in Old English Scriptural Verse' *Speculum* 47 (1972) 207–26

Ginzberg
Ginzberg, Louis *The Legends of the Jews*. Vols 1–7. Philadelphia, The Jewish Publication Society of America 1913–38

Hennecke
Hennecke, Edgar *New Testament Apocrypha*. Ed Wilhelm Schneemelcher, trans R. McL. Wilson. 2 vols. Philadelphia, The Westminster Press, London, Lutterworth Press 1963

Herzfeld *Old English Martyrology*
Herzfeld, George, ed *An Old English Martyrology*. EETS OS 116. London, Kegan Paul, Trench, Trübner and Co 1900

Hirn, *The Sacred Shrine*
Hirn, Yrjö *The Sacred Shrine: A Study of the Poetry and Art of the Catholic Church*. 2nd ed London, Faber and Faber 1958. [First published in Swedish in 1909.]

Horstmann 'Questiones'
Horstmann, Carl, ed 'Questiones by-twene the Maister of Oxenford and his clerke' *Englische Studien* VIII (1855) 284–7. [This text is a ME dialogue edited from ms Harley 1304. Another somewhat abbreviated version of the same dialogue was edited by Kemble (pp 216–20) from ms Lansdowne 762, under the title 'The Master of Oxford's Catechism'.]

Hull *Poem Book of the Gael*
Hull, Eleanor, trans *The Poem Book of the Gael: Translations from Irish Gaelic Poetry into English Prose and Verse*. London, Chatto and Windus 1913

Hyde Register, Liber Vitae
Liber Vitae: Register and Martyrology of New Minster and Hyde Abbey,
Winchester. Ed W. De Gray Birch. London, Winchester, Simkin and Co,
Warren and Son 1892

The Irish Liber Hymnorum
The Irish Liber Hymnorum. Ed and trans J.H. Bernard and R. Atkinson. 2
vols. Henry Bradshaw Society 13–14, London, Harrison and Sons 1898

Isidore *Etymologiae*
Isidori Hispalensis Episcopi Etymologiarum sive Originum libri XX. Ed
W.M. Lindsay. 2 vols. Oxford, The Clarendon Press 1911. Also in PL 82 (a
reprint of Arevalo's edition).

Isidore *De natura rerum*
Isidore *De natura rerum.* Ed Jacques Fontaine *Traité de la Nature.* Bibliothèque de l'école des hautes études hispaniques. Fascicle XXVIII. Bor-
deaux, Féret et Fils 1960. Also in PL 83

James
James, M.R. *The Apocryphal New Testament.* Oxford, The Clarendon
Press 1924

JEGP
Journal of English and Germanic Philology

JWCI
Journal of the Warburg and Courtauld Institutes

Kålund. See *Alfræði Íslenzk*

Kemble
Kemble, John M. ed *The Dialogue of Salomon and Saturnus: with an
Historical Introduction.* Printed for the Ælfric Society. London, Richard
and John E. Taylor 1848

Ker
Ker, N.R. *Catalogue of Manuscripts Containing Anglo-Saxon.* Oxford,
The Clarendon Press 1957

Klinck
Klinck, Roswitha *Die Lateinische Etymologie des Mittelalters.* Medium
Aevum. Philologische Studien. Band 17. München, Wilhelm Fink 1970

'Land of Cockaygne'
'The Land of Cokaygne' ed J.A.W. Bennett and G.V. Smithers in *Early*

Middle English Verse and Prose. Oxford, The Clarendon Press 1966, pp136–44. [The most convenient and thoroughly annotated edition.]

Lapide
Cornelius a Lapide *Commentaria in Scripturam Sacram.* Amsterdam 1681

Leabhar Breac. See *Passions and homilies from Leabhar Breac*

Lebor Gabála Érenn
Lebor Gabála Érenn. Ed and trans R.A. Stewart Macalister. Irish Texts Society, 34, 35. Dublin, Educational Company of Ireland Ltd 1938–9, parts I and II

Legenda aurea
Voragine, Jacobus a *Legenda aurea.* Ed Theodor Graesse. 1890; rpt Osnabruck, O. Zellner 1965

Liber de ordine creaturarum
Liber de ordine creaturarum: Un anónimo irlandés del siglo VII. Ed and trans Manuel C. Díaz y Díaz. Monografias de la Universidad de Santiago de Compostela no 10. Santiago de Compostela 1972. Also in PL 83

Lowe *Bobbio Missal*
Lowe, E.A. ed *The Bobbio Missal.* vol I, Text. Henry Bradshaw Society 58. London, Harrison and Sons 1920. [On pp 5–7 Lowe edits an eighth-century text of the *Joca Monachorum* listed as JM B by Suchier.]

Macrobius
Macrobius *Commentarium in somnium scipionis.* Ed Iacobus Willis. [Vol II of the Opera] Bibliotheca Teubneriana. Leipzig; Teubner 1970

MacCulloch *The Harrowing of Hell*
MacCulloch, John Arnott *The Harrowing of Hell, A Comparative Study of an Early Christian Doctrine.* Edinburgh, T. and T. Clark 1930

McNally *Liber de Numeris*
McNally, R.E. *Der irische Liber de Numeris; Eine Quellenanalyse des pseudo-isidorischen Liber de numeris.* Inaugural-Dissertation zur Erlangung des Doktorgrades der Philosophischen Fakultät der Ludwig-Maxmilians-Universität zu München. München 1957

Napier *Anglia* XI
Napier, A. 'Altenglische Kleinigkeiten' *Anglia* XI (1889) 1–10

Napier *Anglia* XI/I
Ibid no 1, pp 1–4. Text edited from ms Cotton Tiberius A iii, fols 43r–44r

Napier *Anglia* xi/3
Ibid no 3, pp 4–5. Text edited from ms Cotton Vespasian D vi, fol 69v

Napier *Anglia* xi/4
Ibid no 4, pp 5–6. Text edited from ms Cotton Julius A ii, fol 140v.

Napier *Anglia* xi/5
Ibid no 5, p 6. Text edited from ms Cotton Titus D xxvii, fol 55v

Napier *Anglia* xi/6
Ibid no 6, pp 6–7. Text edited from ms Cotton Caligula A xv, fol 139v

Napier *Anglia* xi/10
Ibid no 10, pp 9–10. Text edited from ms Harley 3271, fol 128v

NQ
Notes and Queries

Omont Interrogationes
Omont, H. 'Interrogationes de Fide Catholica (Joca monachorum)' *Bibliothèque de l'école des chartes: Revue d'érudition consacrée spécialement a l'étude du moyen âge* 44 (1883) 58–71

Omont *Interrogationes* I
Ibid pp 60–2. *Joca monachorum* dialogue listed by Suchier p 90 as JM H; Autun, Grand Séminaire, Nr G III, ninth century

Omont *Interrogationes* II
Ibid pp 62–70. *Joca monachorum* dialogue listed by Suchier p 90 as JM K$_1$; Paris Bibliothèque nationale, nouv. acq. lat. 2171, eleventh century

Omont *Interrogationes* III
Ibid pp 70–1. Dialogue listed by Suchier p 90 as JM K$_2$; Paris Bibliothèque nationale, nouv. acq. lat. 2171, eleventh century

Passions and Homilies from Leabhar Breac
The Passions and the Homilies from Leabhar Breac. Ed and trans Robert Atkinson. Royal Irish Academy. Todd Lecture Series II. Dublin, Published by the Academy 1887

Patch *The Other World*
Patch, H.R. *The Other World According to Descriptions in Medieval Literature*. Smith College Studies in Modern Languages ns I. Cambridge Mass 1950; rpt New York, Octagon Books 1970

PG
Patrologia Graeca ed J.P. Migne. 161 vols. Paris 1857–66

PL
Patrologia Latina, ed J.P. Migne. 221 vols. Paris 1844–64. [Individual volumes were sometimes reissued with different pagination so that any given reference may not be correct for a specific set of the PL in a given library. In the event of an apparently inaccurate reference check the entry in the CPL, which gives full publication data for the PL.]

PL *Supplementum*
A.O.F.M. Hamman ed *Patrologiae Latinae Supplementum*. 4 vols. Paris, Éditions Garnier Frères 1959–71

PMLA
Publications of the Modern Language Association

Piers Plowman
Langland, William *The Vision of William concerning Piers the Plowman*. Ed Walter W. Skeat. 2 vols. London, Oxford University Press 1886

PQ
Philological Quarterly

PRIA
Proceedings of the Royal Irish Academy

Purity
Purity: A Middle English Poem. Ed Robert J. Menner. Yale Studies in English LXI. New Haven, London, Yale University Press, Oxford University Press 1920

RC
Revue celtique

Sabatier
Sabatier, Pierre *Bibliorum sacrorum Latinae versiones antiquae*. 3 vols. Reims 1743–9. [Cornell University Library lists Sabatier as Sabbathier. The edition at Cornell was printed at Paris: Apud Franciscum Didot 1751. Our bibliographical information and spelling derives from the *Oxford Dictionary of the Christian Church*.]

Saltair na Rann
Saltair na Rann. Ed Whitley Stokes. Anecdota Oxoniensia, Mediaeval and Modern Series, vol I, part III. Oxford, The Clarendon Press 1883

Singer
Singer, Samuel *Sprichwörter des Mittelalters*. 3 vols. Bern, Verlag Herbert Lang 1944–7

Smith *Dict Bible*
Smith, William ed. *A Dictionary of the Bible comprising its Antiquities, Biography, Geography and Natural History.* 2 vols. Boston, Little, Brown and Co 1860

Spicilegium Solesmense
Pitra, Jean Baptiste, ed *Spicilegium Solesmense.* 4 vols. 1852–8; rpt Graz, Akademische Drück u. Verlagsanstalt 1962–3

Stokes 'Evernew Tongue'
Stokes, Whitley, ed and trans 'The Evernew Tongue' *Ériu* 2 (1905) 96–162

Stokes RC 12
Stokes, Whitley, ed and trans 'The Second Battle of Moytura' *Revue celtique* 12 (1891) 52–130

Suchier
Suchier, Walther, ed *Das mittellateinsche Gespräch Adrian und Epictitus: nebst verwandten Texten (Joca Monachorum).* Tübingen, Max Niemeyer 1955

Suchier AE_1a
Ibid pp 11–16. [*Adrian and Epictitus* and dialogue based on ms version A in Suchier's listing p 2, Arras bibliothèque du ville ms 636, tenth century.]

Suchier AE_1b
Ibid pp 16–19. [End of variant AE_1 based on ms version F in Suchier's listing p 2, ms 239 Balliol College, Oxford, fifteenth century.]

Suchier AE_2
Ibid pp 30–6. [A somewhat different version of the *Adrian and Epictitus* dialogue edited on the basis of ms version C in Suchier's listing p 2, ms 2245 in the Austrian Nationalbibliothek, twelfth century.]

Suchier JM_1
Ibid pp 114–19. [*Joca monachorum* dialogue on the basis of ms D in Suchier's listing p 90, Einsiedeln Stiftsbibliothek, nr 281, eighth/ninth century.]

Suchier JM_2
Ibid pp 123–7. [*Joca monachorum* dialogue on the basis of ms version L in Suchier's listing p 91, Munich Staatsbibliothek, lat 21576, thirteenth century.]

Suchier JM C
Ibid pp 108–11. [*Joca monachorum* dialogue on the basis of ms version C in Suchier's listing p 90, St Gall Stiftsbibliothek, nr 908, eighth century.]

Suchier, JM I
Ibid pp 119–21. [*Joca monachorum* dialogue from ms version I in Suchier's listing p 90, Florence, Laurenziana, Plut. XVIII dextr. 10, tenth century.]

Suchier JM J
Ibid pp 122–3. [A brief *Joca monachorum* dialogue edited from ms version J in Suchier's listing, p 90, St Gall Stiftsbibliothek, nr 196, tenth century.]

Suchier, JM P
Ibid pp 130–3. [A *Joca monachorum* dialogue from ms version P in Suchier's listing p 91, Stiftsbibliothek St Peter, nr a III 13, fifteenth century.]

Suchier *L'Enfant sage*
Suchier, Walther, ed *L'Enfant sage (Das Gespräch des Kaisers Hadrian mit dem klugen Kinde Epitus)*. Gesellschaft für romanische Literatur. Band 24. Dresden, Max Niemeyer 1910. [Collection of over twenty versions of the *L'Enfant Sage* dialogue, mostly in medieval Romance languages, but including some Latin, ME, and Welsh material. We cite by dialogue number (I–XXIV), but we list here only those dialogues which we have cited. We identify these dialogues by language and Suchier's suggested date, but we do not cite the mss from which these dialogues are edited since they are almost all much later than either AR or SS.]

Suchier *L'Enfant sage* I
Ibid 'Gespräch zwischen Adrian und Epictitus (AE)' pp 265–72. [Latin, fifteenth century]

Suchier *L'Enfant sage* II
Ibid 'Disputatio Adriani Augusti et Epicteti philosophi (DAE)' pp 277–8. [Latin, eleventh/twelfth century. Also ed in Daly-Suchier pp 111–13]

Suchier *L'Enfant sage* III
Ibid 'Erschaffung Adams aus acht Teilen' p 279. [Latin, ninth century]

Suchier *L'Enfant sage* IV
Ibid 'Urfassung ES auf Grund der katalanischen Hs. E' pp 286–301. [Catalan, fourteenth century]

Suchier *L'Enfant sage* V
Ibid 'Kritischer Text der provenzalischen Fassung ES_1' pp 311–31. [Provençal, late thirteenth century]

Suchier *L'Enfant sage* VI
Ibid 'Text des franzöischen Druckes F' pp 337–46. [French, about 1480]

Suchier *L'Enfant sage* VIII
Ibid 'Text des kastilianischen Druckes o' pp 365–91. [Castilian, 1540]

Suchier *L'Enfant sage* IX
Ibid 'Kritischer Text von *Titulo. vj. der Historia dela donzella Theodor* (DT)' pp 395–404. [Spanish, sixteenth century]

Suchier *L'Enfant sage* X
Ibid 'Text der provenzalischen Handschrift D' pp 407–17. [Provencal, 1373]

Suchier *L'Enfant sage* XI
Ibid 'Text der französischen Handschrift G' pp 422–44. [French, fifteenth century]

Suchier *L'Enfant sage* XII
Ibid 'Kritischer Text der französischen Fassung ES₂' pp 428–44. [French, first half of fifteenth century]

Suchier *L'Enfant sage* XIII
Ibid 'Kritischer Text der französischen Fassung ES₃' pp 449–61. [French, fifteenth century]

Suchier *L'Enfant sage* XIV
Ibid 'Hss. A₂ and C₁ des mittelenglischen *Ipotis* (Y)' pp 466–89, [ME, fifteenth century]

Suchier *L'Enfant sage* XV
Ibid 'Modern englische Übersetzung von Handschrift o der kymrischen Prosaauflösung des mittelenglischen *Ipotis* (Y)' pp 492–504. [Trans of a fifteenth-century Welsh dialogue]

Suchier *L'Enfant sage* XVIII
Ibid 'Text der englischen Übersetzung von Druck L der französischen Fassung ES₃' pp 525–35. [English, sixteenth century]

Suchier *L'Enfant sage* XIX
Ibid 'Kritischer Text der Version y der französischen Fassung ES₃' pp 539–49. [French, eighteenth century]

Sutphen
Sutphen, Morris C. 'A Further Collection of Latin Proverbs' *American Journal of Philology* 22 (1901) 240–60

Sydracke and Boccus
The History of Kyng Boccus and Sydracke. Translated by Hugo of

Caumpeden out of frenche into englysshe. London, Thomas Godfray [1532?]

Tertullian *De anima* ed Waszink
Tertullian *De anima*. Ed J.H. Waszink. Amsterdam, J.H. Meulenhoff 1947

Stith Thompson
Thompson, Stith *Motif-Index of Folk Literature*. 6 vols. revised and enlarged edition Copenhagen, Rosenkilde and Bagger 1955–8

TLL
Thesaurus Linguae Latinae, Leipzig, Teubner 1900 seq

Utley *Chy*
Utley, Francis Lee 'The Prose Salomon and Saturn and the Tree Called *Chy*' *Medieval Studies* 19 (1957) 55–78

Vercelli Homilies
Die Vercelli Homilien. Ed Max Förster. I. Halfte. Bibliothek der angelsächsischen Prosa. XII Band. Hamburg, Verlag von Henri Grand 1932. (Vercelli Homilies I–VIII). Repr 1964, Wissenschaftliche Buchgesellschaft, Darmstadt. The citations of Vercelli Homily XIX in the commentary can be read in M. Förster *Il Codice Vercellese* (facsimile) Roma 1913.

Visio Pauli
'Visio Pauli.' Ed M.R. James in *Apocrypha Anecdota: A Collection of Thirteen Apocryphal Books and Fragments*, pp 11–42. Texts and Studies II, no 3. Cambridge, Cambridge University Press 1893.

Walther
Walther, Hans, ed *Proverbia sententiaeque latinitatis medii aevi*. 6 vols. Göttingen, Vandenhoeck and Ruprecht 1963–9.

Warner *Early English Homilies*
Warner, Rubie D-N. *Early English Homilies from the Twelfth Century MS. Vesp. D. XIV*. EETS OS 152. London, Kegan Paul, Trench, Trübner and Co 1917

Whiting
Whiting, Bartlett Jere, and Helen Wescott Whiting. *Proverbs, Sentences and Proverbial Phrases from English Writings mainly before 1500*. Cambridge, Mass, The Belknap Press, Harvard University Press 1968

Wilmanns *Fragebüchlein*
Wilmanns, W., ed 'Ein Fragebüchlein aus dem neunten Jahrhundert'

Zeitschrift für deutsches altertum 15 (1872) 166–80. [Munich Staatsbibliothek, lat 19417, ninth century. Suchier p 90 lists as JM G.]

Wölfflin-Tröll
Wölfflin-Tröll, E. 'Joca monachorum, ein Beitrag zur mittelalterlichen Rathsellitteratur' *Monatsberichte der Preuss. Akademie der Wissenschaften, aus dem Jahre 1872* (Berlin 1873) 106–15. [Schlettstadt Stadtbibliothek, nr 2 (formerly 1073) ninth century. Suchier p 90 lists as JM E.]

Wright-Wülker *Vocabularies*
Wright, Thomas, and Richard Paul Wülker, eds *Anglo-Saxon and Old English Vocabularies*. 2 vols. London, Trübner and Co 1884

Wulfstan ed Bethurum
Wulfstan *The Homilies of Wulfstan*. Ed Dorothy Bethurum. Oxford, Oxford University Press 1957

Commentary

The commentary for each question is divided into three sections. In the first section the OE questions and answers are cited in modern English translation and are identified by dialogue (ss, AR) and by number of question. The second section normally contains parallels within the other extant dialogues, and/or other relevant illustration. Such parallels in Latin and in vernacular languages are cited in the forms given by the editors, even though there may appear to be scribal and/or grammatical error on occasions. In the third section we normally consider only the reason for, and explanation of, the OE question and answer, although on occasions parallels are discussed if relevant for the explanation of the OE, or if generally interesting and capable of brief discussion.

Here it makes known how Saturn and Solomon disputed about their wisdom. Then Saturn said to Solomon:

ss 1 Tell me where God sat when He made the heavens and the earth.
I tell you, he sat on the wings of the winds.
AR 4 Tell me where Our Lord sat when he made heaven and earth and all creations.
I tell you, on the wings of the winds.

I:i
Dic mihi ubi sedit Deus, quando creavit coelum et terram? Super pennas ventorum; *Collectanea Bedae* PL 94, col 543B. Cf also Suchier JM₂ 44, 126; Daly-Suchier DAE [variant text] 21, 113.

I:ii
Item dic mici quando fecit Deus celum et terram, ubi se continuit ipsa majestas? R /. Super pinnas ventorum, unde dicit in Psalmo xvii°: Et volabit super pinnas ventorum; Omont *Interrogationes* II 4, 63.

I:iii
A. Ubi fuit Deus quando scripte sunt [tabule Moysi]?
E. In loco *gethrom ems*, qui interpretatur penne ventorum; Suchier AE₁b 59, 17.

II
Utley (*Chy*, 57, and note 14) referred to Psalms 17:11 and 103:3 as the basis for this answer. Psalm 17:11 describes how God '*volavit* super pennas ventorum,' and Psalm 103:3 celebrates the Lord 'qui *ambulas* super pennas ventorum.' This suggestion would have satisfied the question-master (under I:ii above) who cited Psalm 17:11. But there must have been other influences also since both ss and Latin versions of this question, such as the one cited from the *Collectanea Bedae* (I:i above) agree that God *sat* on the wings of the winds in the act of creation. We suggest also a reminiscence of Proverbs 8:27–8 in which a personified wisdom speaks of its close association with God at creation: 'When he prepared the heaven, I was present with him; and when he prepared his throne upon the winds; and when he strengthened the clouds above; and when he secured the fountains of the earth.' This translation of the Septuagint is reflected in the Latin of Fulgen-

tius of Ruspe: '*cum pararet caelum* aderam illi, et cum segregabat *sedem suam super ventos*' (PL 65, col 248). He uses this text as testimony when identifying the 'sapientia' as the Son in a discussion of the consubstantiality of God the Father and God the Son at the creation of the universe. Although Sabatier's text of the Vetus Latina differs from that of Fulgentius and the Septuagint in separating 'sedem suam' and 'super ventos' into different clauses, it would appear that the formulation of this question is a conflation of ideas from this Septuagint/Old Latin text (for God's sitting) and from the citations from Psalms (for the phrase 'on the wings of the winds').

The frontispiece illustration to the Bodleian Library ms Junius 11 ('The Cædmon Manuscript') has exactly the details which we see in the statements of ss 1, AR 4. There God sits on a structure which appears to be a throne, placed on two winged but disembodied faces from whose mouths air is blown. It is obviously difficult to say which came first, the riddling presentation of question and answer in the Latin analogues (1:i) to ss and AR, or the pictorial predecessors to the illustration in the Cædmon manuscript, although the *Collectanea Bedae* text is, at present, the earliest record of the information. But both illustration and dialogue-questions are based ultimately on the conflation of ideas from the Old Latin Proverbs and the Psalms. It is interesting to see that Barbara Raw's recent discussion (*Anglo-Saxon England* 5, 1976) of the analogues to the illustration notes differences between the Junius illustration and its analogues which highlight the correspondence of detail between the Junius picture and the written dialogues. The illustration from the late tenth-century Boethius manuscript from Fleury (Raw, 138) apparently has no winged heads (Raw, 143), and in the illustration from the ninth-century Utrecht Psalter God is '*walking* above the winds' (Raw, 143).

SS 2 Tell me what command first proceeded from the mouth of God.
   I tell you: Fiat lux et facta est lux.
AR 31 Tell me what command was first.
   I tell you, the Lord said: Let there be light.

1:i
Quid primum a Deo processit? Verbum hoc, Fiat lux; *Collectanea Bedae* PL 94, col 539D. Cf also Suchier JM₁ I, 114, JM₂ I, 123; JM P I, 130.

ı:ii
Lærisvein spyr: Hvert ord mælti gud fyrst?
Meistari svarar: Verdi lios. [The pupil asks: What command did God speak
first? The master answers: Let there be light] *Alfræði Íslenzk* ııı 38.

ı:iii
Adrianus inquit: Quid primum processit de ore Dei?
Respondit: Verbum de principio.
Adrianus: Quid in secundo locutus fuit? Respondit: Fiat lux; Suchier AE₂ 9,
10, 31. Cf also Suchier JM I 2, 120; Suchier *L'Enfant sage* I 9, 10, 266 et
passim.

II
The source of the answer in ss 2 is Genesis 1:3: 'Dixitque Deus: Fiat lux. Et
facta est lux,' an extension on the actual first words of God in scripture,
'Fiat lux,' as translated in AR 31. The OE version seems to be a straightforward question on scripture unlike the Latin catch questions (ı:iii) which play
on the implications of the phrase 'verbum Dei' as a name for Christ in John
1:1: 'In principio erat verbum, et verbum erat apud Deum, et Deus erat
verbum.'

SS   3 Tell me for what reasons is Heaven called 'Heaven.'
      I tell you, because it conceals everything that is above it.

ı:i
H. Quid est celum? E. Culmen immensum; Daly-Suchier AHE 42, 106.

ı:ii
Quid est caelum? Epict. respondit: Sicut pellis extensa; Suchier AE₁a 8, 12.
See Psalm 103:2.

ı:iii
Dis l'emperador: Doncas, quina causa es lo cel? L' efant dis: Causa setjada
es de nostre senhor dieu [The emperor said: Then, what thing is the sky?
The child said: it is a secret (*or* hidden) thing of our Lord God's] Suchier
L'Enfant sage v 6, 313. Cf ibid ıv 6, 287; ibid x 4, 408.

I:iv

Lærisvein spyr: þvi er himen kalladur? Meistari svarar: þvi att hylr undir sig allt þad i veraulldinne er [The pupil asks: Why is heaven (so) called? The teacher answers: Because it hides under it everything that is in the world]; *Alfræði Íslenzk* III, 38.

II

Although we have not found a parallel in the Latin lists, it is clear that our answer is based on a medieval etymology, not of OE 'heofon,' as Utley (*Chy*, 58, and note 17) suggests, but of Latin 'caelum.' Kemble (193) speculates correctly on this: 'that is, *coelum* from *celare* (to conceal), an etymology worthy of Isidor or Hierome.' Isidore, however, preferred an alternative etymology, from 'caelatum' (stamped) in the *Etymologiae* III.xxxi.1 and XIII.iv.1 for which he quoted Ambrose as his authority when he used this etymology again in the *De natura rerum* XII.2. Ambrose, in the *Hexaemeron* II.iv.15, explains the etymology of 'caelum' as follows: 'nam caelum, quod graece συ ρανος dicitur, latine, quia inpressa stellarum lumina uelut signa habeat, tamquam caelatum appellatur, sicut argentum, quod signis eminentibus refulget, caelatum dicimus' (CSEL 32.1, 54; PL 14, cols 164–5). Yet Isidore records our alternative: 'alias autem a superiora *celando*' (*Etymologiae* XIII.iv.1). Roswitha Klinck (Klinck, 87) gives her view of this development as from Varro *De lingua latina* V.18: 'caelum ... contrario nomine celatum, quod apertum,' an etymology *per antiphrasin* (by opposite) which became in, for example, Cassiodorus on Psalm 113:24 (CCSL 98, 1035; PL 70, col 816D): 'caelum ... quod intra se celet universa,' an etymology *per efficientiam* (by function). It was widely attested as the examples in Klinck show. Roberta Frank (Frank, 207) comments on our question and remarks that the Anglo-Saxon question-master has 'managed to recapture the sounds of *heofon* in his etymological explanation (*he behelað ... ufan*)'. This is an interesting suggestion and yet, since this is apparently the only example of vernacular paronomasia in either SS or AR, it is difficult to tell whether we are dealing with deliberate word play or simple coincidence.

SS   4 Tell me what is God.
   I tell you he who has all things in his power is God.

I:i

In primis michi dicito quid est Deus. Qui omnia creavit, tenet, regit et gubernat; Daly-Suchier M3, 130.

I:ii

A. Quid est Deus? E. Qui omnia continet; Daly-Suchier DAE 21, 113.

I:iii

L'empereur dist: Que est dieu? L'enfant respont: Celluy est dieu qui tout le monde a fait donner et *qui tout tient en son pouoir* [The emperor says: What is God? The child replies: He is God who has created all the world and who holds everything in his power; our italics]; Suchier *L'Enfant sage* XI 5, 422, cf IV 8, 288, V 8, 313.

I:iv

Lors l'empereur demande: Quelle chose est dieu?. L'enfant dist: Cellui est dieu qui a creé toute chose de nyant, qui est seigneur tout puissant et sçait toutes choses qui furent jamais ne seront [Then the emperor asks: What thing is God? The child says: He is God who has created everything from nothing, who is omnipotent lord and knows all things that ever were or will be]; Suchier *L'Enfant sage* VI 7, 338.

II

The answer of ss 4 is the same as part of I:iii (italicized), but the references in I:iii are to *L'Enfant sage* versions in Catalan (IV 8, fourteenth century), Provençal (V 8, thirteenth century), and French (as cited I:iii, fifteenth century). Yet the general similarity of ss 4 with all the parallels cited under I, together, paradoxically, with differences of itemization in the answers, allows reasonable speculation on probable origins. The answers in their items are generally similar in stressing the omnipotence of God, one scriptural testimony for which was Hebrews 1:3: 'portansque omnia verbo virtutis suae.' A sequence of commentators, including Hrabanus Maurus (PL 112, col 713) and Haymo of Auxerre (PL 117, col 823), explained the text in similar manner and, on occasions, the same phrases. But we cite Luculentius, who is the most detailed, *In cap. I ad Hebraeos*: 'verbum et veritas Christus est ... portans, inquit, omnia, id est *gubernans. Continet* namque cadentia, et ad nihilum tendentia. Sicut enim absque ullo labore cuncta *creavit* ex nihilo ... sic omnia *regit* et *continet* et portat absque labore ... Neque enim aliquid subsistere poterat, nisi per se omnia contineret' (PL 72, col 856).

The italicized verbs in this passage are those of the Latin answers in 1:i, ii, and the OE answer appears to be based on Hebrews 1:3 modified by such a commentary as this. Ælfric speaks of God's omnipotence in a similar way on two occasions, both without known source at present:

i he hylt [cf *tenet*] mid his mihte heofonas and eorðan and ealle gesceafta butan geswince [cf *absque ullo labore*] [he holds with his power the heavens and the earth and all creations without toil]; CH I, 8.

ii He is butan hefe, forðon þe he hylt ealle gesceafta butan geswince [he is without burden because he holds all creations without toil]; CH I, 286.

SS 5 Tell me in how many days did God make all creations.

I tell you, God made all creations in six days. He created light on the first day. On the second day he created the creations that hold this Heaven. On the third day he created the sea and the earth. On the fourth day he created the lights of Heaven, and on the fifth day he created fish and birds, and on the sixth day he created wild animals and cattle, and Adam, the first man.

1:i

Sex diebus rerum creaturam formavit Deus. Prima die, condidit lucem; secunda, firmamentum coeli; tertia, speciem maris et terrae; quarta, sidera coeli; quinta, pisces et volucres; sexta, bestias ac jumenta; novissime, ad similitudinem suam, primum hominem Adam; *Collectanea Bedae* PL 94, col 545B.

1:ii

Dic mihi de vii diebus quod operatus est Salvator. Primo die facti sunt angeli, unde propheta dicit: Cum fecisset celum et terram, laudaverunt me angeli mei. Secunda die factus est celum et terra. Tercia die segregata est aqua ab arida. Quarta die facte sunt luminaria in celo, id est sol et luna et stellas. Quinta die facte sunt omnia quadrupedia de terra et consilium trinitatis et volatibilibus celi et pisces maris. Sexta die factus est Adam homo de limo terre. Septima die requievit; Suchier JM I 3, 120; cf Suchier *L'Enfant sage* V 13, 314 and other examples passim.

II

This answer is in effect a synopsis of the story of creation, Genesis 1:1–27. The phrase 'þa gesceapu ðe þisne heofon healdað,' describing the work of the second day, presumably is an attempt to render the phrase 'firmamentum coeli' into meaningful OE. As Ambrose remarks 'a firmitate ergo firmamentum est nuncupatum' (*Hexaemeron* II.iv.16; CSEL 32.1, 56, PL 14, col 165) and hence the assumption that the 'firmamentum' serves to support or hold 'heofon' is not unreasonable, particularly so in the light of the belief attested in Genesis 1:7 and elsewhere that there are waters above the visible sky, as well as below the earth (Psalm 135:6). In the OE poem, *The Order of the World*, creation is described as being supported by 'great powerful locks':

Ne waciað þas geweorc,   ac he hi wel healdeð;
stondað stiðlice   bestryþed fæste
miclum meahtlocum   in þam mægenþrymme
mid þam sy ahefed   heofon ond eorþe (86–9)

[These works do not weaken but He holds them well; they stand strongly, firmly fixed with great powerful locks, in that power by which heaven and earth are lifted up].

---

ss   6 Tell me from where was Adam's name created.
         I tell you, from four stars.
ss   7 Tell me what they are called.
         I tell you, Arthox, Dux, Arotholem, Minsymbrie.

I:i
Unde Adam nomen accepit? De quattuor stellas, id est: de stella Anotilis tulit A, de stella Doxis tulit D, de stella Arthus tulit A, de stella Mansimbrion tulit M, et habet nomen Adam; Suchier JM I 5, 120. Cf Suchier JM₁ F 28, 117, JM₂ 8–9, 124.

I:ii
Quomodo constructum est nomen Adam? De quattuor stillis. Ubi sunt stillę? In quattuor angulis celi vel ordine; Suchier JM C 56–7, 111.

II

This is a widely attested motif, particularly so in Hiberno-Latin texts. The names of the stars are the four points of the compass in Greek: 'anatole' (east), 'dusis' (west), 'arktos' (north), 'mesembria' (south), which, in order of their initial letters, spell the name 'Adam.' The motif has been discussed, notably for OE instances, in Förster 'Adams Erschaffung und Namengebung' (see ss 8 and 9), and R.E. McNally provides a long list of Latin examples in his commentary on the Hiberno-Latin *Liber de Numeris* (72). The earliest instance appears to be in *The Book of the Secrets of Enoch* 30:13–14 (Charles II, 449), where all the information in the OE question is present: 'I [God] appointed him a name, from the four component parts, from east, from west, from south, from north, and I appointed for him four special stars, and I called his name Adam.' As Charles notes (II, 426), this passage is strong evidence that the work was originally composed in Greek, since this anagram is impossible in Hebrew or Aramaic. The motif is mentioned also in *The Sibylline Books* III.24–6 (Charles II, 379) but its currency in the west was assured by its acceptance in Augustine's *Tractatus in Iohannis Evangelium* IX.14; X.12 (CCSL 36, 98, 108; PL 35, cols 1465, 1473).

Utley (*Chy*, 58) comments on the 'garbled spelling' of the OE text, but we suspect also a transfer of cardinal points to produce a curious order, against the normal order in the Latin texts. OE Arthox (cf Arthus, 1:i; Arthos, Förster 523) is nearer 'arktos,' 'arctos' (north), and OE Arotholem (cf Anatolem, JM₁ F 28, Suchier 117; Anatholim, Förster 481) is nearer 'anatole' (east), to produce an order: north, west, east, south. We should also note that the Slavic recension of *The Book of the Secrets of Enoch* (which Charles translates and is cited above) also has an abnormal order. Augustine has it right, of course.

---

ss 8 Tell me the substance from which Adam, the first man, was made.
   I tell you, from eight pounds' weight.
ss 9 Tell me what they are called.
   I tell you, the first was a pound of earth from which his flesh was made. The second was a pound of fire; from this his blood was red and hot. The third was a pound of wind; from this his breath was given; the fourth was a pound of cloud; from this his instability of mind was given. The fifth was a pound of grace; from this was given

his understanding and thought. The sixth was a pound of blossoms; from this was given the variety of his eyes. The seventh was a pound of dew; from this he got sweat. The eighth was a pound of salt; from this his tears were salt.

---

i:i

Octo pondera de quibus factus est Adam. pondus limi inde factus est caro. pondus ignis. inde rubeus est sanguis et calidus. pondus salis inde sunt salsae lacrimae. pondus roris, unde factus est sudor. pondus floris inde est varietas oculorum. pondus nubis inde est instabilitas mentium. pondus venti inde est anhela frigida. pondus gratiae inde est sensus hominis; *Durham Ritual*, 192. There is an OE superlinear gloss of this text.

i:ii

Incipit de septem ponderibus, unde factus es Adam, fides: Pondus limis: quia de limo factus est. Pondus maris: inde sunt lacrimȩ salsȩ. Pondus ignis: inde sunt alita caldas. Pondus uenti: inde est flatus frigitus. Pondus rux: inde sudor humano corpore. Pondus floris: inde est uarietas oculorum. Pondus feni: inde est diuersitas capillorum. Pondus nuuium: inde est stauilitas in mente.

Mulier autem ex noue pundura facta est ...; Förster *Gesprächbüchlein* 7, 8, 345 (earliest ms about 700 AD).

i:iii

In corpore etenim humano novem sunt mensurae sine dubio compositae: id est quatuor principales, quae sunt terra, aqua, aer, ignis, et aliae quinque subsequenter species, id est, sal, fenum, flores, lapides, nubes et ut in melius de his omnibus intelligas, lege sic: terra in homine est crassitudo, et gravitas carnis, aqua autem sudor, et salivae. Aer vero ipsa anhelatio humida, frigida, atque calida, spirans per os et nares. Ignis in homine, qui in stomacho coquit cibos, et in calore sanguinis, sal in salsitate sanguinis, et sudoris, et lacrymarum, et urinae, quia haec omnia in homine salsa sunt. Fenum autem in capillis et pilis, flores in varietate oculorum, lapides in gravitate et duritia, quia lapides ossa terrae dicuntur. Nubes instabilitas mentis et cogitationum. Et de his novem mensuris compositum corpus; *Liber de Numeris* PL 83, col 1295 B-C; see also McNally *Liber de Numeris*, 30–2.

II

There are many published instances of this theme from which we present
the two closest to the OE list (I:i–ii) and another early Latin example (I:iii).
The closest examples (I:i–ii) differ in order of item and on occasion in detail
of item, but all the OE statements except one are exactly paralleled in at
least one of the other three lists. This exceptional item: 'a pound of grace,
from this he was given understanding and thought' appears to be an extension on the Latin phrase 'pondus gratiae inde sensus hominis' as represented
in the *Durham Ritual*.

The earliest known example of the theme occurs in *The Book of the
Secrets of Enoch* in which the creation of Adam is described as follows:

> On the sixth day I commanded my wisdom to create man from seven
> consistencies: one, his flesh from the earth; two, his blood from the dew;
> three, his eyes from the sun; four, his bones from stone; five, his
> intelligence from the swiftness of the angels and from cloud; six, his
> veins and his hair from the grass of the earth; seven, his soul from my
> breath and from the wind' (2 Enoch 30:8 A, Charles II, 448–9).

But all these quoted examples illustrate a connection between the con-
stituents of the microcosm (man) and of the macrocosm (universe) which,
in different form, is emphasized in the conception that man was com-
pounded of the four elements, earth, air, water, and fire (eg in Isidore
Etymologiae XI.i.16). Note however that the first four in the *Liber de
numeris* list (I:iii) are exactly these elements.

The extent of our theme is illustrated by the following annotated bibliography of discussion or citation of instances, although some entries dupli-
cate material.

1 Suchier JM P, 46, 131–2; Suchier *L'Enfant sage* III, 279; IV 19, 289; V 21,
316; VI 20, 340; X 16, 409; XII 16, 430; XIV (Ipotis), A_2 9; C_1 15, 473–4; XV
11, 495–6; XVIII 70, 534, XIX 64, 548. Examples in dialogues. See also
Suchier *L'Enfant sage* 79–83 for discussion.
2 T.P. Cross *Motif Index of Early Irish Literature* Indiana University
Publications, Folklore Series no 7, Indiana University, Bloomington,
Indiana, 1952, A1260.0.2. Cross has collected references to examples
both in Irish and Irish-Latin literature.
3 'Catécheses celtiques,' ed A. Wilmart in *Analecta Reginensia, Studi e
Testi* 59, Città del Vaticano, Biblioteca Apostolica Vaticana 1933, 111;
now reprinted in McNally CCSL 108B, 185. This example is close to I:iii.
4 Ginzberg V 72–3. Discussion and citation of instances in the context of
Jewish learning.
5 Jacob Grimm *Teutonic Mythology* trans J.S. Stallybrass, London,

Geogre Bell and Sons 1882–8, II 564–71; IV 1449–50. Grimm gathers many examples, but his assumption that this motif derives from Germanic pagan myth is clearly untenable.

6 Kålund *Alfræði Íslenzk* III, 40; cf also ibid I, 57 for a Latin example in a fourteenth-century Icelandic manuscript.

7 For instances of this theme in early medieval Welsh see the poem 'Eneit kid im guneit' in *The Black Book of Carmarthen*, no VI (fol 12r), ed J. Gwenogvryn Evans, Old Welsh Texts V, Pwllheli, Evans 1906, 23, trans in FAB I, 506, and the poem 'Kanu y byt mawr,' *The Book of Taliesin* no LV (fol 38a), text in FAB II, 214 ff, trans in FAB I, 539–40.

8 Förster 'Adams Erschaffung und Namengebung.' This article is the fullest discussion of the theme, but it is marred by an attempt to demonstrate immediate connections between certain of the cited texts.

9 J.M. Evans 'Microcosmic Adam' *Medium Ævum* 35 (1966) 38–42. On this article see the discussion of ss 7–8 in J.E. Cross 'The Literate Anglo-Saxon – on Sources and Disseminations' *Proceedings of the British Academy* 58 (1972) 8–9.

10 Yvan G. Lapage 'Les versions françaises médiévales du récit apocryphe de la formation d'Adam' *Romania* 100 (1979) 155–64. This article includes references to some recent French discussions of this theme.

SS 10 Tell me at what age was Adam when he was created.

I tell you, he was thirty years of age.

I:i

Adam wæs eac swiðe weorðlic hise rinc þa hine god ærest gehiwad hæfde to mænniscum gesceape on þrytiges wintres ylde [Adam was also a very splendid man when God first had formed him as a human being of thirty years of age]; Napier *Anglia* XI/I, 2. For the assertion that Eve was thirty when she was created, see the *Durham Ritual*, 197.

I:ii

Of what age made God Adam
whan he into this world came?
Adam God made and his fere
at his licknes, for they are to him dere,

and yong, ryght as aungels wyse,
... But whan they mysded at the last,
and of paradyse ware out cast,
theyr here began to wax and sprede,
and to theyr heles doune it yede,
and after, theyr here on to se,
them semed of thyrty yeeres to be
Sydracke and Boccus, Question 241, cited from Kemble, 194.

I:iii
Methodius cwað. adam wæs gesceopa man on wlite of ðritig wintra
[Methodius said. Adam was created man in the form of thirty years (old)];
twelfth-century notes in BL Cotton Claudius B iv, printed in Ælfric *Hep-tateuch*, 419.

I:iv
Ni ba sou ocus ni ba sine nech inas a cheile isin ló sin, uair is a n-áis trichat
blíadan adresit an cinedh dáenna uili .I. i n-áis ina ndernad Adam ocus i
n-áis ina roibhi Ísu intan ro baistedh é [No one on that day will be younger
or older than another, for the whole human race will arise at the age of thirty
years, that is, the age at which Adam was created, and the age which Jesus
had attained when He was baptized]. Whitley Stokes, ed and trans 'The
Fifteen Tokens of Doomsday' *RC* 28 (1907) 316–17. For another instance of
the motif that the human race will be resurrected at the age of thirty years,
see Suchier *L'Enfant sage* I 88, 270.

II
Although this question is not paralleled in the other Latin and vernacular
dialogues, interest in Adam's age at creation is attested in 'insular' vernacular literature (I:i, iii, iv), and is based on Scriptural statement. Adam
was created by God 'ad imaginem suam' (Genesis 1:27) and was clearly
fully formed as man at creation. A variety of scriptural texts attest to the
assumption that a man should be the age of thirty before he should exercise
responsible authority. Joseph was thirty when he received authority from
Pharaoh (Genesis 41:46), David was thirty when he began to rule over all
Israel (2 Samuel, 2 Kings 5:4). Christ was about thirty when he began to
preach (Luke 3:23), and, in the Old Testament, it is repeatedly stipulated
that the Levites who were to serve in the presence of the Lord were to be

'from thirty years old and upward' (Numbers 4:3, 23, 30, 35 etc). It would seem that 'thirty' as an age of responsibility for man was a good figure to choose for the Adam who was created as a full-grown man.

SS 11 Tell me how tall Adam was created in height.
  I tell you, he was one hundred and sixteen inches tall.

I:i
he (Adam) wæs on længe on fif and hund nigontiges fingra lenge ofer þweoras þa fingras on medemre wæstme [he was ninety-five fingers in length across fingers of average size (?), cf Bosworth-Toller, Dict, sv 'þweores' I]; Napier *Anglia* XI/1, 2.

I:ii
Longitudo Adae fuit XCIII digitorum, hoc est VII cubitorum; cubitus XX[I]IIII digitos habet; Baesecke *Vocabularius*, 6.

II
Although no question about Adam's size appears in the other extant dialogues, the idea that Adam was of more than normal human size was attested in the literature discussed by Ginzberg *Legends of the Jews* (see I 59, 76, 86; V 79, 99). He notes that Adam's extraordinary size was reduced or lost at the Fall according to some traditions. But that Adam was above normal stature could be accepted within the Christian belief of the declining world in the last age. Augustine, for example, could speak of the bodies of our ancestors exceeding ours (in *De civitate dei* XV.ix) as did their power and length of life.

SS 12 Tell me how many years Adam lived in this world.
  I tell you, he lived nine hundred and thirty years in toil and in misery, and then he went to hell and there he suffered grim torments for five thousand two hundred and twenty-eight years.

1:i

Quantus annus vixit Adam? Nonugenti xxx; Suchier JM C 5, 108. Cf Suchier JM₁ 4, 114; Suchier JM I 7, 120; Suchier JM₂ 6, 124; Suchier JM P 38, 131.

1:ii

Nigon hund wintra *ond* þritig wintra Adam lifde on þysse worulde on geswince *ond* on yrmþe, *ond* syððan to helle for *ond* þær grimme witu þolode fif þusend wintra [*ond* twa hund wintra] *ond* eahta and xx wintra; Vercelli Homily xix, fol 107r, with the inserted phrase from variant versions of the Vercelli homily in CCCC 303, art 43, 162, art 35, and BL Cotton Cleopatra B.xiii, art 6. The statement above exists independently as a jotting in ms Hatton 115, fol 155, printed by Ker no 332, art 37.

II

Adam's age, 930 years, is scriptural (Genesis 5:5). For the duration of his stay in hell see our commentary on ss 17. After Christ was crucified he harrowed hell and released Adam.

But perhaps equally important here for those who wish to trace manuscript relationships is the fact that the ss text extends the sufficient answer of the Latin parallels in words which echo the statements of the Vercelli homily variants and of ms Hatton 115 almost verbatim. We merely note this detail for those who wish to pursue the point.

ss 13 Tell me how many years old was Adam before he begot a son.

I tell you, one hundred and thirty years before he begot a son; and then in his youth he begot a son who was called Seth; and he then lived in this world for nine hundred and thirty years in all. Then his son Seth lived one hundred and five years before he begot a son; and then in his youth he begot a son who was called Enos, and then he himself lived nine hundred and twelve years in all. Then Enos was one hundred years old when he begot Cainan and then Enos lived nine hundred and five years in all; and then Cainan was seventy years old when he begot Malaleel, and then Cainan lived nine hundred and ten years in all. Then Malaleel was sixty-five years old when he begot Jared, and Malaleel lived for nine hundred and five years in all. Then Jared was one hundred and sixty-two years old when he begot Henoch, and his father Jared lived for eight hundred and sixty-two years in all. Then Henoch was sixty-five years old when he begot Mathusala and Henoch lived for three hundred and sixty-five years in all. Then God took him in body and soul up into heaven. Then Mathusala was one hundred and eighty-seven years old when he begot Lamech, and his father Mathusala lived for nine hundred and sixty-nine years in all. Then Lamech was one hundred and eighty-two years old when he begot Noe, and Lamech lived for seven hundred and seventy-seven years in all. Then Noe was five hundred years old when he begot sons Sem, Cham, Japheth, and Noe lived in this world for nine hundred and fifty years in all.

II

The answer is a paraphrase of selected passages in Genesis 5, 'The book of the generation of Adam,' except for the age of Noe at his death, which is recorded in Genesis 9:29. The comment thus ignores Cain and Abel and, in effect, traces the descent of the 'good' from Seth, who was a replacement for the good Abel (Genesis 4:25) to Noe. Our text follows the Vulgate figures, not the Septuagint/Old Latin which differ, but there are errors. Enos was 90 not 100 when he begot Cainan, Malaleel was 895 not 905 when he died, and Jared lived 962 not 862 years. Errors deriving from Roman numerals however are common in this and other medieval texts.

---

ss   14   Tell me how many nations sprang from his three sons.
   I tell you, there are seventy-two nations; and thirty sprang from his eldest son Sem and thirty from Cham and twelve from Japheth.

1:i

Noe hæfde. iii. suna þus wæron hatene. Sem. cham. Iafeð. of þam þreom awocan and forð coman . lxxii. þeoda. fram Iafeðe. xv. and fram chame . xxx . and from Seme .xxvii; Napier *Anglia* xi/6, 7. Cf also Napier xi/1, 2–3, where exactly the same numbers occur.

1:ii

Quod filios habuit Noe? Tres: Sem, Cham et Japhet, qui inter se diviserunt terram; Sem accepit ab oriente, Cham a meridie, Japhet ab occidente. In tres partes Romani terram diviserunt, id est Asyam, Affricam, Europiam.

De tribus filiis Noe orte sunt generaciones lxxii, unde electe sunt ix: de Sem Caldei, Ebrei et Greci; de Cham Affri, Egyptii et Mauri; de Japhet Ytali, Galli et Hyspanenses; Suchier *L'Enfant sage* I 99, 271 Cf also Suchier JM I 12, 120; Förster *Gesprächbüchlein* 21, 22, 347; Baesecke *Vocabularius* 27, 7.

II

The total (72) of the nations derives from a count of the descendants in the Vulgate, as Augustine, *De civitate dei* XVI.vi, implies, and Isidore, *Etymologiae* IX.ii.2, indicates more fully, although quoting partly from Augustine (as italicized): 'Gentes autem a quibus divisa est terra LXXIII. Quindecim de Japhet, triginta et una de Cham, viginti septem de Sem, quae fiunt septuaginta tres *vel potius, ut ratio* declarat, *septuaginta duae, totidemque linguae per terras esse coeperunt quae crescendo provincias et insulas impleverunt*'.

The difference between 73 and 72 is explained by the presence of the Cainan (recorded in Luke 3:36 within the list of the generations of Christ) who, as Bede points out in his commentary on the verse in Luke, *In Lucam* I.iii.35–6 (CCSL 120, 90; PL 92 col 363) does not appear in the Hebrew (and Vulgate) at Genesis 11:12, but only in the Septuagint/Old Latin as the father of Sale and son of Arphaxad. Augustine was apparently the first to draw attention to this Cainan.

Although the total (72) of ss 14 is accurate by Vulgate count the division of 12 to Japheth and 30 to Sem (Shem) differ from the Vulgate division as recorded in the OE snippets of I:i. The Irish vernacular text, *Lebor Gabála Érenn* I, 148, appears to suggest that there was an alternative tradition of division when it notes that: 'tricha no .uii.xx mac badar ag Sem' (Sem had thirty or twenty-seven sons), but if such a tradition had arisen it could have originated in an error in Roman numeral from a transmitter to the ss figures. Roman 'xu,' with the 'u' in the minim strokes of insular script, is easily misread as 'xii,' to produce the twelve descendants of Japheth, instead of fifteen. In order to agree with the correct total another three descendants would need to be allotted to one of the others, in ss to Sem.

---

ss 15 Tell me who was he who was not born and afterwards was buried in his mother's womb, and was baptized after death.

I tell you, that was Adam.

AR 28 Tell me which man died and was not born, and after death was later
buried in his mother's womb.

I tell you, that was Adam the first man, because the earth was his
mother and he was buried afterwards in the earth.

I:i

Dic mihi quis homo, qui non natus est, et mortuus est, atque in utero matris
suae post mortem baptizatus? Est Adam; *Collectanea Bedae*, PL 94, col
544B.

I:ii

Hwæt wæs se on þissere worulde se ðe acænned næs *and* þeah hwæðere
wæs to men geworden *and* lange lifde *and* þa eft æfter his deaðe *þæt* he
wæs bebyrged innon his moder innoðe *and* æfter þam deaðe eft *þæt* hit
gelamp æfter manegum wintrum *þæt* he wæs gefullwad ... *þæt* wæs adam se
æresta mann [Who was he, in this world, who was not born and yet was
made as a man and lived long and then again after his death was buried in his
mother's womb and, after his death it happened that he was baptized after
many years ... He was Adam the first man]; Napier *Anglia* XI/I, I.

I:iii

Qui est mortuos et non est natus? Adam; Suchier JM C 2, 108. See also
Suchier JM₁ D 2, 114; JM I 18, 120; JM₂ 3, 123; AE₁a 50, 15; AE₁b 39, 16. Cf
also *Alfræði Íslenzk* III, 39, Suchier *L'Enfant sage* I 11, 266, and other
examples passim.

II

This is an 'enigmatic question' fitting the title of one of the Latin lists. The
part of the OE conundrum corresponding to I:iii is clearly based on Genesis
2:7 about Adam's being made 'de limo terrae' and on Genesis 5:5 which
records his natural death. The Latin question (I:iii) appears to be the
earliest form since it is sometimes accompanied by other enigmas of a *natus
et mortuus*, for example, 'Quis fuit natus et non mortuus? Helias et Enoch
(Suchier AE₂ 18, 32) or 'Quis vir mortuus bis et semel natus? Est Laza-
rus ...' (*Collectanea Bedae*, PL 94, col 544B).

The extension in AR 28 that the earth was Adam's mother obviously
reflects the common concept of 'mother Earth,' a concept which is not only
pagan (as Utley suggests, *Chy*, 59) but Biblical as well (eg Ecclesiasticus

40:1). This figure is reaffirmed for Christians in the typological associations between Christ's birth from the Virgin and Adam's birth from virgin soil as for example in Irenaeus *Contra haereses* III.21.10 (PG 7, cols 954–5); Tertullian *Adversus Iudaeos* XIII.11 (CCSL 2, 1387, PL 2, col 675); and Maximus of Turin *Sermo* 50A.2 (CCSL 23, 203, PL 57, col 571).

Adam's baptism after death in ss 15 (and in I:i, I:ii) needs a more detailed explanation since it was a subject of separate questions in some lists, and the answers there indicate knowledge of two different traditions. One question-master places Adam's baptism with that of other patriarchs during the Harrowing of Hell as a necessary act before salvation (on this problem see J.A. MacCulloch *The Harrowing of Hell*, 246 ff):

> Quomodo babtizatus est Adam? Quando Dominus descendit in infernum, et erat ibi Adam et dixit: 'Ego video manus qui me plasmaverunt'; et Dominus collegit eum sub asellam suam, sed de sanguine et aqua que processit de latere Domini baptizatus est; Suchier JM_2 29, 126.

But the mention of the blood and water of baptism from Christ's side, which we have not seen so specified in accounts of the descent into hell, may suggest that this explicator knows also of another tradition which is presented by other question-masters:

i Item dic mici fuit Adam baptizatus aut non? R. Fuit. Dic mici quo ordine? R. Crux Domini, in qua Dominus crucifixus est, super sepulchrum Adam fuit ficta et sanguis et aqua quod ex latus Domini exivit super eum cucurrit, hoc abuit pro babtismo; Omont *Interrogationes* II 10–11, 63.

ii Ubi Adam accepit baptismum? In monte Calvarię, ubi dominus Jesus Christus crucifixus est, de eius sanguine; Wilmanns *Fragebüchlein* 40, 169.

This tradition had wide diffusion even among well-known Christian writers. Its centre is the name Golgotha whose interpretation is: 'quod est Calvariae locus,' Matthew 27:33 etc. Bede *In Lucam* XXIII, 33 (from Jerome *In Mattheum*) (CCSL 120, 401; PL 92, col 615) explains it literalistically, ie, from the skulls of previous malefactors. But a persistent Hebrew tradition, which appealed to typologists, insisted that the skull was Adam's. (Pseudo-)Origen *In Mattheum*, reporting 'a certain tradition,' placed Adam's skull at Golgotha (PG 13, col 1777). So too did Ambrose, once noting that the story was 'as Hebrews argue' (*In Lucam* X, 114, CSEL 32.4, 498; PL 15, col 1925) but another time baldly stating 'ibi Adae sepulchrum' (*Epist.* LXXI 10, PL 16, col 1297) when concerned with the typological association of Adam and Christ. Jerome disagreed since he regarded the Adam named in Joshua 14:15 as the first man, and had chosen Hebron as Adam's burial-place. To him the previous name of Hebron, Cariath-Arbe, meant 'civitas quattuor,' from the four who rested there, Adam, Abraham, Isaac, and Jacob (*Liber de situ ... Hebraicorum*; de Genesi sv 'Arboc,' PL 23, col 906; *Epist.* CVIII 11, PL 22, col 886). But ironically he seems to have aided the dissemination of the tradition that Adam's skull was at Golgotha since he reports it fully, although in benign dismissal: 'Audivi quemdam exposuisse Calvariae locum, in quo sepultus est Adam, et ideo sic appellatum esse, quia ibi antiqui hominis sit conditum caput, et hoc esse quod Apostolus dicat: Surge qui dormis, et exsurge a mortuis, et illuminabit te Christus (Ephesians 5:14). Favorabilis interpretatio et mulcens aurem populi, nec tamen vera' (*In Mattheum* XXVII 33, PL 26, col 217). He is more explicit elsewhere about this 'favorabilis interpretatio, nec tamen vera.' In his commentary on *Epist. ad Ephesios* V 14 (PL 26, col 559) he noted an alternative reading of his Vulgate text 'illuminabit te Christus,' as 'continget te Christus' which he had heard in a sermon on the Pauline text. This stated how Adam was 'touched': 'Quia videlicet tactu sanguinis ipsius ... vivificetur atque consurgat' (PL 26, col 559). Jerome's friends Paula and Eustochium, when telling the story in a letter to Marcella 'about the holy places,' add another detail to aid the association, that Adam's name meant 'sanguis Christi de cruce stillans' (*Epist.* XLVI 3, PL 22, col 485). The tradition was known to the influential Caesarius of Arles: 'et sanguis ille pretiosus etiam corporaliter pulverem antiqui peccatoris dum dignatur stillando contingere redemisse credatur' (Sermo 84, §5, CCSL 103, 347). We note the verb 'contingere.' Pseudo-Tertullian (perhaps another Gaulish writer) turned the story into verse:

Hic patitur Christus, pio sanguine terra madescit,
Pulvis Adae ut possit veteris cum sanguine Christi
Commixtus, stillantis aquae virtute levari
(PL 2, cols 1123–4).

Irishmen later transmit the story in *The Poems of Blathmac* (ed Carney, 21), in *Lebor Gabála Érenn* I, 96, but also in *Saltair na Rann* (as translated by Hull *Poem book of the Gael*, 50) which last says that Adam was buried at Hebron but echoes an early tradition on how his head came to Golgotha: 'The flood of the deluge over every land / many countries did it upturn / it carried his head from Adam / and brought it to Jerusalem. / There the head remained / before Jerusalem; / without grief the cross of Christ afterwards / was planted in the flesh of Adam.'

Such a tradition agrees partly with one recorded in a sermon in Coptic (translated by Budge *Coptic Apocrypha*, 341), supposedly deriving from Chrysostom, which says: 'The waters of the flood rolled over the body of Adam, and they carried it away and deposited it in the midst of Jerusalem.'

But another tradition of removal was recorded in the Syriac *Cave of Treasures* which describes how Adam's body was taken into the Ark and was eventually placed at Golgotha: 'And when blood and water flowed down from his side, they ran down into the mouth of Adam' (Budge *Cave*, 225). This may record the traditions of the Hebrews to which Jerome and Ambrose refer.

We suggest that one other OE writer knew of the tradition about Adam's baptism. The poet of *Christ and Satan* certainly filled out scriptural statement with apocryphal story as is shown in the commentary by M.D. Clubb in his edition of the poem and in recent papers by T.D. Hill (*PQ* 48 (1969), 550–4; *NQ* 216 (1972), 2–4). There may well be one more reference in that difficult collocation from the description of Christ's crucifixion, where, as 'baths of baptism' (l 545), His blood fell to the ground. The 'baths of baptism' could well be for Adam, in view of the persistent emphasis on apocryphal tradition in this poem.

---

ss 16 Tell me how long Adam lived in Paradise.
I tell you ... and on the ... he tasted the fruit of the forbidden fig-tree, and that on Friday, and because of that he was in hell five thousand two hundred and twenty-eight years.

See the commentary on AR I, 2.

---

ss 17 Tell me about St Mary's age.
I tell you, she was sixty-three years old when she died, and she was fourteen years old when she gave birth to Christ, and she was with him on earth for thirty-three years, and she remained sixteen years after him in the world; and from Adam and from the beginning of the world until the great flood of Noe it was two thousand two hundred and sixty-two years by count of number, and from the flood until the birth of Abraham it was nine hundred and forty-two years, and from Abraham thenceforth up to the time of Moses and the departure of Israel out of Egypt it was five hundred and eight years, and from the

beginning of the world up to Christ's passion there were six thousand one hundred and fifty-eight years.

I

Sancta Maria wæs on þreo and sixtigan wintra þa heo of middan gearde ferde and heo wæs feowertyne geara eald þa heo Crist acende and heo wæs mid him xxxiii geara on middan gearde and heo wæs syxtyne gear æfter him on worulde; *Hyde Register, Liber Vitae*, 83.

II:a

There are a number of snippets in OE manuscripts which discuss the Virgin Mary's age in much the same terms and process as SS'17 and the example in I:i. Napier (*Anglia* XI) printed three of these from mss, Cotton Tiberius A iii, fol 44, Cotton Titus D xxvii, fol 55b, and ms Bodley 343, on 3, 6, and 6 footnote 8 respectively. The following table indicates similarities and variants.

	age at Christ's birth	with Christ	after Christ	age at death
SS 17	14	33	16	63
Hyde Register	14	33	16	63
Tiberius A iii	14	33	14	63
Titus D xxvii	14	33	16	63
Bodley 343	15	33	16	63

The consistent total in all texts, which is an acceptable total of the ss items, indicates scribal error of number for individual items in Tiberius A iii and Bodley 343. Only one of the items, the 33 years when Mary was with Christ, is based on scripture. Her age of fourteen at Christ's birth, however, agrees with that in the *Gospel of Pseudo-Matthew* (James, 73), in the *Gospel of the Birth of Mary* (James, 79) and in the *History of Joseph* (James, 84), but disagrees with the *Protevangelium* which gives her age as 16 (James, 44). The length of time she lived after Christ's death varies in the texts we have seen, but it seems probable that our figure was taken from some version of the Virgin's Assumption. The Coptic text (James, 197) gives variants of 10 and 15 for this period. A discourse by Cyril, Archbishop of Jerusalem (in E.A.W. Budge *Miscellaneous Coptic Texts in the dialect of Upper Egypt* (London, Oxford University Press 1915), 649) gives different numbers, 15 at Christ's birth, 60 at death, and 11½ years of life after Christ's passion. An insertion in Eusebius's Chronicle (now apparently regarded as a forgery) says: 'in the year 48 Mary the Virgin was taken up into heaven' (Smith *Dict. Bible* II, 269, col 1). Apparently a Syriac *Transitus B. Virginis* (as noted in *Coptic Apocryphal Gospels*, ed F. Robinson, Texts and Studies IV.2 (Cambridge, Cambridge University Press 1896, 201 note) says Mary was 16 years after Christ on earth. It would appear the originator of the ss statement had some knowledge of Apocryphal stories about Mary.

II:b

The periods demarked represent the first three ages of the world, to the Flood, then to Abraham, and then to the Exodus, together with a total from Adam to Christ's Passion. The numbers for the length of the ages and the total are based on Septuagint figures, although with some scribal error in copying of Roman numerals and, probably, with some misunderstanding. Förster ('Die Weltzeitalter,' 194–8) groups our passage with a chronological piece in ms Cotton Vespasian D vi, fol 69b (printed Napier *Anglia* XI/3, 4–5) and with a possible source, a section of Æthelweard's *Chronicle* (printed Förster, 195). There are agreements between the three texts certainly in choice of period, in some numbers for the periods, and even in form of expression. But there are significant differences (as set out in the table below) which suggest that Æthelweard's text was not the sole source or an immediate source. If we hold merely to the ss piece we may say that it is based, no doubt at some remove, on information from the influential *Chronicon* of Eusebius, as translated and enlarged by Jerome. Eusebius/Jerome sum up information at various points in the chronicle and indicate period viz 'a Diluuio usque ad Abraham anni DCCCCXLII, ab Adam usque ad Diluuium IICCXLII' and 'a nativitate ... Abraham usque ad Moysen et egressum Israhel ex Aegypto conputantur anni DV' (ed Schoene and Petermann II, 149, (cf II, 199) and II, 9 respectively), and the Exodus is also recorded under the year 505 from Abraham (II, 28). These figures and choice of period agree with Æthelweard who is obviously in the Eusebius/Jerome tradition, in opposition to, eg, Bede, *De Temporum Ratione* cap LXVI (PL 90, cols 520–1), whose third age is from Abraham to David, and who agrees with Isidore, *Chronicon* (PL 83, cols 1019–38). The numbers in Æthelweard and in Eusebius/Jerome indicate clearly that there was transposition of x and L in the Roman numeral which produces 2262 for the first age in ss, and suggests strongly an extension and confusion of minim strokes to produce 508 in place of 505 for the third age.

	First age: Adam to Flood	Second age: Flood to Abraham	Third age: Abraham to Exodus	From Creation to Christ
ss 17	2262	942	508	6158 (to the Passion)
ss 12				6158 (to the Harrowing of Hell)
Eusebius/Jerome	2242	942	505	5528 (to the Preaching)
Æthelweard	2242	942	505	5095 (to the Advent)
Vespasian D vi	2242	942	505	5228 (to the Advent)
Harley 3271	2242	940	505 and 100	5028 (to the Advent)
Hyde Register	3676	397	970	6125 and 9 months (to the Nativity) 6158 (to the Passion)
Caligula A xv	796	397	970	6125 and 9 months (to the Nativity) 6158 (to the Passion)

The total 6158 appears to derive from a misunderstanding, but not of Æthelweard's total which is 5095. Eusebius/Jerome (Schoene and Petermann II, 9) give the following figures: from Abraham to Moses and the Exodus 505, to Solomon and the first building of the temple 479, to the restoration of the temple under Darius 512, to the preaching of Christ and the fifteenth year of the emperor Tiberius 547 and, despite the real total (2043), from Abraham to Christ 2044. If we add 2242 from Adam to the Flood and 942 from the Flood to Abraham, the period from the beginning to Christ's preaching is 5228. This total, or an error based on this total, appears elsewhere in OE texts, in ms Cotton Vespasian D xiv (Warner *Early*

English Homilies, 140) as an isolated statement (5528), in Cotton Vespasian D vi and Harley 3271 (Napier *Anglia* XI/3 and 10 resp), and these texts indicate a continuation of the Eusebius/Jerome figures. But another tradition, as indicated in ss 12 above, is attested that Adam lived 930 years, died, and remained 5228 years in hell (presumably until the Harrowing). This statement about Adam, as indicated under ss 12, is found in the exemplar of Vercelli Homily XIX. The new total 6158 is found in texts which Förster prints, 191–3, the Hyde Register, and ms Cotton Caligula A xv, there from the beginning of the world to Christ's passion, as in this ss answer. We may assume two comprehensible misunderstandings of the Eusebius/Jerome comments at some stage, that a limit 'from Adam' was taken by someone to mean 'from Adam's death,' and a limit 'to Christ's preaching' was taken to mean 'to Christ's passion.'

---

ss 18 Tell me how long was Noe's ark being made.
   I tell you, eighty years, from the wood that is called Sem.

I:i
Quod anni ędificauit Noë arca? ci; Suchier JM C 70, 111.

I:ii
Dic mihi, quantos annos habebat Noę, quando cepit fabricare archam? c.
In quantos annos fabricavit archam? In c.
Quo tempore fuit in archa? Annos i; Suchier JM I 8–10, 120. Similar sequences of questions are found in versions of *L'Enfant sage* (Suchier passim).

I:iii
Quot annis edifficata est arca Noë? c; Suchier JM_1 34, 117.

I:iv
Unde facta fuit arca Noë? De lignis sethim imputribilis nature; Suchier JM_1 61, 118, mss D and E. As Suchier observes (119, note 61) ms F of this text substitutes 'arca testimonii' for 'arca Noë' within the question.

II
The answer contains two separate statements, on the length of time taken to build Noah's ark and on the wood from which it was made.

On the wood Utley (*Chy*, 77) speculated variously within the text of his paper but eventually came to the simplest explanation on p 77 (note 160) when he saw Suchier's Latin list (1:iv). OE 'sem' clearly derives, by scribal corruption, from the Vulgate 'setim' (Deuteronomy 10:3), the wood from which ark of the covenant was made. The scribe of JM F (1:iv) corrected the error implicit in this question by substituting 'arca testimonii' for 'arca Noë.' But the form of this question which we have quoted (1:iv) is interesting since it collocates the alternative 'setim' (Vulgate) and 'de lignis imputrilibus' (Old Latin/Septuagint) of Deuteronomy 10:3 for the ark. Augustine in the *Tractatus in Ioannis evangelium* VI.19 (CCSL 36, 63; PL 35, col 1434) says: 'In ipsa ergo arca ligna imputribilia erant' in describing *Noah's ark* as a figure of the church, although Noah's ark (Gen. 6:14) was made 'de lignis laevigatis' (Vulgate), 'de lignis quadratis' (Old Latin/Septuagint). It would seem that the importance of the two arks within the faith allowed a transfer of quality (or, simply, epithet) from one to the other.

We have no exact numerical parallels to the OE figure for the time taken in building the ark. The variants 'c' and 'ci' (1:i–iii) in the parallel Latin questions give no hint of progressive scribal error towards the OE figure of 'lxxx.' Indeed the popular figures for the time it took Noah to make the ark were 100 and 120 (see Ginzberg V, 174) and, among those who could have influenced the Anglo-Saxons, Augustine implies 120 in *De civitate dei* XV.24 and Bede in commenting on Genesis chose 100 years (*In genesim* II, vi, 13–14; CCSL 118A, 103; PL 91, col 85).

SS 19 Tell me what Noe's wife was called.
   I tell you, she was called Dalila.
SS 20 And what was Cham's wife called.
   She was called Iaitarecta.
SS 21 And what was Japheth's wife called.
   I tell you, she was called Catafluuia; and they are called by other names, Olla and Ollina and Ollibania, so these three are called.

1:i
Octo itaque hominum animae in arca Noe sunt salve reperte, id est IIII viri et IIII feminae.
Viri vero hii sunt: Noe et filii eius tres: Sem, Cham, Iafed.

Nomina autem feminarum, ut littere tradunt, hec sunt: Olla, Oleva, Ollina. Uxor vero Noe Percova vocabatur; McNally *Liber de Numeris* VIII, I, 128. McNally (127) cites three other instances of the names, Olla, Oliva, in relation to Noah's sons in Irish vernacular literature and one in Latin.

I:ii

Percoba cainiu cachfiach,
setig Noe meicc Lamhiach,
mna natrimac monar ṅgle,
Olla, Oliua, Oliuane.

Olla ben Sem, soer friaháil,
Oliua ben Chaim choemnáir,
Oliuana baigthi treith
asósser ben Iafeith

[Percoba, lovelier than all due rewards (?) was the wife of Noe son of Lamech; the wives of the three sons – bright the undertaking – Olla, Oliua and Oliuane – Olla was the wife of Sem – she was generous to supplication; Oliua was the wife of fair, modest Cham; Oliuana – extolled by princes (?) – the youngest of them, was the wife of Japheth]; *Saltair Na Rann* 2485–88, 2497–500, trans N.J.A. Williams.

I:iii

Percoba ben Noe co nnaíri: cen choi, cen gári, ba gand
Copa seím ba comsech ca cáem-fhir: toirsech ca coiniud a cland
Olla setig Seím blaíth bíthi. Ben Chaim Oliuan o hAís.
Commam Iafeth Oliuane: na tarat bari for baís.

[Percoba was wife of shame-faced Noah. She was poor without murmur or complaint. Though she was mild she had power with her gentle husband. Her children were weary with lamenting her. Olla was the blooming womanly spouse of Shem. Ham's wife was Olivan from Asia. Jafeth's consort was Olivane who did not conquer death]; The *Ban-Shencus* ed and trans M.C. Dobbs *RC* 47 (1930) 290 and 316.

I:iv

Ða wæs se snotra   sunu Lamehes
of fere acumen   flod on laste
mid his eaforum þrim,   yrfes hyrde
(and heora feower wif;
nemde wæron   Percoba, Olla,
Olliua, Olliuani)

[Then the wise son of Lamech, guardian of the heritage, came from the ship, as the flood receded, with his three sons (and their four wives; they were called Percoba, Olla, Olliua, Olliuani)]; *Genesis A*, 1543–8.

I:V

Cata Rechta ba ben Sem,
Cata Chasta ben Iafeth,
Cata Flauia, co n'grād ngrinn,
Ainm mnā Caim, nocho celim
[Cata Rechta, she was the wife of Sem, Cata Casta, the wife of Jafeth, Cata Flavia, with pleasant love, was the name of Cham's wife, I conceal it not]; *Lebor Gabála Érenn* I, 188–9.

II

Echoes of two groupings of names occur in our text, ie Iaitarecta, Catafluuia, and Olla, Ollina, Ollibania, together with an isolated name, Dalila. Utley lists many recorded and some speculated names for the scripturally nameless wives of Noah and his sons in 'The One Hundred and Three Names of Noah's Wife' *Speculum* 16 (1941), 426–52. To these lists a few more names and instances could be added. But by listing separately against the individual men Utley obscured the distinctiveness of groupings. We add one grouping (I:i) from the eighth-century Hiberno-Latin *Liber de Numeris* which may well be near the origin of the grouping in the Irish vernacular and OE passages I:ii–iv, and helps to explain one of the groupings in our text. As Israel Gollancz noted (in *The Caedmon Manuscript* (Oxford, Oxford University Press 1927), lxiii–iv) Oolla, Ooliba are names in Ezekiel 23:4 (Vulgate spelling) and an Oolibama is Esau's wife in Genesis 36:2. As he speculated, these names were probably taken and linked with Noah and his sons from some alphabetical onomasticon where they appeared in sequence. The variant forms in our vernacular texts may be explained as through the common medieval Latin orthographic variant of medial 'u' and 'b,' together with scribal error of minim strokes in insular script, thus ss Ollina for Vulgate Ooliba (b/u-n) and Ollibania (ni/m) for Vulgate Oolibama. Doubling of single vowels and consonants and simplification of double vowels and consonants is common in vernacular and Latin texts of this period. It thus appears that these names derive ultimately from scripture, but the application as a group is through Irish influence. The other group also now has an Irish parallel. Utley on Iaitarecta (440) and Catafluuia (442) had no parallel to the former and regarded the Cataflua,

Cathaflua, of the later Peter Comestor (440) as parallel to the latter. Now, with reference to the citation in I:v, we suggest that the names reflect another Irish grouping which disseminated to Comestor as well as to our text. Catafluuia is near enough to Cata Flavia of the *Lebor Gabála Érenn* and, for Iaitarecta, a scribal confusion of an upright C (with a strong straight downward stroke) as a capital I, would make the OE word similar to Cata Rechta. Cata Rechta in the Irish text is the wife of Sem, whose name is missing from the OE series, but this merely confirms that the sequence of names was regarded as a group.

The isolated name of Dalila (in Vulgate spelling) is obviously a transfer of a well-known scriptural name, but not necessarily by our scribe.

---

ss   22   Tell me how long was Noe's flood on the earth.
     I tell you, forty days and nights.

I:i
Quantos dies fuit diluuium? XL dies et XL noctes; Quandos dies natauit archa super aquas in diluuio? CL; Baesecke *Vocabularius* 19, 20, 7.

I:ii
Quot dies facta est pluvia? Diebus XL et noctibus; Suchier JM$_1$ 35, 117.

I:iii
Dic mihi, quantos dies fuit archa super aquas? CL; Suchier JM I 11, 120.

II
Utley (*Chy*, 59) notes that the question reports 'the Bible faithfully' and he is correct in relation to Genesis 7:17: 'factumque est diluvium quadraginta diebus super terram,' but the 'diluvium' here is the 'pluvia' (super terram) of Genesis 7:12 (as in I:ii). In relation to the Latin lists and despite Genesis 7:17 we suggest that the Anglo-Saxon (or a predecessor) conflated sequential questions by omission. The ark was floating on the flood (on the earth) for a much longer time, 150 days say I:i and I:iii, although certain versions of Suchier *L'Enfant sage* (eg I 97, 271, IV 69, 297) offer an error by saying that the period was forty days.

---

ss 23 Tell me how long was Noe's ark in length.
I tell you, it was three hundred fathoms long and fifty fathoms broad and thirty fathoms high.

I:i

Noes arc wæs III hundfeðma lang *and* fiftig wid *and* þrittig heah; Napier *Anglia* XI/4, 5.

I:ii

Also the emperour hym demaunded how longe, how large and how hye the sayd arche was. And the chylde him answered that hit had .ccc. fadome in lengthe, .ccxxx. of heyght and a .clx. in largenes; Suchier *L'Enfant sage* XVIII 50, 532, and other examples passim.

II

The information in the OE question is exactly as in scripture (Genesis 6:15). The translation of Latin 'cubitum' by 'fæðm' is well attested (sv 'fæðm' III, Bosworth-Toller Dict).

---

ss 24 Tell me how many sons Adam had.
I tell you, thirty sons and thirty daughters.

I:i

Adam hæfde lii suna *and* lxx dohtra; Napier *Anglia* 11/6, 7.

I:ii

Quot filios habuit Adam? Triginta filios et triginta filias. Aliter. Filiorum Adam computatio, ut alii dicunt, sexaginta duo, et filiarum computatio, quinquaginta tres sunt; *Collectanea Bedae* PL 94, col 544B.

I:iii

Et ipsus Adam quantus filius habuit excepto Cain et Abel et Sedh? .xxx. filius et .xxx. filias; Suchier JM C 6, 108. Cf also Suchier JM₁ 5, 114; JM P 48, 132; Wilmanns, *Fragebüchlein* 21, 168; Omont *Interrogationes* II 78, 69;

and Suchier AE₂ 14, 32. Versions of Suchier *L'Enfant sage* passim record examples.

II

The Bible, of course, does not specify the number of children born to Adam and Eve. The OE statement of 1:i together with the Latin alternative of 1:ii suggest that there were more traditions than one. But such texts as the *Life of Adam and Eve* (24, 2) (Charles II, 139) and the *Apocalypse of Moses* (5, 1) (Charles II, 139) imply that Adam had thirty sons and thirty daughters apart from Cain, Abel, and Seth. This statement appears in most of the answers of the dialogue lists (1:iii), the only variant being the omission of Seth's name from the exceptions, probably by error. Our OE answer has probably omitted the named exceptions by error also.

SS 25 Tell me which man first built a city.

I tell you he was called Enos, and Ninive was the city, and there were one hundred and twenty thousand men in it and ... twenty thousand, and the city of Jerusalem was the first built after Noe's flood.

I

It is more convenient to cite Latin parallels within the discussion for this question.

II

The question and answer reveal an intricate confusion of information which is only partly considered by Utley (*Chy*, 59–60). He rightly suspects an error in Kemble's *Knos* for *Enos*, in fact a misreading of the ms which originated with Thorpe (see textual note to ss 25). He also comments on a confusion of Enos (son of Seth, ss 13, Genesis 5:6) with Henoch (son of Cain), after whom the first city was named by its builder Cain (Genesis 4:17). There is, however, no confusion of people, since Henoch (Vulgate) was alternatively called Enos (as in the OE poem *Genesis A*, 1055, and as a Latin text, 'De inventione nominum' (PL Suppl. IV** col 907), puts it: 'Duo sunt Enos, unus est de Cain, alter de Seth.') But obviously the name of the city (Enos) has been substituted for its builder (Cain), as in the *Alfræði Íslenzk* III, 38: 'Hver gerde fyrst borg i veraulldine? Enos son Kainn' [Who made the first city in the world? Enos, son of Cain]. The text JM₂ 14, Suchier 124, records the correct form of question and answer: 'Quis primus edificavit civitatem? Cain, quam vocavit Enos.' But these are only the beginnings of errors. The problems are:

1 the linking of Enos (for Henoch) with Ninive;
2 the implication that Ninive was built before the flood;
3 the unusual way of numbering its inhabitants as the ms text reads in sequence;
4 the choice of Jerusalem as the first city after the flood.

1 / On the linking of Enos with Ninive the Latin parallels allow construction of a sequence of error, and illustrate attempts to avoid it. There were undoubtedly two quite separate questions or sequences of questions in the lists originally. One was:

Who was the first 'princeps'? Ninus.
What city did he build? Ninive.

The other was:

Who built the first city? Cain, which he called Enos [Henoch]

But at a date earlier than our extant texts an extension was made on the Ninus sequence, as illustrated both in the *Collectanea Bedae* (PL 94, col 544C):

Quis primus princeps factus fuit? Ninus, filius Beli.
Quae prima civitas? Ninive.
Quis eam aedificavit? Ninus.

and in Lowe, *The Bobbio Missal*, 6:

Qui prius factus est precepes [for 'principes,' a vulgar form of 'princeps']? ninius.
Qui [for 'Que'] ciuitas priu facta est. niniuin.

In both these cases, Ninive has become the first city, instead of simply the city which the first 'princeps' built, by a thoughtless extension from the question on the first 'princeps.'

Ninus as first 'princeps' often appears in a sequence naming also the first 'rex,' Saul, and the first 'imperator,' Julius Caesar. Such a sequence is recorded in two manuscripts, D and E, of Suchier's text JM₁, 12, 13, 14, 115, including the erroneous extension on Ninus the first 'princeps' (as no 10): 'Int.: Quę civitas prima facta est? Resp.: Ninivę.'

As a result, when the scribes of these manuscripts (and their exemplar) wish to speak of Cain as first builder this question is altered: 'Quis primus edifficavit *maceriam*? Cain, civitatem Enoch'; Suchier JM₁ 31, 117.

'Maceriam' (enclosure, stronghold) is clearly an alteration from an original 'civitatem' as indicated by the answer which includes 'civitatem' and by the fact that the word 'maceria' has no authority from the text of Genesis 4:17, either in the Vulgate or in the variants noted in the construction of the Old Latin by Bonifatius Fischer. The other ms (F) of this text JM₁ answers the question (no 10 above) on the first city differently (and corruptly, but in which enough sense can be seen): 'Ciuitas cain quam edifficaui ex noe [probably for 'nomine'] filii enoch' (Suchier, 115 note 10), and, having made this correction, omits the other question about Cain building a 'maceria'.

2 / The implication, in the OE answer, that Ninive was built before the flood obviously accompanies the inaccurate connection of Ninus with the city called Henoch built by Cain.

3 / The information on the city, in the OE answer, is about Ninive with some accuracy but with various errors. The Latin lists tell us that Ninus built Ninive which is at variance with scriptural statement, that Assur was its builder (Genesis 10:11), but in agreement with Augustine *De Civitate Dei* XVI.3. Augustine explains that where scripture says that Assur was the builder, this was long after ('longe postea') and he states that Ninus 'Beli filius' was 'conditor Nineuae ciuitatis magnae' which was named after him.

Its size is noted by population in Jonas 4:11 which says of Ninive: 'in qua sunt plus quam centum viginti millia hominum' (Vulgate) to give authority and origin for the OE answer of 'one hundred and twenty thousand' (via Latin lists). But the number, 'twenty thousand,' which appears to be another portion of the population in the manuscript reading, is unlikely to be so. It would be unique for an Anglo-Saxon to express one hundred and forty thousand in this way, and Latin parallels, which are no later than the ninth century, indicate a scribal omission of phrase from the OE text. One such parallel, Suchier's text JM₁ 11, 115 reads:

Int.: Quod mansiones habet ut illam totam cercis?

Resp.: xv; una mansio xxx milia, hoc est lequas xx.

Another list printed by Wilmanns *Fragebüchlein*, 168, asks:

Quales primi civitas fuit? Ninnivę.
Qui eam edificavit? Nimo; ubi fuerant c viginti milia hominum.
Quod mansiones habet? Ut illa tota circis XII, una mansio triginta milia habet pedes.

Yet another, printed by Wölfflin-Troll, 109, runs:

In.: Quo prima ciuitas facta est? R.: Nineuae.
In.: Quod mansiones habet uillam totam.
R.: Quindecim milia; una mansio xxx, allequas xx.

It appears that the OE scribe (or a predecessor) has omitted the question about the 'mansiones' ('mansio,' a station, a day's journey) and has picked up part of the answer which defines the length of a 'mansio' in paces ('pedes'). The loss of a Roman numeral x explains the difference of OE 'twenty thousand' and Latin 'thirty thousand.' The physical size of the city is not scriptural but probably derives from some geographer or historian. Diodorus Siculus, in his *Library of History*, describes the founding of Ninive by Ninus and notes its size II.3 and III.I.

4 / Jerusalem's primacy among cities after the flood is not mentioned in any of the extant Latin lists, but the information could well have derived ultimately from Isidore *Etymologiae* xv.i.5. Isidore's categorizing is very similar to questions about the first city. In xv.i.3 he notes that: 'primus ante diluvium Cain civitatem Enoch ... condidit,' but that: 'primus post diluvium Nemrod gigas Babylonem urbem ... fundavit,' xv.i.4 (cf Genesis 10:10 and Orosius *Historia adversus paganos* II.vi.7), yet that: 'Judaei asserunt Sem filium Noe ... post diluvium, in Syria condidisse urbem Salem ...' xv.i.5 (cf Jerome, *de situ ... Hebraicorum*, sub. *Salem*, citing Josephus *Antiquitates* I.xi) '... Hanc postea tenuerunt Jebusaei, ex quibus, et sortitia est vocabulum Jebus, sicque duobus nominibus copulatis, Jebus et Salem, vocata est Hierusalem.' Thus he says that a Jewish tradition gave Salem primacy and this Salem became Jerusalem. One can understand why a Christian question-master would award Jerusalem the primacy before Babylon, built by Nemrod.

---

ss 26 And what is the city called where the sun rises in the morning.
I tell you, the city is called Iaiaca.
ss 27 Tell me where does the sun set in the evening.
I tell you, the city is called Garita.

AR 29 Tell me the name of the city where the sun rises.
I tell you, it is called Iaiaca.
AR 30 Tell me what is it called where it sets.
I tell you, it is called Iainta.

II

These questions are found elsewhere only in AR and in the two manuscripts of the ME 'Questiones bytwene the Maister of Oxenford and his clerke.' For the city of sunrise the ME text has no answer by omission, and for the city of sunset the ME text has 'Garica' (Harley ms), and 'Sarica' (Lansdowne ms). Utley has discussed these names in 'Jaiaca, the city of sunrise,' *Names* 5 (1957) 208–21, and has certainly identified the city of sunset as modern Cadiz, ancient Gadeira (Gadir, Gades), at the Pillars of Hercules, the western limits of the ancient world. Anglo-Saxons who know that Spain and England are at the end of the world include the writer of the *Old English Martyrology* (Herzfeld, 128) speaking of James the apostle preaching in Spain, 'in the western part of the world near the setting of the sun,' and Ælfric (*Lives of Saints*, I, 290) who calls England 'the outer edge of the breadth of the earth' although he knows Ireland to the west.

The answer 'Janita' (Utley), *recte* 'Iainta' to the corresponding question in AR, together with the answers 'Garica,' 'Sarica' of the ME dialogue, are regarded as possibly paleographical derivations from 'Garita,' by Utley (209). It is difficult to decide on the original form, even if there are close connections between ss and the others. Probably all we should say is that, in relation to the Latin forms, the word began with 'Ga.'

The naming of the city of sunrise as Iaiaca in both ss and AR is more puzzling. The most promising suggestion is Utley's (220) as the Homeric 'Aiaia' where 'Helios [has] his place of rising.' 'Aiaia' as Utley indicates, has variant forms: 'Αἴα' and 'Γαῖα', and 'since the Greek *gamma* regularly becomes in mediaeval Greek a tailed i or j, the variant 'Γαῖα' may lie behind our Jaiaca.'

---

ss 28 Tell me which plant is best and most blessed.
I tell you, the plant is called the lily, because it signifies Christ.
ss 29 Tell me which bird is best.
I tell you, the dove is best; it signifies the Holy Ghost.

ss 31 Tell me what water is best.

I tell you, the River Jordan is the best because Christ was baptized in it.

ss 40 Tell me which tree is the best of all trees.

I tell you, it is the vine.

1:i

Int. Quit obtimum lignorum?

R. Vinea, quia vinea in typpum sanguis Christi intelligitur, quando venit Christus ad Iohannem et vidit spiritum descendentem de celo quasi columbam.

Int. Quit obtimum erbarum?

R. Lilia in typpo spiritu sancti intelligitur; Daly-Suchier k 62–3, 121.

1:ii

And I said: O Lord my Lord, out of all the woods of the earth and all the trees thereof thou hast chosen thee one vine; out of all the lands of the world thou hast chosen thee one planting-ground; out of all the flowers of the world thou hast chosen thee one lily; out of all the depths of the sea thou has replenished for thyself one river; out of all the cities that have been built thou hast sanctified Sion unto thyself; out of all birds that have been created thou hast called for thyself one dove; out of all the cattle that have been formed thou hast provided thee one sheep; and out of all the peoples who have become so numerous thou hast gotten thee one people: and the law which thou didst approve out of all (laws) thou hast bestowed upon the people whom thou didst desire; 4 Ezra 5:23–27 (Charles ii, 571).

1:iii

Is e tra fáth ar-a n-abar airchindech re Míchel archangel; uair in tan do-rígne Dia in domun, rochoraig airchindech airithe do na hulib dúileb saindredach: – Lucifer do na demnaib, grian do na rendaib, sliab Sioin do na slebtib, sruth n-Iordanen do na srothaib, finemain do na crandaib, colum do na henaib, in leoman do na biastaib, in lebedan do na bratanaib, Crist uas doinib [Now the reason why the Archangel Michael is called the Chief is the following. When God made the world he appointed a determinate chief to all creatures separately: Lucifer for the demons; the sun for the stars; Mt Sion for the mountains; the river Jordan among rivers; the vine among trees; the dove among birds; the lion among beasts; the leviathan among fishes; Christ over mankind]; *Passions and the Homilies from Leabhar Breac* 218–19, 456.

II

These four questions are considered together since they are obviously related and, as a group, may well have derived ultimately from a common source, the passage from 4 Ezra cited above. The point, however, of this passage in 4 Ezra is to suggest Israel's special role among the nations. But the question-master who originally shaped the questions as we now have them may have followed the tradition of this text for the general concept of the 'best' plant etc, but then proceeded to justify his selection in terms of traditional Christian symbolism. Thus the dove is best because it represents the Holy Spirit in the gospels (see Matthew 3:16 etc). The lily is best because of such texts as Canticles 2:1 'Ego flos campi et lilium convallium' and Ecclesiasticus 39:19 'Florete flores quasi lilium' which were consistently glossed in terms of their Christological significance (see the commentaries of Cornelius a Lapide for a convenient summary of patristic opinion on these verses). And, of course, Christ's baptism in the Jordan and his own description of himself as the 'vitis vera' (John 15:1) provide a reason for the answers on Jordan and the vine.

The fact that the original creator of these questions found it so easy to reinterpret a Jewish apocalyptic text in terms of Christian symbolism illustrates how dependent both the New Testament and texts such as 4 Ezra were upon a common stock of Old Testament imagery.

It is interesting here that the OE list, for once, helps to explain a muddle in a Latin dialogue (1:i) when normally the aid is from Latin lists for the OE. Daly-Suchier (124) are puzzled that the lily is said to be 'in typpo spiritu sancti,' since they can find no parallel for this particular signification. But the muddle is more fundamental, as the OE list and a knowledge of scripture show. A question on the dove has been omitted and there has been some curious interchange. The Latin would make sense if it had read:

Int.: Quit obtimum lignorum?
R.: Vinea, quia vinea in typpum sanguis Christi intelligitur ...
Int.: [Quit obtimum avium?]
R.: [Columba, quia columba] in typpo spiritu sancti intelligitur, quando venit Christus ad Iohannem et vidit spiritum descendentem de celo quasi columbam.

Int.: Quit obtimum erbarum?

R.: Lilia ...

The vine is a type of the blood of Christ, not when Christ is baptized (when the Holy Ghost descends as a dove) but at the Last Supper, when Christ breaks bread and drinks saying: 'Hoc est corpus meum ... Hic est enim sanguis meus' (Matthew 26:26, 28).

In the OE list the 'wintreow' is not typified. We speculate that if a pedantically logical transmitter looked at such a question as the Latin which asks 'quid optimum *lignorum*?' and answers 'vinea' which, in signification, clearly becomes liquid wine, he might have pondered and omitted the signification especially since OE 'wintreow' is clearly different from 'win.' This would allow his readers to recall another scriptural text where Christ says of himself: 'ego sum vitis vera' (John 15:1). In doubt leave out, the Anglo-Saxon (or his predecessor) may have thought.

SS 30 Tell me where does lightning come from.

     I tell you, it comes from wind and from water.

I

There are no parallels in the Latin lists.

II

This answer appears to reflect the old notion about the cause of lightning such as is presented by Isidore *De natura rerum*: 'Fit enim fulmen nube, imbre et vento. Nam cum ventus in nubibus vehementer agitatus est, sic incalescit ut incendatur. Dehinc, ut praedictum est, fulgura et tonitrua simul exprimuntur' (XXX, 3; PL 83, col 1002). Since lightning (and thunder) were thought to result from the crashing of clouds blown together by a high wind, it seems that a necessary ingredient 'cloud' is omitted from the OE answer.

---

ss 31 Tell me what water is best.
I tell you, the River Jordan is the best because Christ was baptized in it.

See the commentary on ss 28, 29.

---

ss 32 Tell me where did the angels go who rejected God in the kingdom of heaven.
I tell you, they divided into three parts; he put one part in the region of the air, the second part in the region of the water, the third part in the abyss of hell.

I
C.: Where becom thangels þat god put owte of heven and bycom develen?
M.: In thre parties were þei partid: some in to hell, and some regnen in the skye, and som in waters and in wodis; Horstmann *Questiones*, 286.

II
The text cited here is not really a parallel since it is the ME derivative of ss 32 or a predecessor but, in this instance, it contains a noteworthy extension, 'woods.' But we have found a parallel statement which may hint at the kind of literature which the original creator of our question may have used. The Hiberno-Latin hymn *Altus Prosator* includes a stanza which speaks of a 'draco magnus' who 'tertiam partem siderum traxit secum in barathrum' (*The Irish Liber Hymnorum* I, 69). This verse refers to the 'draco magnus' (Apocalypse 12:3 and 12:9) whose tail 'trahebat tertiam partem stellarum coeli, et misit eas in terram' (Apocalypse 12:4). But an Irish glossator explains 'tertiam': 'a tri ernaile forahintinn ... trian dib in aere ocus trian ... maris et terrae ocus trian in barathro. i. in inferno' (I, 69) translated as 'there are three modes of explaining it, one third *in aere* and one third *maris* ... *et terrae* and one third *in barathro*, viz. *in inferno*' (II, 157; our italics). *Piers Plowman* (B. Passus I.123) has a similar division of the fallen angels: 'somme in eyre, somme in erthe and somme in helle depe.' We suggest that

the Irish glossator points to a commentary, as yet unseen, on Apocalypse 12:4 as the ultimate source for the particular division.

Such a summary, in commentary, would not explain why the fallen angels were so divided. We would normally expect them to fall to hell, as so vividly expressed in the OE poem *Genesis B*. But there was debate about other possible places for their ultimate station. It was commonplace that demons *are* in the air around us, based on explanation of Paul's comment on the demonic 'powers of the air' (Ephesians 2:2), as eg expressed by Haymo of Auxerre: 'ut philosophi dixerunt et doctores nostri opinantur' (PL 118, col 809 B), and the Hiberno-Latin *De ordine creaturarum liber* notes that the 'plurimi catholicorum auctorum' state that angels, at apostasy, fell to the 'aer' from the 'aether' (PL 83, col 927). But 'wæteres gedrif' is a tradition for which we have no satisfactory precedent. There is a brief reference in Job 26:5 to the 'gigantes qui gemunt sub aquis' and Gregory does gloss these giants as apostate angels (*Moralia in Job* XVII.xxi.30; PL 76, col 25). Gregory, however, is here interested in morality rather than cosmology and also glosses these giants as 'proud men.' Yet one may suppose that such an explanation could suggest the third place to a commentator on Apocalypse 12:4, in the curious world of medieval exegesis. Certainly, the sea is frequently associated with chaos in the Bible (Job 38:8–11; Proverbs 8:29; Apocalypse 21:1) and could be a suitable realm for the apostate angels.

The extension to this question in the ME version of SS 32, in which the redactor says that the fallen angels are in hell, the air, the waters, and *the woods* (1:i), suggests another perspective on this question. For Christians the innumerable local deities of the classical world (who inhabited, among other locations, waters and woods) were demons (on this problem see Martin of Braga *De correctione rusticorum* 8, ed C.W. Barlow (New Haven, Yale University Press 1950), 188). And the ME redactor seems to have assumed that the question reflects the belief that fallen angels distributed themselves throughout the world 'aut in mare aut in fluminibus aut in fontibus aut in silvis' (ibid). As a final parallel we cite a modern Irish folkloristic analogue: 'The angels who sided with Lucifer were expelled from heaven. The Archangel Michael pleaded with God not to empty heaven, and God relented, saying that all things should remain as they then were: the fallen angels in the *air* and on the *earth* became the fairies, and those who had fallen into the *sea* became the under-water beings' (italics ours); Seán Ó. Súilleabhain 'Etiological Stories in Ireland' *Medieval Literature and Folklore Studies: Essays in Honor of Francis Lee Utley*, ed

Jerome Mandel and Bruce A. Rosenberg (New Brunswick, Rutgers University Press 1970) A 6, 258.

---

ss 33 Tell me how many are the waters of the world.
     I tell you, there are two salt seas and two fresh.

I

Aquae mundi quot sunt? Duae: sal et aqua; *Collectanea Bedae* PL 94, col 543D.

II

The Latin parallel reveals the error in the OE answer. There are two kinds of water in the world, salt and fresh, but not two salt seas and two fresh.

---

ss 34 Tell me what man was the first (to be) talking with a dog.
     I tell you, Saint Peter.

I

Qui cum cane locutus est? Sanctus Petrus. Qui cum asina locutus est? Balaam propheta; Suchier JM C 27–8, 109–10; cf Wilmanns *Fragebüchlein* 30–1, 168.

II

This question is based on an episode in the apocryphal 'Passion of the Apostles Peter and Paul,' to which Utley (*Chy*, 62) refers, and for which Kemble, 196, cites an account from an English version of the *Legenda Aurea*. Unfortunately Kemble's version, which reports no direct speech, misses the unusual point of the dialogue questions about speaking animals and conversations with them. Balaam's ass (Numbers 22: 28–30) follows Peter's dog in the Latin parallels.

The story goes that Simon Magus had a fierce dog bound to lie in wait for and kill Peter. But when Peter came the dog spoke, asking him what his commands were. Peter told the dog to relay a message to Simon Magus, which it did. See Hennecke II 291–2. Ælfric (*CH* I 372–4) also tells the story but, in his account, the dog's speeches are missing.

---

ss 35 Tell me which man first thought of tilling with a plough.
    I say to you it was Cham, the son of Noe.

I:i
Quis primus excogitavit aratum? Cham; Suchier JM J 7, 122.

I:ii
Dic mihi quis primus excogitavit aratrum? Cham, filius Noe; *Collectanea Bedae* PL 94, col 539 D.

I:iii
Adr. d. Qui primus iniciavit aratrum? Ep. r.: Noë; Suchier AE₁a 37, 14.

I:iv
Quis primum inchoavit arare? Ante diluvium Neptare, post diluvium Noë; Suchier AE₂ 75, 35.

II
Although some answers in the dialogue lists illustrate thoughtless extension of essentially accurate information (as happens here, we think, for the OE and I:ii) there may also be a change which reflects a more 'modern' tradition. The Vulgate Genesis 4:2 names Cain simply as 'agricola' but in the Old Latin, reconstructed by Sabatier and more fully by Fischer, it says: 'Cain autem operabatur terram.' Among the texts cited in support for the Old Latin reading we note Ambrose calling Cain 'operator terrae, operarius terrae,' an anonymous text naming him 'terrae cultor,' and the fifth-century Cyprianus Gallus describing him 'super aratrum,' and saying of him, 'curvo terram vertebat aratro.' It is clear that 'working the earth' was taken to mean 'working with the plough.' So an answer based on the Septuagint/Old

Latin would be Cain (as probably in 1:i). Since Cham was an alternative name for Cain, but also for Ham, son of Noe, a thoughtless extension was made both in the OE answer and in the Latin of 1:ii. It is relevant to note that the OE question is verbally closer to the Latin of 1:i and ii than to the phrases of 1:iii and iv. But a pedantic reader of the Vulgate text, on seeing this answer before him, could say that Cain is simply an 'agricola.' Noah was the first man to work the earth, Genesis 9:20: 'coepitique Noe vir agricola exercere terram' (Vulgate). So he would 'modernize' the answer and change it to Noah (as in 1:iii and 1:iv).

---

ss 36 Tell me why stones are not fruitful.
    I tell you, because Abel's blood fell on a stone when his brother
    Cham killed him with the jawbone of an ass.

1:i
Rogab Cāin n-a lāim luind
lecain cintaig in chamuill:
co Haibēl lēim co luindi,
conid ro marb d'āen-builli.

Adberait rind na heōlaig,
lucht in ēcnai il-cheōlaig,
nach fāsait na clocha ō chēin –
ō'n lō rosfer fuil Aibēil

[Cain brought in his savage hand the guilty jaw-bone of the camel to Abel –
a violent attack – and killed him with a single blow ... The wise men tell us,
those of wisdom of varied melody, that, from of old, stones are not fruitful
since he spilled the blood of Abel] *Lebor Gabála Érenn*, I, stanzas 20, 22,
text 180, trans N.J.A. Williams.

1:ii
Quis primus holocaustum obtulit Deo? Abel agnum, unde occidit eum
frater eius Cain. Unde decollavit illum? Quia ferrum non habuit, dentibus
suis et fodit eum in terram duodecim pedes; Suchier JM$_2$ 12–13, 124.

II

The question is not found in the extant Latin dialogues, but the phrasing of the Irish vernacular parallel suggests that in Ireland, at least, this reason for the unfruitfulness of stones was an older tradition. Utley (*Chy*, 63) speculates that 'the unfruitful stone merely collected on itself all the curse which God laid on the ground as a whole in Genesis 4:11.' According to Jewish legend about the murder of Abel, part of the punishment which God inflicted upon Cain was a diminution of the earth's fertility (Ginzberg I 110–11; V 140). But, at present, the motif, in our OE form, appears to be linked with the Irish.

The other extra-scriptural statement is the naming of Cain's weapon, which has been discussed by the scholars cited in Utley (*Chy*, 63 note 59), and, more recently, by George Henderson 'Cain's Jaw-Bone' *JWCI* 24 (1962), 108–14, and by A.A. Barb 'Cain's murder-weapon and Samson's jawbone of an ass' *JWCI* 35 (1972), 386–9. It has also been noted, but only with reference to the illustration of the murder of Abel in the British Library ms Claudius B iv, by C.R. Dodwell and Peter Clemoes in their 1974 facsimile edition (see 'Old English Texts' above, note 10). Commenting on 'the fact that the instrument of murder is a jaw-bone of an ass' in the illustration, Dodwell and Clemoes indicate that it 'derives ... from a play of words in Old English.' They referred to a paper by M. Schapiro in *Arts Bulletin* 24 (1942), 210–11 which suggested a link between the 'cinbān' (of ss, actually 'cyngbān,' jawbone) and 'Cāin bana' (Cain the slayer?). The later art historians, Henderson and Barb, rightly dispute this suggestion, (Henderson in convincing detail), since to philologists a play on such words would be somewhat fanciful, whether in sound or spelling.

Henderson considers literature and iconography and argues that the specification of the weapon derives from representations of the death of Abel in art. On the origin he suggests the possibility either that the story of Samson's slaughter of the Philistines, pictorially represented, was a model, or that an artist who depicted Abel's murder had misunderstood his exemplar which gave Cain a type of short-bladed coulter (Cain was a ploughman, ss 35) easily confused with a jawbone.

Barb, noting (without reference) that 'it has been established that both the literary tradition [ie in ss], and the artistic representation, originated in early medieval Hiberno-Saxon Insular art and spread thence to the continent,' argues that Cain's weapon was a sickle (of wood) in original representation.

We cannot be certain, but a picture or an elaborating commentary on Genesis 4:11 could have decided the weapon. As Utley says (*Chy*, 63) other weapons were chosen, such as stone, sword, axe or hoe, cane or rod, club, ploughshare, but those who chose iron weapons had forgotten their scripture as the dialogue-question (1:ii) implies: 'How did he cut his head off?' 'With his teeth because he did not have "ferrum" (sword or iron).' It was Cain's descendant Tubalcain who was presumably the first 'malleator et faber in cuncta opera aeris et ferri' (Genesis 4:22).

SS 37 Tell me what is best and worst among men.
I tell you, word is best and worst among men.
AR 43 Tell me what is best and worst.
I tell you, the word of man.

1:i
Quid est optimum et pessimum? Verbum; *Collectanea Bedae* PL 94, col 545A. See also Daly-Suchier DAE 10, 113; ibid AHE 19, 104; Suchier *L'Enfant sage* IV 36, 294; V 36, 321 and other examples passim.

1:ii
El emperador le pregunto: Infante, qual es la mejor cosa y peor del mundo? El infante le respondio: La palabra, ca conella puer hazer mucho mal y mucho bien [The emperor asked him: Child, what is the best and worst thing in the world? The child replied: The word because with it much evil and much good can be done] Suchier *L'Enfant sage* VIII 133, 384; cf XI 11, 423.

1:iii
Quid est lingua? Optimum et pessimum; Daly-Suchier M 24, 131.

II
The OE question is based on what is, or becomes, a proverb. Whiting lists SS 37 and AR 43 in his *Proverbs* (W 635) and notes some similar ME proverbial expressions eg 'For a tonge ys the best membyr of a man whyll hit ys rewlet, and the worst when hit yis out of rewle' (T 387, Mirk *Festial* 161.6–8, cf also T 371). Daly-Suchier (86 with other references) explain their similar answers (AHE 19, DAE 10 (1:i), and M 24 (1:ii)) by citing a story of Plutarch about a certain Bias (or Pittacus in alternative versions) who, when asked for the best and worst meat, sent a tongue. The point of the

riddle answered by 'verbum' or 'lingua' is the double function of speech which can establish and disrupt concord, as certainly in I:ii above. Utley (*Chy*, 63) suggests that the 'best *verbum*' may bear the connotation of 'logos.' This is, of course, possible but unlikely in view of the development in I:ii and in the proverb cited above.

---

ss 38 Tell me what is most evident for men on earth to know.
　　　I tell you, nothing is so evident to any man as that he must suffer death.

I:i
H. Quid est certissimum? E. Mors; Daly-Suchier AHE 22, 104. See also Daly-Suchier DAE 13, 113, Suchier *L'Enfant sage* passim.

I:ii
P. Quid est mors? A. Inevitabilis eventus etc; Daly-Suchier DPA 7, 138.

II
This question is based on a proverb which was widely current; often, however, the concept that death is certain is linked with the idea that the time of death is uncertain. Thus, to quote an instance from the Pseudo-Augustinian *Liber de spiritu et anima* cap xxxi, 'nihil enim morte certius et nihil hora mortis incertius' (PL 40, col 800). For instances see Sutphen, 249, Singer III 109–10, Walther, nos 12179, 15117, 15123, 15133, and 15134, and Whiting D 96, 121–3.

---

ss 39 Tell me what are the three things without which no man can live.
　　　I tell you, one is fire, the second is water, the third is iron.
AR 39 Tell me what are the three things that no man can be without.
　　　I tell you, they are water and fire and iron.

I

Qui sunt tres amici et inimici, sine quibus vivere nemo potest?
Ignis, aqua et ferrum; *Collectanea Bedae* PL 94, col 541A.

II

This question is based on Ecclesiasticus 39:31: 'Initium necessariae rei
vitae hominum, aqua, ignis, et ferrum ...' The selection of only the first
three items, from ten in the scriptural statement, is explained by the Latin
question (I) which names 'water, fire, and iron' as both 'friends and
enemies.' The other items in the Ecclesiasticus list, such as 'salt, milk,
honey,' would not suit such a conundrum.

---

ss 40 Tell me which tree is the best of all trees.
I tell you it is the vine.

See the commentary on ss 28, 29.

---

ss 41 Tell me where does man's soul rest when the body sleeps.
I tell you, it is in three places; in the brain, or in the heart, or in the
blood.

I:i

Dic mihi ubi sit anima hominis, quando dormiunt homines? In tribus locis:
aut in corde, aut in sanguine, aut in cerebro; *Collectanea Bedae* PL 94, col
539D.

I:ii

Int. Requiescit anima hominis in somno in tribus locis? R. In cerebro, vel in
corde, vel in sanguine; Daly-Suchier K 64, 121. See also Daly-Suchier G 20,
127, Suchier AE₁b 86, 18.

1:iii

Lærisveinn spyr: Hvar hvilir sala manz þa er hann sefur? Meistare svarar: I þrim stodum, i heila, i hiarta, i blode [The pupil asks: Where does a man's soul rest when he sleeps? The teacher answers: In three places, in the brain, in the heart, in the blood]; *Alfræði Íslenzk* III 37.

II

The identity of idea together with slight variations in formulation between ss 40 and the Latin examples of 1:i, ii confirm the accuracy of transmission of this OE question. The Latin questions, however are ambiguous in that 'anima' can mean either 'soul' (as the OE question-master translates it) or 'vital spirit.' Again, both the Latin and OE questions are ambiguous in that it is impossible to tell, as the questions are now phrased, whether the question-masters were proposing three different possible answers to this question or rather suggesting that any given moment when a man is asleep his 'anima' is either in the brain or in the heart or in the blood. In classical Latin this distinction would have been indicated by using 'aut … aut' (either … or) or 'vel … vel' (or … or) but, as a glance at the Latin examples shows, the question-masters were either unaware of this distinction or else did not themselves understand the question. Given these problems in translation, the only simple solution would be for us to cite some specific text from a recognized and generally accessible authority which is clearly the source of these questions, but unfortunately we have not found such a source. In Hellenistic philosophy and medicine the question of 'the seat of the soul' was a recognized problem and a variety of answers was suggested. Tertullian (*De Anima* 15.1–5, 18–20, ed J.H. Waszink) had his own views and, selecting scriptural testimonies, chose the heart but, in condemning other Greek opinions, conveniently summarized them: 'ut neque exstrinsecus agitari putes principale istud secundum Heraclitum, neque per totum corpus ventilari secundum Moschionem, neque in capite concludi secundum Platonem, neque in vertice potius praesidere secundum Xenocraten, neque *in cerebro* cubare secundum Hippocraten, sed nec circa cerebri fundamentum, ut Herophilus, nec in membranulis, ut Strato et Erasistratus, nec in superciliorum meditullio, ut Strato Physicus, nec in tota lorica pectoris, ut Epicurus, sed quod et Aegyptii renuntiaverunt … namque homini *sanguis circumcordialis* est sensus' (our italics). Waszink (219–20) informs us that Tertullian took his material from Soranus, and he cites

Caelius Aurelianus *Acut. Morb.* I, 8, 53/4 (who translates Soranus) and gives the varying opinions.

These opinions are too many for our question. But we have seen a 'triplex opinio' which, though in a text later than ours, nevertheless may derive from earlier material, and may suggest the kind of scriptural and physiological speculation which underlies it. It is a comment (on Christ's giving up his 'spiritus' at crucifixion) in an anonymous sermon preserved in a fourteenth-century ms (printed in *Bibliotheca casinensis* I 271–7) and runs: 'De anima sunt tres opiniones, ubi scilicet anima habeat principalem sedem, scilicet vel in corde propter illud de corde exeunt male cogitaciones etc. [Matthew 15:19 etc]; vel in sanguine propter illud levitici anima omnis carnis in sanguine est [Leviticus 17:11]; vel in capite propter illud et inclinato capite tradidit spiritum [John 19:30]. Hanc triplicem opinionem iudei saltem ipso facto videntur scivisse, nam ut eius animam a corpore avellerent, quesierunt ipsam in capite cum spinas usque ad cerebrum infixerunt; quesierunt in sanguine cum eius venas in pedibus et manibus aperuerunt; quesierunt in corde cum eius latus perforaverunt' (273, punctuation normalized).

While this specific sermon appears to be relatively late, it quotes a number of patristic authorities, and is, in fact, a pastiche of traditional material rather than an original composition. If we could trace the patristic sources for this passage, we should have, we believe, the sources for this group of questions. The one aspect of these questions which the passage does not deal with, where the soul of a man is when he is asleep, is problematic to some degree. Lucretius in the *De natura rerum* IV, 916 ff suggests that the 'vis animae' withdraws within the body during sleep and is 'rekindled' upon awaking, a belief which could be related to the assumption that there is a specific 'seat' of the 'anima' during sleep, but we are unable to provide a real answer to this problem.

---

ss 42 Tell me why the sea became salt.
I tell you, from the ten commandments which Moses collected in the old law at God's decree, and he threw those ten commandments in the sea, and he poured out his tears into the sea; thus it became salt.
AR 25 Tell me why the sea is salt.
I tell you, because Moses threw the ten commandments of the old

law into the sea, when he made the tablets, because the people of Israel were worshipping idols.

I

Laerisvein spyr: þvi er sior salltur? Meistare svarar: Af x laugmaalum, er Moyses kastaði ut aa sioin [The pupil asks, Why is the sea salt? The teacher answers, From the ten commandments (lit, lawsayings) which Moses cast out into the sea]; *Alfræði Íslenzk* III 37.

II

Although there is an Icelandic parallel, we have no reasonable explanation for the origin of this question. Stith Thompson A 1115.1–3 records a variety of answers from folklore to the question 'Why is the sea salt?' but none corresponds with ours. The originator of our answer obviously seeks a scriptural reason, but there are some removes from scripture in the statement. Moses was inland when he broke the tables of the law (Exodus 32:19) and the only thing that he put into water was the golden calf, beaten into powder.

---

ss 43 Tell me what were the commandments.

I tell you, the first commandment was, 'Non habeos deos alienos,' that is 'Do not love another God before me'; the second commandment was 'Non adsumes nomen domini in uanum:' 'Do not call upon the name of God in vain;' the third commandment was 'Keep the holy day of rest;' the fourth commandment was, 'Honour thy father and thy mother;' the fifth commandment was, 'Non occides;' 'Do not kill an innocent man;' the sixth commandment was, 'Non mechaberis;' 'Do not commit adultery;' the seventh commandment was, 'Do not steal;' the eighth commandment was, 'Do not bear false witness;' the ninth commandment was 'Non concupiscens rem et omnia proximi tui;' 'Do not desire another man's possessions wrongly;' the tenth commandment was, 'Non concupiscens uxorem proximi tui;' 'Do not desire another man's wife wrongly.'

I

There are no Latin parallels in the extant dialogues.

II

The answer is obviously the ten commandments which are presented in scripture within Exodus 20:3–17 and Deuteronomy 5:7–21, but with difference of some phrasing. Indications within the Latin citations of ss (although these are sometimes inaccurate) suggest that the list is based on Exodus 20:3–17 in Vulgate form.

There are, however, adaptations both in the Latin and in the OE. The Latin for the ninth commandment in ss is a summary of the detailed list in Exodus 20:17 but such summary was not uncommon. Caesarius of Arles, *Sermo* 100 §11 (CCSL 103, 411–12), gave a similar form as his tenth commandment: 'non concupisces ullam rem proximi tui' (cf Augustine *Contra Faustum* XV.7, PL 42, col 311) and Wulfstan, although quoting Deuteronomy 5:21 (equivalent in idea to Exodus 20:17) in full in the Latin version given in his *De Christianitate*, summarises in a manner similar to Caesarius in his OE version (Bethurum edition, 194, 201 resp). Our OE list reverses the order of the ninth and tenth commandments in comparison with these others. But these commandments are included within a single scriptural verse, Exodus 20:17, Deuteronomy 5:21. In Exodus 20:17 only, 'domus' precedes 'uxor' and could lead to the prohibition on coveting other possessions being given priority in the ss list.

On some occasions the OE seems to be more a gloss than a translation. The fifth commandment 'non occides' (Exodus 20:13, Deuteronomy 5:17) is rendered 'do not kill an innocent man' (see textual notes to ss 43) to agree with Ælfric's comment on this dictate 'that is the greatest sin that an innocent man be slain' (for the Latin and OE see textual notes to ss 43). The distinction is presented in another way in Wulfstan's rendering: 'Ne beo ðu ænig manslaga,' (nor be any homicide, 201). In this variation the Englishmen accepted the medieval Roman view that certain kinds of killing were permissible (see Cross 'The ethic of war in Old English' *England before the Conquest* ed Peter Clemoes and Kathleen Hughes (Cambridge, Cambridge University Press 1971), 269–82).

The first commandment in Latin: 'non habeos [sic] deos alienos' (Exod. 20:3) is also adapted in OE as: 'do not love another God before me.' This may indicate some influence of the New Testament dictates of 'caritas' (Matthew 22:37 and 39 on love of God and neighbour) especially since these precepts were occasionally joined to the ten commandments within homilies (see *Wulfstan* ed Bethurum, 323, where examples are cited). As Bethurum says, the Biblical model for this was Romans 13:8–9 where the precepts are linked with some of the commandments. But an interesting substitution by Augustine and Ælfric may hint at another influence. They replace Exodus 20:3 with Deuteronomy 6:4: 'Audi Israel, Dominus Deus noster, Dominus unus est,' Augustine (*Contra Faustum* xv.5) exactly and Ælfric (*CH* II, 198) with some adaptation. But the following verse (6:5) is the well-known command: 'Diliges Dominum tuum ex toto corde tuo etc.' A recall and an adaptation within the presentation of the decalogue is obviously permissible in this period.

Finally the phrase 'on unriht' (wrongly) appears to be added gratuitously to the ninth and tenth commandments, but it is paralleled in other OE versions of the scriptural verse, for example, Wulfstan (201) and *The Laws of Alfred* cited in A.S. Cook *Biblical Quotations* (1898) 61.

SS 44 Tell me where is the grave of the king Moses.

I tell you, it is by the house which is called Fegor and there is no man who may know of it before the great judgment.

I:i
Lærisveinn spyr: Hvar er grauf Moysi? Meistare svarar: I stad þeim er Sieth heitir, hia huse þvi, er Fiegor heitir, ok veit eingen nema gud allt til þessa dags [The pupil asks: Where is the grave of Moses? The master answers: In that place which is called Sieth, beside that house which is called Fiegor, and no-one knows it, except God, right up to this day]; *Alfræði Íslenzk* III 37–8.

I:ii
Cuius sepulchrum non est inventum? Moysi; Suchier *L'Enfant sage* I 34, 267; other examples are recorded passim and in Omont *Interrogationes* I 43, 61.

I:iii
Cuius sepulchrum non est inventum in terra? Moysy; Wilmanns *Fragebüchlein* 25, 168; cf also Lowe *Bobbio Missal*, 7.

I:iv

IN. Cuius sepulchrum quaesitum et non inuentum?
R. Moysi, quia dixit ei deus: uade in montem, elevare et morere; et adsumptus est ibi Moyses; Wölflinn-Troll 81, 114.

II

Although the Latin of I:ii, iii could be based on the Vulgate statement that God buried Moses 'in valle terrae Moab contra Phogor; et non cognovit sepulchrum eius usque in presentem diem' (Deuteronomy 34:6), both the OE and the Icelandic (of I:i) echo the Septuagint/Old Latin (the Icelandic text very closely), 'et sepelierunt eum in Geth prope domum [translating the Hebrew prefix 'Beth'] Phegor et nemo scit sepulchrum eius usque in diem istum.' Utley (*Chy*, 64 note 67), omitting reference to the Old Latin, comments on the Hebrew Beth-peor (of the Authorized Version) and a development from 'peor' to OE 'Fegor;' but a Latin intermediary Phegor should be assumed for the OE form.

The OE answer, although echoing the 'hus' of 'domus' makes slight adaptations, that the grave of Moses will be revealed 'at the great judgment,' and it calls him a king. The former is presumably an adjustment to conform with the scriptural idea that all will be revealed at judgment; the latter, though minor, is more puzzling. Moses of course was raised by the daughter of Pharoah, but he had to flee Egypt and is never called king in scripture. The prophet Samuel establishes a king over Israel only after warning the people of the consequences of this new and momentous step in the history of Israel (I Samuel, I Kings 8:1–22). The term 'king' in our question may be an unthoughtful adaptation or a variant of the term 'ruler' or 'leader' at some stage in the transmission of this question.

The Latin of I:iv has a different answer, possibly linked with the apocryphal *Assumption of Moses*, of which we have only a fragmentary text (Charles II, 407–24).

SS 45 Tell me for what reasons was this earth cursed or afterwards blessed.
I tell you, it was cursed because of Adam and because of Abel's blood and afterwards it was blessed because of Noe and because of Abraham and because of baptism.

I:i
Dic mihi quot vicibus maledicta est terra. Duabus: per Adam primo et secundo pro Cain.
Quot vicibus benedicta est terra? iiii: per Noë, per Abraham, per baptisma, per sanguinem Christi; Suchier JM₁ 62–3, 118.

I:ii
Pro quibus benedicta est terra, pro quibus maledicta est? E. Pro Noë benedicta est terra, pro Adam maledicta est et pro Cain, qui occidit Abel fratrem suum; Suchier AE₁ b 99, 19.

I:iii
Lærisvein spyr: Hversu oft var iord blezud eda bolvod? Meistare svarar: Iord vard bolvod fyri blod Abels, enn blezud fyri Abrahaam ok Isaac ok skirn drottins vors [The pupil asks: How often was the earth blessed or cursed?' The master answers: The earth was cursed because of Abel's blood, but blessed because of Abraham and Isaac and our Lord's baptism]; *Alfræði Íslenzk* III, 38.

II
Our text for this answer is reconstructed from what can still be seen in the manuscript in relation to the Latin parallels.

The answer draws on scriptural information, for the cursing of the earth because of Adam, Genesis 3:17, and because of Abel's blood, Genesis 4:11. In both these cases the physical earth is cursed, Genesis 3:17: 'maledicta terra in opere tuo' (Vulgate), and, though the curse is on Cain in the Vulgate Genesis 4:11: 'maledictus eris *super* terram,' Jerome himself, on Ezekiel, cites a relevant variant of this verse in which the earth is cursed: 'maledicta terra quae aperuit os suum et hausit sanguinem fratris tui' (PL 25, col 257C).

But for the blessings there are no specific scriptural texts of this nature. For Noe, Genesis 6:12 says that the earth was corrupted and clearly the flood destroys that corruption. But the actual blessing by God is on Noe and his sons (Genesis 9:1). For Abraham the blessing is on the people of the earth through him (Genesis 12:2–3). For baptism also we must assume benefits to the people of the earth also, unless the blood and water which baptized Adam at Calvary (see ss 15) is assumed to baptize the earth which covers him.

---

ss 46 Tell me who first planted a vineyard.
I tell you, it was Noe the patriarch.
AR 17 Tell me who first planted vineyards, from which who first drank wine.
I tell you, Noe.

1:i
Quis primus plantavit vineam post diluvium? Noë; Suchier AE₂, 16, 32. See also Baesecke *Vocabularius* 26, 7.; Suchier *L'Enfant sage* I 15, 266, and other examples passim.

1:ii
IN. Qui primus plantavit uineam? R. Noe post diluuium introiuit in paradiso, colligit uitis qui fuerunt plantatas de manu domini, adportans in scapulis suis; plantauit eas in terra Senaar ...; Wölfflin-Troll 49, III. Cf also Suchier JM P 61, 133.

II
This question is based on Genesis 9:20: 'Noe ... plantavit vineam.'

---

ss 47 Tell me who first named the name of God.
I tell you, the devil first named the name of God.
AR 40 Tell me who first named the name of God.
I tell you, the devil.

1:i
Quis primus nomen Dei dixit? In quo loco terrarum dixit? Qua causa dixit? Id est, diabolus perhibetur nomen Dei primus dixisse, quando ad Euam locutus est dicens: Quid *precepit uobis Deus ut non* aedatis *de* hoc *ligno*; McNally *Comm. in Epist. Cath., Iac.* 77–80, *Scriptores Hiberniae Minores* 5 (CCSL 108B).

1:ii
Et quis primus Deus dixit? Respondetur. Est diabolus in paradyso. Dixit Adae, [sic] ut: *Cur praecepit uobis Deus ne comederitis de* hoc *ligno*?;

McNally *Praefacio secundum Marcum* 27, *Scriptores Hiberniae Minores* 224 (CCSL 108B).

1:iii
Discipulus spyr, Hver nefndi fyrst nafn guds? Meistare svarar, Fiandi gjorde þad [The pupil asks, Who first named the name of God? The teacher answers, The Devil did that]; *Alfræði Íslenzk* III 38.

II
Utley (*Chy*, 64) refers to the relevant scriptural text, Genesis 3:1 (cited in Vulgate form in 1:ii) where the serpent uses the name 'Deus' when Eve is asked why God has forbidden her to eat the fruit. The Latin parallels (1:i, ii) now presented, however, are not from the normal dialogue-lists, but from Hiberno-Latin catechism and commentary on scripture. This question may have been taken from such a catechism. 1:ii presents the question without hint of enigma: 'and who first said *Deus*?' but 1:i, the OE and the Icelandic, adapt a little to present a slight puzzle, as in 1:i: 'who first said the name of God?' If there is more to this question than a demand for detailed knowledge of scripture, it may have been influenced by the idea that knowing the name of a person or a god gives one special power (a prominent idea in the Old Testament in the taboos centred on the name Yahweh). The cosmic struggle between God and Satan is begun by the serpent's casual allusion to God and his commands.

SS 48 Tell me what is heaviest to bear on earth.
        I tell you, man's sins and his Lord's anger.
AR 32 Tell me what is heaviest for men on earth.
        I tell you, his Lord's anger.

1:i
Quid est gravissimum terre? Cor hominis, ira regis; Suchier *L'Enfant sage* I 36, 267. cf *Alfræði Íslenzk* III 38, for a similar question which omits, however, the crucial word 'gravissimum.'

1:ii
Quid gravissimum est terre? cor hominis; Suchier AE₂ 46, 33; cf Suchier *L'Enfant sage* IV 53, 296.

II
The difference of answer in AR 32 and SS 48 from those of the Latin parallels (1:i, ii), all to the same questions, suggest that the OE answers are those of a Christian and based on scripture. The answer in AR 32: 'his lord's anger' is ambiguous, but the difference from the unambiguous 'rex' of the Latin is a hint; and the additional phrase of SS 48, 'man's sins,' makes 'his Lord's anger' unambiguously a reference to God in that answer. SS 48 is certainly based on scripture.

Isaisas 30:27 says of the Lord: 'ardens furor eius, et gravis ad portandum' (cf 'hefegost to berende' of SS 48), and the *gravitas* of sin is clearly expressed in Psalm 37:5: 'quoniam iniquitates meae supergressae sunt caput meum: et sicut onus grave gravatae sunt super me.' The common patristic figure of the 'weight' of sin (still implicit in the phrase 'a grave sin') reinforces the choice of answer. On this see, for example, Gregory *Moralia in Job* VIII, xxxii.52 (PL 75, col 834).

SS 49 Tell me what it is which pleases one (some) and displeases another (others).
I tell you, that is judgment.

1:i
Quid est quod uni placet et alteri displicet? Judicium; Wilmanns *Fragebüchlein* 17, 168.

1:ii
Quid est quod alii placet, alii displicet? Vita; *Collectanea Bedae* PL 94, col 545A. see also Daly-Suchier AHE 20, 104; ibid DAE 11, 113.

1:iii
Lærisvein spyr: Hvat er godum ok illum iafnheimellt?' Meistare svarar: Upprisa enn efzsta, ero godir menn innleiddir i saelu, enn illir til kvala [The

pupil asks: What is equally ready for good and evil men? The teacher answers: The last resurrection, good men are brought into joy and wicked to torment]; *Alfrœði Íslenzk* III 38–9.

II

This question reflects the influence of early Latin dialogues such as AHE in which the point of the exchange is chiefly to illustrate the verbal wit of the narrator. It could, however, readily be rewritten in Christian terms as our Icelandic parallel (1:iii) illustrates.

---

ss 50 Tell me what are the four things which were never satisfied, nor ever will be.
I tell you, one is earth, the second is fire, the third is hell, the fourth is a man greedy for worldly wealth.

1:i
Tres sunt qui numquam satiantur: Infernum et terra, que non satiatur aqua et ignis qui numquam dicit sufficit; ita et cupiditas hominum insatiabilis est; Wilmanns *Fragebüchlein* 19, 168. See also Daly-Suchier DAE [variant text] 17, 113. *Alfrœði Íslenzk* III, 39 has this item in abbreviated form.

1:ii
Tria sunt insaturabilia, et quartum quod nunquam dicit, Sufficit: infernus et os vulvae et terra. Aqua [sic] non saturatur aqua: ignis vero nunquam dicit, Sufficit; *Collectanea Bedae* PL 94, col 541B.

1:iii ――
Quid nunquam saciatur. Terra, aqua, ignis et os vulve; nunquam dicunt: sufficit; Suchier *L'Enfant sage* I 37, 267.

II
This question is based on Proverbs 30:15–16, from which three of the four insatiable things derive: 'Tria sunt insaturabilia, et quartum, quod nunquam dicit: Sufficit. Infernus, et os vulvae, et terra, quae non satiatur aqua: ignis vero nunquam dicit: Sufficit.' These scriptural verses were accepted

with minor adaptation in the statements and question of 1:ii and 1:iii. But the substitution of 'cupiditas hominum' for 'os vulvae' of scripture appears already in the ninth-century text of Wilmanns, perhaps, as he suggests (172–3), under the influence of Proverbs 27:20, 'Infernus et perditio nunquam implentur: similiter et oculi hominum insatiabiles,' although this cupidity is more pointedly described in Ecclesiasticus 14:9: 'Insatiabilis oculus cupidi in parte iniquitatis; non satiabatur ...' Walther lists some Latin proverbs (23673; 23696) which derive from these scriptural statements.

SS 51 Tell me how many kinds of flying birds there are.
   I tell you, fifty-four.
SS 52 Tell me how many kinds of fish there are in water.
   I tell you, thirty-six.

See the commentary on AR 33–6.

SS 53 Tell me which man first built a monastery?
   I tell you, Elias and Eliseus the prophets, and, after baptism, Paul and Antony the first hermits.

I
We cite two early examples only but consider relevant variants of this popular question within the discussion.

1:i
Quis prius monastirio fecit. elias et eliseus. Iam post eliam paulus erimita et antonios habas; Lowe *Bobbio Missal* 6.

1:ii
Quis primus monasterium construxit? Ante adventum Elias et Eliseos et post adventum Paulus heremita et Antonius abba; Wilmanns *Fragebüchlein* 27, 168.

II

Among the extant examples a variation of the verb of the question indicates a changing conception of the term 'monasterium' and also that the ss form of the question is a later development. The verb 'fecit' of 1:i occurs also in Omont *Interrogationes* 1 62, 62, in Suchier JM₂ 22a, 125, and in the *Alfræði Íslenzk* III, 39 ('gerdi'). Suchier JM C 14, 109 reads 'constituit.' Suchier AE₂ 25, 32, and Suchier, *L'Enfant sage* 1 24, 266 have 'construxit.' The 'hecdificavit' of Suchier JM 1 14, 120 agrees with the 'getimbrode' of ss 53. Such neutral words as 'fecit,' 'constituit,' which do not imply a tangible building but merely a place where a monk is, are later replaced by 'edificavit,' 'construxit' as the 'monasterium' came to be regarded as a building.

Isidore, in his chapter on monks, *De ecclesiasticis officiis* II.xvi.1 (PL 83, col 794), echoing Jerome, *Epist. 58 ad Paulinum* (PL 22, col 583), not only names Elias and Eliseus as prototypes of monastic life, but, with reference to the Rechabites of Jeremias chapter 35, emphasizes their rejection of permanent buildings: 'Quantum attinet ad auctoritatem veterum Scripturarum, hujus propositi princeps Elias et discipulus eius Elisæus fuerunt [3 Kings 19:19], sive filii prophetarum, qui habitabant in solitudine, urbibusque relictis, faciebant sibi casulas prope fluenta Jordanis.'

Some forms of the answer have either only 'Elias and Eliseus' or 'Paul and Antony' so it is impossible to speculate whether the two pairs of names are a later development or, if so, which pair were in the original answer. But they are balancing pairs. As Eliseus was the disciple of Elias, so Anthony was the follower of Paul. As Jerome describes, *Vita S. Pauli* 7–13 (PL 23, cols 22–7), Anthony visited Paul in the desert in order to be instructed in the religious life.

The pair of names may indicate a subtlety in the question 'who made the first "monasterium,"' since the fact that this question is consistently answered by *two* names in the dialogues implies that a 'monasterium' does not exist until there is an abbot and a monk, a teacher and a disciple. Despite the etymology of the words 'monachus' and 'monasterium' (both are related to Greek 'monos,' 'single' or 'alone'), Benedict is emphatic in insisting that monks should live together under the rule of an abbot and according to fixed discipline. While he grants that some monks might choose to be anchorites or hermits, he insists that monks should not attempt the solitary life until they have lived under 'monasterii probatione diuturna' (Benedict *Regula* 1.3, CSEL 75, 17, italics ours).

ss 54 Tell me what are the streams and rivers which flow in Paradise.
I tell you, there are four of them. The first is called Fison, the second
is called Geon, and the third is called Tygres, the fourth Eufraten,
that is, milk and honey and oil and wine.

i:i
Quot sunt flumina paradisi? Quattuor: Phison, Geon, Tigris, Euphrates;
lac, mel, vinum et oleum; *Collectanea Bedae* PL 94, col 543D. Cf the
Alfræði Íslenzk III, 36 whose composer adapts the answer, 'they are like
milk and sweeter than honey or wine or oil,' and seems not to have
understood the tradition.

i:ii
IN. Dic mihi flumina, qui sunt in paradisu. R. Unus est uini, alter est oleum,
tertius mel, quartus lac. Uero dicitur Eufratis, quia iusti, cum exierint de
saeculo, super ipsa flumina habent habitationes; Wölfflin-Troll 41, 110–11.

i:iii
Dic mihi de iiii fluminibus qui inrigant de paradyos [sic] omnem terram.
Geon, Fison, Tigris, et Eufrates; Suchier JM 54, 118.

II
The names of the rivers are obviously scriptural (Genesis 2:11–14, named
in I:i and I:iii as in Vulgate and Old Latin) but the identification of the rivers
of paradise with milk, honey, oil, and wine appears to derive originally from
The Book of the Secrets of Enoch VIII.5 (Charles II, 434): 'And two springs
come out which send forth honey and milk; and their springs send forth oil
and wine, and they separate into four parts ... and go down into the paradise
of Eden.' As Charles notes they are taken over into the *Apocalypse of Paul*
(James, 539–40). The rivers become a common motif in descriptions of
Paradise as for example in the ME poem *The Land of Cockaygne*.

ss 55 Tell me why the sun is red in the evening.
I tell you, because it looks on hell.
ss 56 Tell me why does the sun shine so red in the morning.
I tell you, because it doubts whether it can or cannot illuminate this
earth as it is commanded.

AR 7 Tell me why the sun shines so red in the early morning.
       I tell you, because it comes up from the sea.

AR 8 Tell me why the sun is so red in the evening.
       I tell you, because it looks down on hell.

II

These questions about the redness of the sun are not paralleled in the extant dialogue literature and it is most convenient to comment on the variant answers as a group.

The statement that the setting sun is red because it looks on hell (ss 55, AR 8) is found in Jewish lore: 'Dawn is a reflection of the roses of paradise; the evening twilight of the fire of hell' (cited by Utley, *Chy*, 65, from Ginzberg v 37). Hell in the west is implied in the *Visio Pauli* 31 (James, 542).

The reasons for the redness of the rising sun are less easy to parallel. Certainly (as in AR 6), to medieval people, the sun moving around the fixed earth, came up from the sea, Oceanus, which was believed to encompass the earth. As Isidore says: 'Sol oriens per meridiem iter habet, qui post-quam ad occasum venerit, et Oceano se tinxerit, per incognitas sub terra vias vadit, et rursus ad orientem recurrit' (*Etymologiae* III.lii.1, cf *De natura rerum* XVII.2). When Isidore here says 'et Oceano se tinxerit' he is taking up a point made by Ambrose (*Hexaemeron* II.iii.14, but deriving from Basil) that the sun absorbs water from the sea: 'Unde frequenter et solem madidum atque rorantem. In quo evidens dat indicium, quod elimentum sibi aquarum ad temperiem sui sumserit' (Ambrose, ibid II.iii.13, cf Isidore *De natura rerum* XV.2). A moist sun is not a red sun necessarily, but it may be, and, in the spirit of the catch-questions, we speculate. If a well-nourished man, either from excessive drink or food, may have a flushed face, so presumably may the sun, by such analogy as accepted by humorists. Another possibility for a link is that the verb 'tingo,' used by Isidore above, can mean generally 'to wet, moisten, bathe' but specifically 'to soak in colour, to dye, to tinge.' In the same spirit we consider ss 56 where the rising sun is worried whether it can do its job, and recall that Isidore *Etymologiae* V.xxxi.3 noted that the sun was tired after its day's journey. Perhaps a similar tiredness of an animate sun after a night's journey is implied in this answer. But we doubt whether more than one medieval person, the man who asked the question, would have given this answer to the question of ss 56.

---

ss 57 Tell me the four waters which feed the earth.
I tell you, it is snow and water and hail and dew.

I:i
A. Quibus fluminibus irrigatur terra? E. .iiii. : aqua, grandine, nive, rore;
Daly-Suchier DAE (variant manuscript) 16, 113.

I:ii
Lærisvein spyr: 'Hver ero þesse iiii korn, er bleyta iordina?' Meistari
svarar: Vatn ok hagl, snior ok daugg [The pupil asks: What are the four
grains (seeds) which moisten the earth? The master answers: Water and
hail, snow and dew]; *Alfræði Íslenzk* III, 37.

I:iii
C.: Whech ben the foure waters þat weyen [bear] the erthe?
M.: That on is snow, the other is occian [ocean] waters, þe III^{de} is haill, þe
IIIIth is dewe; Horstmann *Questiones*, 287.

II
The variation in keywords in the questions of ss I:i and I:ii (waters, rivers,
grains, or seeds) to exactly the same answers may indicate, paradoxically,
an error in the answers and adjustments of question in two cases. The
repetition of 'water,' of the question, in the answer of ss points to the error
since 'water,' of both question and answer, is the common property of the
other three items of the answer 'snow, hail, dew.' We suggest, therefore,
that ss represents the original form of the question but that, at some stage of
transmission, a Latin 'aqua' of the answer became a substitute by error for,
probably, 'pluvia.' It probably read:
Tell me the four waters which feed the earth.
I tell you, snow, rain, hail, and dew.
The two other questioners reacted variously to the puzzling answer, the
Icelander noting, at least, the common properties of hail and dew, and the
metaphorical use of 'korn' (grain, but, also hail), the Latin writer probably
thinking rather of the four rivers of Eden (Genesis 2: 11–14) which were
said to irrigate the world.
The ME writer (I:iii) confirms the 'waters' of the question but reacts quite
differently to, presumably, 'water' which he saw in the answer, by defining
it as 'occian waters.' Then, we suggest, he changes the verb of the question

to fit the function of ocean waters, which were believed to 'bear' the earth. But he forgot or did not care about the nonsense he left for the three other liquids.

---

ss 58 Tell me who first established letters.
        I tell you, Mercury the giant.
AR 16 Tell me who first wrote letters.
        I tell you, Mercury the giant.

I:i
Adr. d.: Qui primus fecit litteras. Ep. r.: Mercurius gigans; Suchier AE₁ a 38, 14; cf Suchier AE₁ b 66, 17.

I:ii
Quis primus litteras didicit? Mercurius gigans et Enoch filius Iareth. Incertum est; Suchier JM₁ 32, 117.

I:iii
Quis primus litteras Gregas inuenit? Quononoel. Quis primus litteras Latinas inuenit? Carmitis nepha. Quis primus litteras Guticas inuenit? Goulphyla Gothorum episcopus; Förster *Gesprächbüchlein* 26, 29, 39, 347, 348.

I:iv
Quis primus fecit litteras? Seth; Suchier *L'Enfant sage* I 62, 268; cf IV 45, 295 and other examples passim.

I:v
Discipulus spyr: Hver gerdi fyrst bok eda stafi? Meistare svarar: Mercurius enn ille [The pupil asks: Who first made a book or letter? The teacher answers: Mercury the wicked]; *Alfræði Íslenzk* III, 37.

II
There were a number of people named Mercury/Hermes in the ancient world. But this Mercury, by his description as 'gigans' (I:i), 'gygand' (ss), is Hermes Trismegistus whose by-name was given, according to Isidore, 'ob

virtutem multarumque artium scientiam,' and was interpreted 'ter maximus' (*Etymologiae* VIII.xi.49). Clearly the by-name indicated intellectual stature but apparently it was taken more literally in the dialogue tradition. This Hermes was the one on whom was foisted the so-named hermetic writings.

Quintillian mentions Mercury as the originator of letters (*Institutio oratoria* III.7, 8) and, among Christian authorities, Tertullian also twice mentions that Mercury was reputed to have been the originator of letters among pagans (*De testimonio animae* V.5, CCSL I, 181; PL I, col 690; *De corona* 8, CSEL 70, 169; PL 2, col 107).

Among the various biblical and classical figures whom the question-masters cited as originators of writing, one, at least, has some historical claim to be celebrated as a man who 'invenit litteras,' that is Ulfilas the Goth (1:iii) who, according to the Greek ecclesiastical historians Philostorgios and Sokrates, invented the Gothic alphabet.

---

ss 59 Tell me what kinds of books and how many there are.

I tell you there are seventy-two canonical books in all; there are just as many nations in number and just as many disciples beside the twelve apostles.

A man's bones are in all two hundred and eighteen in number.

A man's veins (*or* sinews) are three hundred and sixty-five in all.

A man's teeth are thirty-two for all his life.

In twelve months there are fifty-two weeks and three hundred and sixty-five days. There are eight thousand and seven hundred hours in twelve months. In twelve months you must give to your servant seven hundred and twenty loaves besides morning and afternoon meals.

1:i

Dic mihi. Quanti libri intellecuntur in nouum testamentum? Respondit. Vigenti VII. Et in uetus testamentum lex Moysi XLV libri sunt. Iuxta septuagenta duae linguas, septuagenta duo libri intellecuntur; McNally *Questiones sancti Hysidori* 3, *Scriptores Hiberniae Minores*, 197 (CCSL 108B).

I:ii

Quot linguae? Septuaginta duae; *Collectanea Bedae* PL 94, col 544C; cf Wölfflin-Troll 16, 109 where the answer is: XXII.

I:iii

Veteris Testamenti sunt libri quinguaginta quinque, Novi autem viginti septem; *Collectanea Bedae* PL 94, col 542A.

I:iv

Interrogatio: Quot sunt linguę in mundo? R.: Septuagintę duę. Int.: Cur non plures uel pauciores? R.: Propter tres filios Noe: Sem. Cham. & [I]afeht; Sem habuit filios xxvii; Cham habuit filios xxx; Iafeth habuit filios xv. His simul iunctis fiunt lxx duę; *Hyde Register … Liber Vitae* 168.

I:v

Quod sunt ossa hominis? Numerorum CCXVIII. Numerus uenarum CCCLXII; Baesecke *Vocabularius*, 6.

I:vi

Man hafað bana twa hundred and nigontine and he hafað æddrena þreo hundred and fife and sixti and swa fæla daga beoð on twelf monðum [A man has two hundred and nineteen bones and he has three hundred and sixty five veins and there are as many days in twelve months]; Napier *Anglia* XI/4, 6.

I:vii

On oðrum monþe þa ædron beoð geworden on lxv *and* þreo hundræd scytran *and* lengran hi beoð todælede and þæt blod þonne floweð on þa fet *and* uppan þa handa [In the second month the veins are formed; they are separated into three hundred and sixty five, shorter and longer, and the blood then flows into the feet and up into the hands]; T.O. Cockayne *Narratiunculæ Anglice conscriptæ* (London, J.R. Smith 1861) 49, printing a piece on the gestation of a baby from ms Cotton Tiberius A iii, fol 38b ('recte' 40v). Cockayne reprints the text (used above) in his *Leechdoms, Wortcunning and Starcraft of Early England* (London, Longmans 1866) III, 146.

I:viii

XXXII teth, that beþe full kene,
CC bonys and nyntene,
CCC vaynys syxty and fyve,

Euery man haþe, that is a-lyve.
Förster 'Kleiner mittelenglische Texte' 215.

II

The series of assertions which conclude ss give the impression of being material added at some stage rather than the conclusion of the ss dialogue. Such gathering and presentation of scraps of information is not uncommon, as Napier illustrated in his paper 'Altenglische Kleinigkeiten' *Anglia* XI (1889), by printing such snippets.

The first three items (on canonical books, nations, and disciples) are sometimes linked elsewhere as here. Isidore, *De ecclesiasticis officiis* I.xi.7 (PL 83, cols 746–7) says: 'Hi sunt libri canonici septuaginta duo, et ob hoc Moyses elegit presbyteros qui prophetarent. Ob hoc et Jesus Dominus noster septuaginta duos discipulos praedicare mandavit. Et quoniam septuaginta duae linguae in hoc mundo erant diffusae, congrue providit Spiritus sanctus, ut tot libri essent quot nationes, quibus populi ad percipiendam fidei gratiam aedificarentur.' In OE, Ælfric (*Heptateuch*, 69–70) links all three in a similar manner to Isidore, and associates nations with disciples in *Sigewulfi Interrogationes* ll.375–8 (ed. Maclean, *Anglia* 7 (1884) 40).

For a discussion of some of the problems relating to the number of canonical books, see Cassiodorus *De institutione divinarum litterarum* 12–13 (PL 70, cols 1123–5), and of the seventy-two nations see the commentary to ss 14. The number of disciples is scriptural (Luke 10:1).

The number of bones in the human skeleton is approximately right, according to medical colleagues who, nevertheless, point out that it has been difficult to decide what is an individual bone. Teeth however can be counted and the number is correct. The figure, 365, for the veins or sinews is less realistic. We suggest that it derives from the Irish habit of using this figure to indicate totality in contexts where a precise or naturalistic figure cannot be obtained. The Hiberno-Latin *Liber de Numeris* speaking of Adam, says: 'et ... ossibus majoribus et minoribus constitutum, conjuncturis principalibus numero CCCLXV. Aliis vero minoribus vix invenitur numerus. Similiter et venis principalibus CCCLXV, minores vero venae innumerabiles sunt' (PL 83, col 1295C). For more examples of this concept in an Irish context see Binchy *Ériu* 19, 58–9, Stokes *RC* 12, 68 ff, and Calder 150; for further discussion of the anatomical information in this question see G. Eis 'Der anatomische Merkspruche des angelsächsischen Salomon und Saturn' in *Forschungen zur Fachprosa* (Bern and München, Franke Verlag 1971), 9–11. The most interesting parallel which Eis cites is a few verses from the 12th century *Schola salernitana, sive de conservanda valetudine praecepta metrica*:

Ossibus ex denis bis centenisque novenis
constat homo, denis bis dentibus, et duodenis,
et ter centenis decies sex quinque venis. (Eis 10)

The information on hours in a year probably records an error of scribal omission, not of multiplication. The number should be 8760 not 8700. But the reference to the rations for a servant, 720 loaves in twelve months and two meals a day, is more interesting. We suggest first the probability of scribal error in number 720, for 730, as the annual figure, which would be at the rate of two loaves a day, since it is unlikely that a cataloguer would be concerned with a five-day fast. If this is so, the statement may have a relationship with the rations prescribed for monks in the Rule of St Benedict. In cap 39 this suggests two meals and a pound weight of bread as a daily ration, but the monks engaged in hard physical labour were to get more, according to the abbot's discretion. If the pound of bread were equivalent to one loaf this extra ration for the labourers could be the basis for the statement in ss. But, obviously, if the OE 'loaf' were half a pound in weight the ss statement could refer to the ordinary ration for monks.

Adrian said to Ritheus:
AR 1 Tell me how long Adam was in Paradise.
   I tell you, he was thirteen years.
AR 2 Tell me on what day he sinned.
   I tell you, on Friday, and he was previously created on that day, and
   he later died on that day, and because of this Christ later suffered on
   that day.
SS 16 Tell me how long Adam lived in Paradise.
   I tell you ... and on the ... he tasted the fruit of the forbidden fig-tree,
   and that on Friday, and because of that he was in hell five thousand
   two hundred and twenty-eight years.

I:i

Adam vixit annos quindecim in paradiso, Eva quatuordecim, alii dicunt
septem, sine uxore quadraginta dies. Die sexto manducavit Adam de ligno
scientiae boni et mali, decimo quinto anno aetatis suae; *Collectanea Bedae*
PL 94, col 547D.

I:ii

A. In qua die clamavit diabolus de ligno in paradiso quando seduxit Evam?
E. In sexta feria hora sexta et in ipsa die conceptus est et crucifixus est
Christus; Suchier AE_1a 101, 19.

I:iii

Quod annis fuit per prevaricationem in paradiso? Dimidium. Qua hora
comedit fructum? Per horam terciam, et ad horam nonam eiectus est de
paradiso (cf Suchier AE_2 13, 31). Quod annos fuit in inferno? V. milia.
ccxxviii; Suchier JM_2 11, 124.

II

AR 1, AR 2, and SS 16 comment on Adam in paradise and in hell after his
death, but the only relevant scriptural information is that he was created on
the sixth day (Genesis 1:26 and 31) and that he ate the forbidden fruit
(Genesis 3:6). The remaining ideas about his time in paradise, the kind of
fruit, the naming of the day of creation and fall, its association with the
crucifixion and the period of Adam's stay in hell are found in statements
made by previous Christian and/or rabbinic writers. These views obviously
interested other compilers of lists as illustrated under I above.

No text which we have seen states that Adam was in paradise thirteen years, as in AR 1, but we have noted that numerals, particularly Roman numerals, facilitate error, and there appears to be no dominant tradition about the period of his stay. Pseudo-Athanasius, in his *Quaestiones ad Antiochum Ducem*, answers a question 'Quantum temporis in paradiso mansit Adam?' with 'Rem de qua non consentiunt Patres proponis. Alii enim sex menses, alii diutius mansisse existimant, alii tot horas (nec amplius) quot Dominus in ligno crucis mansit, quod arbitror verius esse. At alii vero novem tantum horas' (PG 28, col 629).

The variant opinions noted by Pseudo-Athanasius, and more, are attested in texts of the Middle Ages. A seven-hour period is recorded in a twelfth-century OE note: 'Me [Methodius] cwæð þæt hi wære inne neorxnawange vii tide' (Ælfric *Heptateuch*, 419). Peter Comestor agrees with this: 'Quidam tradunt eos fuisse in paradiso septem horas' (*Hist. schol.*, *Liber Genesis* xxiv); so too does Dante:

'Nel monte che si leva più da l'onda
fu'io, con vita pura e disonesta,
de la prim'ora a quella che seconda,
come'l sol muta quadra, l'ora sesta'

[On the mountain which rises highest above the sea I lived pure, then guilty, from the first hour to that which follows the sixth, when the sun changes quadrant]; *Paradiso* XXVI, 139–42.

The period (7 hours) is noted also in *Sydracke and Boccus* and Andrew of Wyntoun (Kemble, 208). According to Ginzberg V, 106, some church fathers and rabbinic writers agree that Adam sinned on the first day of his creation, so that would be a matter of hours. But, as in AR 1, years are suggested in the OE snippet printed by Napier *Anglia* XI/1, 1 which says that Adam sinned 'in the sixteenth year from his creation' (cf 1:i above). Even days occur, in the Irish *Book of Lecan* (15 days, see Seymour, *PRIA* 36, C, 127).

The naming of the fruit as from a fig-tree is more commonly attested. That same Pseudo-Athanasius answers the question 'Quale lignum fuit, cujus fructus Adamus comedit?' with 'Nec hac iure consentiunt Patres, et merito. Quod enim divina Scriptura sponte occultavit, nemo exquisite potuit dicere. Unde alii ficum fuisse illum fructum putant; alii fructum spiritalem, alii Evae contemplationem. Nonnullis etiam videtur nihil in paradiso comedisse Adamus. Forte tamen verior est prima sententia quae ficum fuisse defendit, quia scilicet huius foliis usi sunt primi parentes ad se tegendum [Genesis 3:7] et quod postea ficus a Christo maledicta fuerit [Matthew 21:19]' (PG 28, col 629). Isidore of Pelusium also chooses the fig (PG 78, col 214) saying that he had the information 'a senibus sapientibus.' One of these could have been the *Apocalypse of Moses* (20:4; Charles II, 146). But the choice and the reasons of Pseudo-Athanasius appear in the Hiberno-Latin *Liber de ordine creaturarum* X.13 (PL 83, col 941), a text which was known in Anglo-Saxon England (see Cross *Anglia* 90, 132–40). The tree is also a fig-tree in the exemplar of Vercelli Homily XIX, as indicated by variant texts (noted under ss 12, I:ii). An edited version (XIX, fol 107r) reads: '*And* him God forgeaf þæt hie ealles geweald agan moston þe on eorðan wære butan anes treowes bleda þe is genemned lifes treow (*and* we hit nemnað fic treow]; þæt treow ys on middan neorxnawange.'

The linking of Adam, the 'old man,' and Christ, the 'new man,' is commonplace among exegetes who seize on all possible details of connection. Irenaeus *Contra Haereses* V.23 (PG 7, col 1185) for example, has our detailed connection: 'The Lord, therefore ... underwent his sufferings on the day preceding the Sabbath, that is, the sixth day of creation, on which day man was created.' Among Anglo-Saxons, Bede *In Marcum* XV, 33 (CCSL 120, 634, PL 92, col 290) noted: 'et qua hora primus Adam peccando mortem huic mundo inuexit eadem hora secundus Adam mortem moriendo destrueret;' cf Ælfric, *De passione domini* (*CH* II, 260).

For the period which Adam spent in hell see the illustrative note to ss 17.

AR 3 Tell me from which side of Adam did our Lord take the rib from which he made woman.
I tell you, from the left.

I:i
Unde facta est Eva? De costibus Ade; Suchier JM I 4, 120.

I:ii
D. Où la premiere femme fut-elle créée? R. Dans le paradis terrestre d'une côte d'Adam.
D. Pourquoi fut-elle faite de la côte d'Adam? R. Afin qu'ils fussent par dilection tout d'un cœur et d'une même affection; Suchier *L'Enfant sage* XIX 17–18, 542–3.

II

Scripture (Genesis 2:21) does not identify the position of the rib from which Eve was formed, but others speak of the left side. In 'The Mysteries of John the Apostle and the Holy Virgin' (Budge *Coptic Apocrypha*, 251) it is noted that 'she [Eve] was, of a surety, hidden in the rib of the left side.' In OE, Vercelli Homily XIX (fol 107r) says: '*and* Dryhten ælmigtig of Adames wynstran sidan genam þæt ribb þe he þæt wif of geworhte þe Eua hatte.' And finally a tenth-century medical text preserved in Monte Cassino Codex LLXCVII speaks of the descent of the 'due vene maiores per duo latera spinalis ... usque dum veniant *ad costam que dicitur Eva*' (*Bibliotheca Casinensis, Florilegium* V.314; italics ours). We assume that the rib 'which is called Eva' is on the lower left-hand side and that the ascetic attitude toward Eve, which would wish to connect her with the 'sinister' side, influenced the OE question. The French question (1:ii, which is translated into sixteenth-century English, XVIII 19–20, 529) is irrelevant but interesting in showing a favourable attitude to Eve.

AR   4   Tell me where our Lord sat when he made heaven and earth and all creations.

I tell you, on the wings of the winds.

See the commentary on SS 1.

AR   5   Tell me where the soil is on which the sun never shone, nor the moon, and on which the wind never blew, at any hour of the day, neither before nor after.

I tell you, the soil is in the Red Sea over which the people of Israel went from the captivity of Egypt.

1:i

Discipulus spyr: Seg mier til landz þess, er alldri skijnn sool aa eda tungle ok blaess vindr sky. Meistare svarar: þar er land þad, er I[s]raelis lydur geingu þurrum fotum um rauda haf [The pupil asks: Tell me about that land where the sun never shines nor the moon and the wind blows the cloud. The teacher answers: There is that land, where the people of Israel went over with dry feet through the Red Sea]; *Alfræði Íslenzk* III, 36.

1:ii

Quę fuit terra quę nunquam visit solem nec ventum nisi in una hora diei, nec antea nec postea? Terra est quam populus Israeliticus in mari rubro siccis plantis calcavit; Suchier JM J 5, 122. Cf Suchier AE₁b 46, 16 and *Collectanea Bedae* PL 94, col 540, where the same ideas are presented, apart from 'siccis plantis,' in almost the same words.

1:iii

Qui terra semel vidit solem? Viam maris; Suchier JM C 11, 109.

II

This item depends on the scriptural description (Exodus 14: 22) of the crossing of the Red Sea by the Israelites, but a transmitter, and thus the OE scribe, has made nonsense of the idea by muddling the Latin phrase 'nisi in una hora diei' (except for one hour of the day). The Icelandic version of this question similarly confuses the riddle by omitting the crucial exception.

AR 6 Tell me where the sun shines at night.
I tell you, in three places; first on the belly of the whale which is called Leviathan, and, in the second period, it shines on Hell, and the third period it shines on the island which is called Glið, and the souls of holy men rest there until Doomsday.

1:i

Quid agit sol in nocte? Sex horas illuminat gentem illam ubi habitatio peccatorum est; tres horas illuminat mare infernum; tres horas illuminat *emanechan*, ubi justorum habitatio est; et postea insurgit et sic illuminat totum mundum; Suchier *L'Enfant sage* I 103, 271.

1:ii

Item dic mici sol lucet in nocte aut non? R. Lucet. Dic mici quo ordine? R. iii oras in abissum, iii in mare, iii. in Nataleon civitate et iii in Jherusalem, deinde revertitur in oriente ora prima diei et lucet diei oras xii^m et revertitur in occasum; Omont *Interrogationes* II 28–9, 65.

I:iii
L'emperador li demana: Que fa lo sol de nit? L'infant respos: Ores hi ha que illumina porgatori, e ores hi ha que illumina la mar, e puixs ix en orient e illumina tot lo mon [The emperor asks him: What does the sun do at night? The child replies: For a time it shines on purgatory and for a time it shines on the sea, and then it goes in the east and shines on all the world]; Suchier *L'Enfant sage* IV 59, 296; cf also V 59, 325, and other examples passim.

I:iv
Ubi es sol in nocte? In ventre coeti qui dicitur Leviathan; Suchier JM J 10, 123.

I:v
The sages of the Hebrews asked: 'Tell us of those twelve plains that are under the flanks of the earth and against which the sun shines for light every night; since knowledge thereof is obscure to us.' Then the Evernew Tongue answered: 'This is [the way] the sun goes in the eve of every night. In the first place he illumines the transmarine stream with tidings of the eastern waters. Then he illumines the ocean of fire at night and the seas of sulphurous fire around the red tribes. Then he shines on the hosts of the children in the pleasant fields, who send the cry towards heaven for dread of the beast that kills many thousands of hosts under waves in the south. Then he shines on the mountain with streams of fire which traverse (?) the ... plains, with the hosts of guardian (demons) in them. Then shine the ribs of the great beast at which the four and twenty champions arise ... glen of the torments. Thereafter he (the sun) shines over against the awful, many-trooped fence which has closed around ... of the hell-dwellers in the north. He shines in the dark glens with the sad streams over their faces. So he illumines the ribs of the Beast that distributes the many seas around the flanks of the earth on every side, that sucks in the many seas again till it leaves the shores dry on every side. Then he illumines the fiery mountain which has been formed of the fire of Doom ... every element. Then he illumines the many beasts who, from the beginning of the world, sleep the tearful sleep in the Glen of the Flowers. Then he shines on the gloomy tearful plain with the dragons that were set under the mist. Then he illumines the flocks of the birds, which sing together the many melodies in the Glens of the Flowers. Thereafter he shines on the radiant plains with the wine-flowers that irradiate the Glen. After this he shines against Adam's

Paradise, till it rises up from the east in the morning' Stokes *Evernew Tongue* §§65–80, 125.

II

The question 'where does the sun go at night' reflects a genuine cosmological problem. Isidore suggests that night comes either because the sun is weary after its day's work and quenches its own fire or alternatively that 'eadem vi sub terras cogitur, qua super terras pertulit lumen, et sic umbra terrae noctem facit' (*Etymologiae* v.xxxi.3). The OE question-master and the authors of the Latin and vernacular parallels above accept the second of these options and describe the course of the sun 'sub terras.' The problem which this question raises was a real issue for Anglo-Saxons who were concerned with cosmology, as for example the poet of 'The Order of the World' ll.76–81 who states that no man alive knows about the sun's journey at night under the waters.

The answer to this question in AR, however, implies that the sun moves from west to east under the earth and, in its course, shines on the realm of the dead, since hell is one of the places illuminated, and what is clearly the earthly paradise is lighted at the sun's rising in the east to begin a new day. Hell appears under various names in the parallels as 'habitatio peccatorum' (I:i), 'abissus' (I:ii), and as different places of 'sadness' in the *Evernew Tongue* (I:v). The earthly paradise is identified in the OE partly because 'the souls of holy men rest there until Doomsday,' as in the OE prose text of *The Phoenix* (the phoenix lives in the earthly paradise), printed in N.F. Blake's *The Phoenix*, 94–6, and in *The Apocalypse of Paul* (James, 536), where the souls of the righteous go after death to the earthly paradise which is situated by Oceanus, the river-sea surrounding the earth. Its description in OE as 'an island' is also a distinguishing feature as noted in the OE poem on *The Phoenix* l.9 and as indicated in Patch's comment (in *The Other World*, 153) that the earthly paradise often had physical features which emphasized its inaccessibility to men such as its frequently being an island. Two of the parallels also choose the earthly paradise as the last place on the sun's journey: 'emanechan ubi justorum habitatio est' (I:i), and 'Adam's paradise' (I:v). It must also be certain that the 'Jherusalem' of I:ii is not the earthly Jerusalem.

A problem, however, is the name of the place which Franciscus Junius read as 'glið,' but which we now read as gl[i]ð. We speculate that since it describes the earthly paradise this should be a word with 'good' meaning.

At a meeting of the Dublin Mediaeval Society, Mr Pheifer of Trinity College suggested that there could have been a sequence of scribal errors from OE 'gliew, gleow' (joy, delight). This is a possibility since ð and þ are interchangeable symbols in OE texts and scribal errors on þ and ƿ (= w) are exemplified in mss. The name 'emanechan' may be a parallel but if, as Suchier suggests (*L'Enfant sage*, 276), it is based on the Hebrew word 'menachem' it is not a precise parallel, since Suchier notes its meaning as 'tröster' (comforter, consoler).

We are left with the 'belly of the whale Leviathan' which is exactly paralleled in ı:iv, but without helpful identification. Nevertheless the other parallels offer water in which it might gambol, 'mare infernum' (ı:i), 'in mare' (ı:ii), 'la mar' (ı:iii), which are clearly the waters under the earth (Genesis 1:7). But the great fish of Jonah is regarded as a figure of hell in scripture (Jonas 2:3) and the image of a monster with gaping mouth swallowing sinners is a commonplace of medieval art. If there is meant to be a distinction between the 'whale's belly' and hell it is just possible that it is an attempt to distinguish between the place of purgatory and hell, as often in medieval authors.

AR 7 Tell me why the sun shines so red in the early morning.
    I tell you, because it comes up from the sea.
AR 8 Tell me why the sun is so red in the evening.
    I tell you, because it looks down on hell.

See the commentary on ss 55, 56.

ı:i
The emperour þan seide: Sekirleche,
þan is a sterre wele moche
þat hedir doun to grounde ritht
ʒeueþ to vs so moche light.

The childe þan answerde anone:
þe leest sterre of eueryone
Is as moche, as men rede,
As all myddelerth of lenþe and brede;
þan is the mone, I telle the,
As moche as sterres þre;
þan is þe sonne, I telle þe sone,
As moche as twys þe mone.
Suchier, *L'Enfant sage* xiv (Ipotis) c 10, 470.

i:ii
Quid est parvus in aspettu et cruciet mundum? Sol; Suchier JM I 31, 121.

i:iii
Quid est aspectum parvissimum, tota[m] contegit terram et totam illuminat orbem? Sol; Wilmanns *Fragebüchlein* 3, 167. Cf *Alfræði Íslenzk* III, 38.

i:iv
Quid est quod aspectu totam terram illuminat, quod numquam crescit nec decrescit? – Sol; Suchier JM₂ 45, 126.

II
The size of the sun was a concern of Hexaemeral writers, for example Ambrose *Hexaemeron* IV.6.25–6 [CSEL 32.1, 132–3; PL 14, col 214), who drew on Basil's work for his comment. Ambrose, however, demonstrates the size by stating that the sun is seen from every country, an idea presented in the riddling question (i:iii). But, before his proof, he does comment: 'Possumus accipere non tam aliorum comparatione magna, quam suo munere, ut est caelum magnum, et mare magnum. *Nam et magnus sol, qui conplet orbem terrarum suo calore*, vel luna suo lumine, nec solum terras, sed etiam aerem hunc et mare, caelique faciem' (IV.6.25, copied almost verbatim by Bede, *in Genesim* I.i.16, CCSL 118A, 17; PL 91, col 23; our italics). A question-master who knew such a writer on creation and also the Vulgate Psalm 18:7 on the course of the sun: 'A summo coelo egressio ejus: et occursus ejus usque ad summum ejus; *nec est qui se abscondat a calore ejus*,' could easily shift the emphasis to the ubiquity of the sun's heat as in AR 9.

AR 10 Tell me what the sun is?
    I tell you, the magician Astriges said it was burning stone.

II

There is no parallel to this answer in the printed dialogues but there are other questions on the sun, and this could be a rare addition. The reason may have been the concern whether heavenly bodies were animate. Isidore, *De natura rerum* XXVII.1–2, (PL 83, cols 1000–1), proves from scripture to his own satisfaction that the sun has a soul and raises the further question of what will happen to the heavenly bodies at the final resurrection. In his *Enchiridion* XV.58, Augustine does not commit himself, but refers to those who think that the sun, moon, and stars are inanimate bodies (CCSL 46, 80–1, PL 40, cols 259–60). But in *De civitate dei* XVIII.41 he recalls the Greek philosopher Anaxagoras who 'solem dixit esse lapidem ardentem' and notes that he was accused by the pagans for this belief. Augustine could have been the transmitter for this information to the creator of our question, but Anaxagoras' theory was well known. Anaxagoras had predicted a fall of meteoric stone to prove his theory and this event was recorded in various kinds of literature, for example, in the *Chronicle* of Eusebius/Jerome (ed Fotheringham, 192), in Pliny, *Naturalis Historia* II.lix.149 and in Diogenes Laertius, *Lives of philosophers* II.10.

    The name 'Astriges' is a problem. The name in AR 10 is that of the pagan king who martyred the apostle Bartholomew, 'Astriges' (Ælfric *CH* I, 468, 524), so our 'Astriges' could have been a scribal substitution. It is nevertheless clear why an authority on a problem of this kind should be called a 'dry' since 'dry' is a gloss on 'magus,' and the scriptural magi who followed the star were the most famous astrologers known to early medieval Europe.

AR 11 Tell me what the glory of the living man is.
    I tell you, the blood of the dead one.

I:i

L'emperador li demana : Qual es la cosa que mes desplau al hom? L'infant respos : La vida de son enemich [The emperor asks him: What is the thing that displeases a man most? The child answers: The life of his enemy];

Suchier *L'Enfant sage* IV 37, 294; cf also ibid IX 53, 403; XII 26, 432; XIII 58, 458.

II

We cite the sanguinary question and answer from the Romance dialogues (I:i) even though it is unlikely that this exchange is really an analogue of our question. If our question is simply a secular statement of the ethic of blood vengeance, the Romance parallels illustrate that similar proverbial ideas were assimilated into the dialogue tradition. But in the religious context of the AR dialogue a secular proverb (particularly one which violates elementary norms of Christian morality) seems strikingly incongruent. We therefore speculate that what we might have here is a transformation or adaptation of an originally religious statement expressing the conception that the blood of Christ crucified is the glory of every living Christian.

AR 12 Tell me which son first avenged his father in his mother's womb?
I tell you, the son of the serpent, because the mother killed the father before and the children kill the mother afterwards.

I:i
Qui uindicant patrem mortuum, antequam nati fuerint? Hoc est serpentes. Quia pater mortuus fuit generando per linguam, et filii occidunt matrem nascendo quia rumpendo matrem nascunt serpentes; McNally *Prebiarum* 76 (*Scriptores Hiberniae Minores*, 167 (CCSL 108B).

I:ii
Dic mihi qui sunt filii qui vindicaverunt patrem suum in utero matris suae? Filii viperae; *Collectanea Bedae* PL 94, col 540D; cf also *Alfræði Íslenzk* III, 37.

I:iii
Quis vindex est patris in utero matris? Vipera que effodit latera matris; Suchier JM₁ 57, 118. Cf also Suchier JM J 4, 122; Omont *Interrogationes* II 23, 64.

II

This question is based on a widely diffused medieval and Renaissance belief that the male viper is killed by the female after he has succeeded in impregnating her and that the female viper in turn is destroyed by her own offspring who must gnaw through the flesh of their own mother in order to be born. See, for example, Pliny *Naturalis historia* x.lxxxii.170 or Isidore *Etymologiae* XII.iv.10–11. Shakespeare knows of the belief as in *Pericles* I.i: 'I am no viper, yet I feed/On mother's flesh which did me breed.' But, more relevantly, the viper's habits are the subject of one of the *Ænigmata* (no xv) of Symphosius: 'Non possum nasci, si non occidero matrem,/Occidi matrem, sed me manet exitus idem./Id mea mors patitur quod iam mea fecit origo (*Collectiones ænigmatum* pars II, CCSL 133 A, 636). The AR question however is not pointed since it substitutes the OE term 'næddre' which is equivalent to the similarly general word 'serpens' of the Hiberno-Latin example (I:i) not to the specific term 'vipera' of the other dialogues (I:ii, iii).

AR 13 Tell me which bishop was first in the old law before the advent of Christ.
     I tell you, Melchisedech and Aaron.
AR 14 Tell me which bishop was in the new law.
     I tell you, Peter and James.

I:i

Dic mihi quis primus sacerdos in Veteri Testamento fuit? Melchisedech. In Novo? Petrus et Jacobus, frater Domini; *Collectanea Bedae* PL 94, cols 539D–40D.

I:ii

A. Quis primus fuit episcopus in Veteri Testamento? E. Abiud.
A. Quis in Novo? E. Petrus et Iacobus, frater Domini, quia matres amborum erant sorores.
A. Quis fuit primus sacerdos? E. Melchisedech et Aron; Suchier AE₁ b 72–4, 18.

I:iii

  8 Quis primus clericus? Petrus.
  9 Quis primus diaconus? Sanctus Stephanus.

10 Quis primus ante diluuium obtullit holocaustum? Abel.
11 Quis post diluuium (primus) obtullit holocaustum? Habraham.
12 Quis primus panem et vinum obtulit in sacrificiom? Melchisedec sacerdos.
13 Quis primus martir ante diluuium? Habel.
14 Quis primus martir post adventum Christi? Sanctus Stefanus.
15 Quis primus episcopus? Sanctus Iacob.
(Baesecke *Vocabularius*, 7; cf Omont *Interrogationes* III 8, 9, 10, 12, 70–1 for some parallels to this list.

I:iv
Quis primus episcopus fuit in Veteri Testamento? Abiuth. Quis in Novo? Petrus et Iacobus, frater Domini; Suchier JM₂ 36–7, 126.

I:v
Quis prius sacerdus fuit semper ipsem melcesedic. Quis primus clerecos factus est petros; Lowe *Bobbio Missal*, 7. (These two questions are not in sequence.)

II

The variant forms of the questions and answers in the Latin lists may depend on varied applications of the Latin names 'sacerdos,' 'episcopus,' 'pontifex,' and, for the OE, on a dual application of the term 'the old law,' probably also on conflation and adaptation and perhaps on a desire to balance the answers.

Beginning with simple facts we can say that Melchisedech (Genesis 14:18) and Aaron (Exodus 28:1) are 'sacerdotes' (as in I:ii), the former being the first named priest of the Gentiles, the latter of the Israelites. Isidore, however, notes: 'initium quidem sacerdotii Aaron fuit. Quanquam et Melchisedech prior obtulerit sacrificium,' *De ecclesiasticis officiis* II.v.1, PL 83, col 780 (cf I:iii, no 12), thus giving priority to Aaron although recognising some claim of priority for Melchisedech. But 'caeterum Aaron primus *in lege* sacerdotale nomen accepit, primusque pontificale stola infulatus' (II.v.2), referring to Exodus 29 on the vesting and consecration of Aaron. Isidore continues: 'Quo loco contemplari oportet, Aaron summum sacerdotem fuisse id est, *episcopum*' (II.v.3). Thus to Isidore (and following him Ælfric in *Hirtenbriefe* ed Fehr, Latin 2.93, 46, OE 2.119, 112) Aaron was the first bishop within 'the old law,' that is, the law of Moses for the Israelites. But 'the old law' meaning 'in Veteri Testamento' allows the question in 1:i to be answered by Melchisedech as the first priest. It is possible, for the answer in AR, that Aaron and Melchisedech were associated as first priests, then, with the naming of Aaron as 'episcopus,' Melchisedech remained with him in the double answer. There would also be some reason for Melchisedech's elevation, however, in the words of Paul (?) about Christ: 'appellatus a Deo *pontifex* juxta ordinem Melchisedech' (Hebrews 5:10).

For the New Testament Peter is clearly the first 'clericus' (as in 1:iii, no 8) as the one first called by Christ (Matthew 4:18 etc) and because of his primacy over the apostles (Matthew 10:2 etc). But Isidore, in the same discussion, notes: 'In Novo autem Testamento post Christum sacerdotalis ordo a Petro coepit. Ipsi enim primum datus est *pontificatus* in Ecclesia Christi' (II.v.5), referring to Matthew 16:18–19 on Peter, the rock of the church who is given the keys of the kingdom of heaven. James, the son of Alphaeus, the brother of Christ, was the first bishop of Jerusalem (Eusebius *Eccles. Hist.* II.23.1, I, 56) and, as Ælfric says, 'he succeeded to Christ's seat after his passion' (*CH* II, 298). James chiefly served the Jewish community, while Peter, who received the office of 'pontifex' in Isidore's words above, was bishop of the whole church and later, as bishop of Rome, served the Gentiles. Whether fortuitously or not there is a balance of 'bishop' of Jew and Gentile for the Old and New Testament.

AR 15 Tell me which man first prophesied.
    I tell you, Samuel.

1:i
Adr*ianus* d*ixit*: Quis est qui primus fuit propheta? Ep*ictitus* r*espondit*: Samuel; Suchier AE₁ a 53, 15.

1:ii
Dic mihi. Qui[s] primis prophetauit? Respondit. Adam, quando dixit: *Hoc nunc hos ex ossibus meis et caro de carne mea*; McNally *Questiones* 53, *Scriptores Hiberniae Minores*, 204 (CCSL 108B); cf *Collectanea Bedae* PL 94, col 540D.

1:iii
Quis primus prophetavit in seculo? Gallus prophetans lucem; Suchier JM J 3, 122.

I:iv

Duo prophetae, quorum alter prophetavit post mortem, alter vero ante nativitatem, sunt Samuel et Joannes; *Collectanea Bedae* PL 94, col 544B.

II

Suchier's note (p 24) to the Latin parallel I:i refers to I Kings (I Samuel) 28:19, which records Samuel's actual prophecy when he was recalled after death by the woman of Endor for Saul. But it does not explain why Samuel could be regarded as the first 'propheta.' The letter of scripture, which is often a crucial factor in the dialogues, indicates that the word 'propheta' was applied to other men before Samuel, for example, Abraham (Genesis 20:7) and an unnamed man (Judges 6:8). The answer, Adam, of I:ii, to the question 'who first prophesied?' is more understandable since Adam speaks of a present and future situation in Genesis 2:23–4.

There are two possible reasons for the answer in I:i and AR. One is that the question originally made a further distinction: who first prophesied after death? – to which the answer could be Samuel. The statement of Pseudo-Bede (I:iv) indicates that Samuel was remembered in this way.

But, without our assuming an omission, Peter's reference in Acts 3:24 to 'omnes prophetae a Samuel et deinceps' and Paul's comment in Acts 13:20: 'et post haec dedit judices usque ad Samuel prophetam' could have provided the kind of scriptural support for the answer which the question-masters accepted.

AR 16 Tell me who first wrote letters.
        I tell you, Mercury the giant.

See the commentary on ss 58.

AR 17 Tell me who first planted vineyards, from which who first drank wine.
        I tell you, Noe.

See the commentary on ss 46.

AR 18 Tell me who was the first doctor.
     I tell you, he was called Aslerius.

I
We have seen no parallels in the dialogue literature.

II
Isidore asserts that Aesculapius was the first man to practise medicine
(*Etymologiae* IV.iii.1–2). Aesculapius (Greek, Asklepios), son of Apollo,
was educated by Chiron who taught him the art of medicine.

It is probable that the otherwise unattested 'Aslerius' is the result of
scribal variation and error. Various pennings of Franciscus Junius suggest
that he came to the same conclusion. Ms Junius 45 transcribes 'Aslerius' in
the text but has 'Asclepius, Aesculapius' in the right-hand margin as if
trying out the possibilities of scribal error. Ms Junius 61 has 'Asclepius' in
the text and 'Aesculapius' immediately below and between the lines. OE 'r'
for 'p' is a known scribal error, and 's' for 'sc' is an attested variation in
twelfth-century OE manuscripts (see textual note to ss 10).

For discussion of the legend of Aesculapius and his reputation in the
ancient and early Christian world see E.J. and L. Edelstein *Asclepius* 2 vols
(Baltimore: The Johns Hopkins University Press 1945).

AR 19 Tell me who are the two men in Paradise, and these continually
     weep and are sorrowful.
     I tell you, Henoch and Elias. They weep because they must come
     into this world and die, although hitherto they have long delayed
     death.

I:i
Adrianus: Quis fuit natus et non mortuus?

Respondit: Elyas et Enoch; Suchier *L'Enfant sage* I 17, 266; cf Wölflinn-Troll 7, 109; Wilmans *Fragebüchlein* 47, 169 (with John the Evangelist).

I:ii
Also the emperour hym demaunded: Who be those that shall never deye tyll unto the ende of the worlde? And the chylde answerde hym that it was Enoch and Helie, the whiche ben in the yate of paradys terrestre, holdyng every of them a swORde brennynge in theyr mouthes; Suchier *L'Enfant sage* XVIII 65, 534.

I:iii
Dic mici qui sunt duo vetus et nobo testamento, qui dormiunt in paradiso usque in odiernum diem? R /. Enoc et Elias; Enoc de vetus testamento, David de prophetas qui adventum Domini omnia pronuntiaberunt. De nobo et vetero testamento Elias est qui visu vidit Dominum et apostolis est; Omont *Interrogationes* II 67, 68.

II
Scriptural statements about Henoch and Elias caused traditions to be created about them. Henoch 'walked with God and was seen no more: because God took him' (Genesis 5:24), a text which Paul (?) explained as 'by faith Henoch was translated, that he should not see death' (Hebrews 11:5), and he was 'translated into paradise, that he may give repentance to the nations' (Ecclesiasticus 44:16). Elias 'went up by a whirlwind into heaven' (4 Kings 2:11, Vulgate), but was to return, 'behold, I will send you Elias, the prophet, before the coming of the great and dreadful day of the Lord' (Malachias 4:5). Common tradition, following scripture, placed them both in paradise (as in I:ii, iii above) defined as the earthly paradise by Gregory (*Homilia* 29 *in Evang.* s5, PL 76, col 1216) and others. Tradition also associated these men, and taking hints from scripture (above), identified them with the 'two witnesses' of Apocalypse 11:3, against whom 'the beast that ascendeth out of the abyss shall make war' (11:7) at the end of the world (as in Bede, *In Genesim*, II.v.23–4, CCSL 118A, 96, PL 91, cols 80–1; see also generally W. Bousset *The Antichrist Legend* trans. A.H. Keane (London, Hutchinson 1896), 27 note, and 203–8; and Wulfstan ed Bethurum, 284). The beast, or Antichrist, was to 'overcome them and kill them' (Apocalypse 11:7).

Their sorrow in their temporary resting place is not scriptural but may be assumed from their future fate, and is attested. It is stated early in the

Coptic History of Joseph the Carpenter XXXI (summarized in James, 86), and later in the Irish 'Fis Adamnáin,' 46, and it is elaborated in the Irish 'Dá brón flatha nime' ed and trans G. Dottin as 'Les deux chagrins du royaume du ciel' *RC* 21 (1900) 349–87. For a parodic treatment of this motif see the ME *Land of Cockaygne* ll7–156.

AR 20 Tell me where they live.
    I tell you, Malifica and Intimphonis; that is in Simfelda and in Sceanfelda.

I
There are no parallels in the dialogue literature.

II
We suspect some corruption in transmission here and our commentary is partially speculative. Traditionally, Enoch and Elias await their final death in the earthly paradise (see AR 19) but our text appears to record two locations. One of these, the association of 'Intimphonis' and 'sceanfelda,' can be explained by common tradition and by two helpful glosses which read: 'In Tempis, on scenfeldum' (Wright-Wülcker *Vocabularies*, 425, l 19 and 518, l 28). The second of these citations occurs in a sequence of glosses on Aldhelm's poem *De Virginitate*, speaking of Elias: 'Sed manet in tempis paradisi hectenus heros/Heliseum colit ut superis in sedibus Enoch' (ll272–3). The sequence of contacts between the glossed Aldhelm on Elias and Enoch and the one part of the AR answer are too many to be coincidental. We should not hold back from concluding that the original creator of the OE answer saw the Aldhelm comment in context but also glossed in this unusual way. Aldhelm's classical bent could allow him to use 'in tempis paradisi' as a name for the earthly paradise, since Tempe, originally a real valley in Thessaly, had become a name for a 'locus amoenus' wherever it might be (eg Virgil *Georgics* 2,469; Ovid *Fasti* 4,477). The glossator may, as Wülcker suggests (518 note 10), have 'interpreted the word as a general term' signifying 'bright fields,' or, as H.D. Meritt suggests, he may have been influenced by the nominal qualifier 'paradisi,' and he glossed in terms of his general conception of paradise (*Fact and Lore about Old English words* (Stanford, Stanford University Press 1954), 141).

It would now seem that 'malefica' is a Latin word glossed by an OE 'simfelda,' but, if so, both words are puzzling. 'Malefica' seems to be associated with words connected with 'malefacio' (do evil) such as 'maleficium' (noun; 'sin, vice, injury,' sometimes specifically connected with the magic arts), 'maleficus' (adj.). 'Maleficus' (noun) to describe magicians is used by Augustine (*De civitate dei* x, xi). In 'simfelda' the element 'sim' is not otherwise attested as a word or as a first element of a compound. But if 'malefica' and 'simfelda' are equated we might suggest that 'sim' is a scribal mistranscription of 'sinn' (for 'synn') meaning 'sin.' But why should Enoch and Elias, against the persistent tradition about them, live in a place described by 'malefica,' 'simfelda,' which appear to be places of sin? We think that there has been some omission and conflation to produce the AR statement here (cf comment on ss 25 and others). We speculate that the original creation consisted of two questions, one on where Enoch and Elias live, to be answered 'in tempis' etc, and another on a place where some malefactors remain. The OE scribe or a predecessor conflated the two to produce the partially puzzling answer of AR 20.

AR 21 Tell me why the raven is so black, that was white before.
　　I tell you, because it did not return again to Noe into the ark, from which it previously was sent.

I
Ocus do béndach Náe eisim de sin ocus ra mallach an fiach, ocus tuc Dia de sin a dath-sain forsan fiach ocus taitnem an fiaich fair-sim ar anumlacht in fiaich [And Noe blessed it (the dove), and cursed the raven; and for that, God gave the colour of the former to the raven, and the sheen of the raven to the other, for the insubordination of the raven]; *Lebor Gabála Érenn* I, 120–2, trans 121–3.

II
The origin of the various characteristics of animals is a common theme of folklore and the fact that baby ravens are born with white feathers which then turn black attracted attention and demanded explanation. Classical myth narrated by Ovid, *Metamorphoses* II, 536 ff, explained that the raven

was blackened for revealing the infidelity of Coronis, the nymph whom Apollo loved. Christians, however, found immediate basis for the real nigration of the bird in its disobedience (see AR 22) to Noah at the flood. Christian references include I:i and the ME poem *Purity* ll 455–6 which says that the raven which Noah cursed was 'þat rebel' and 'watz colored as þe cole' (cf also ll 467–8).

AR 22 Tell me why the raven atoned through obedience, which had previously sinned through pride.
I tell you, when it fed Elias, when it went into the wilderness and ministered to him.

I
Corvis [sic] vero ministrare Prophetae praecipitur, ut scilicet culpam, quam in diluvio commiserat in terra, purgare avis illa videretur, dum ut fidelis minister efficitur Eliae, qui negligens et fallax erat ante Noe; *De mirabilibus sacrae scripturae* II, 15, PL 35, col 2180D.

II
The raven (corvus) fails Noah when he is attempting to determine whether the flood has subsided (Genesis 8:7) and yet the raven sustains Elias in the desert (3 Kings 17:4–6). The discrepancy in the raven's role in these two episodes in the Old Testament provides the rationale for the AR question and the passage from the Hiberno-Latin *De mirabilibus sacrae scripturae*. This motif does not occur in any other of the dialogues, but Ambrose in commenting on Luke 3:1–20 does provide an allegorical gloss on the 'corvus' which accepts the explicit idea that the ravens who ministered to Elias were doing penance for their forefather's misdeeds in the ark: 'Sic etiam Helian corui cibo aduecticio et lucratiuo potu inter deserta pauerunt, ut indicio foret populos nationum taetro squalentes colore meritorum, qui ante cibum faetidis in cadaueribus requirebant, nunc de se aduecticiam prophetis alimoniam praebituros ...' (*Expositio Evangelii secundam Lucam* II 72; CSEL 32, 4, 79–80; PL 15, col 1660).

AR 23 Tell me where a man's intellect is.
       I tell you, in the head, and it goes out through the mouth.

1:i

Ubi est memoria? In sensu. Ubi est sensus? In cerebro. Cui non datur sensus, non datur et cerebrum; *Collectanea Bedae* PL 94, col 543D.

1:ii

Quid est cerebrum? Servator memoriae; Daly-Suchier DPA 23, 138. Cf also ibid, 32, 158: 'custos memorie.'

II

The term 'mod' in OE bore a wide range of meanings. We take it here as 'intellect' or 'mind' because this is a well-attested meaning for the word which makes explicable sense in this context, and this translation aligns AR 23 with the statement from the *Collectanea Bedae* (1:i). A passage from Ælfric both illustrates this sense of 'mod' and suggests how a man's head and his 'mod' might be associated: 'on halgum gewrite bið gelomlice heafod gesett for þæs mannes mode, forðan ðe þæt heafod gewissað þam oðrum limum swa swa þæt mod gediht ða geðohtas' [In holy scripture 'head' is very frequently put for man's 'mind,' because the head directs the other limbs as the mind devises the thoughts] (*CH* i, 612). Given our translation of the question, we suggest that it reflects classical and early medieval speculation about the location of man's cognitive faculties. Plato had situated the faculty of reason in the brain but Aristotle maintained it was situated in the heart. (On this problem see Charles Singer *A Short History of Anatomy and Physiology from the Greeks to Harvey* (New York, Dover 1956), 11–20). Both concepts were current during our period. Isidore favoured the heart, *Etymologiae* XI.i.117, but Macrobius, as one would expect from a Neo-Platonist, states in his *Commentarii in somnium Scipionis* that 'soli ergo homini rationem, id est vim mentis, infudit *cui sedes in capite est*' (1.14.10; italics ours). The question-masters, on the basis of our question and 1:i–ii, apparently preferred the Platonic (and correct) answer to this problem. As far as the final extension to our question is concerned, the assertion that 'mod' goes out through the mouth, we suggest a slightly cryptic reference to speech by which a man reveals his 'mod' to another.

AR 24 Tell me what creatures are sometimes female and sometimes male.
I tell you, Belda the fish in the sea, and Viperus the serpent and
Corvus the bird, that is, the raven.

1:i
Dic michi que sunt animalia que sunt aliquando femine aliquando masculi.
Scilicet lepus (hare) et mustella (weasel *or* lamprey) et vipera; Colker
'Anecdota Dublinensa,' 43.

II
The parallel to our question (from a brief dialogue in a thirteenth century
English ms) agrees with AR 24 on Viper, an agreement which is either the
result of common error or some tradition unknown to us. A certain Ar-
chelaus cited by Pliny (*Naturalis historia* VIII.lxxxi.218–19) says that hares
are bisexual, but 'lepus et mustella' are not our problem. Yet they offer us a
clue to our list, since both are among the unclean animals of the Old
Testament along with our 'corvus' (*Leviticus* 11:6, 15, 29). Scripture says
nothing about their change of sex, but one commentator on the unclean
animals, the anonymous author of the apocryphal Epistle of Barnabas, may
take us a stage further. The text offers moral interpretations on the animals
and, in an early Latin version, says 'nor shall you eat the *belua*,' which is
said to represent the adulterer or corrupter 'because that animal continually changes its sex and is at one time male and at another time female'
(Epistle of Barnabas x. 7; *The Apostolic Fathers* I, 377). The Greek text at
this point has the word for 'hyena' but the Latin rendering is permissible
since Jerome on Isaiah and Rufinus take 'belua' an alternative name for
hyena (see *TLL* sv 'belua'). The hyena, which was thought by others in
ancient times to be bisexual (Pliny *Naturalis historia* VIII.xliv.105), is
obviously no fish. Yet an explicable error may have arisen from a different
application of its equivalent 'belua,' normally a general name for 'beast'
including large sea-beasts such as dolphins and whales. But that 'belua' of
Barnabas is among the 'unclean' animals. We think that 'corvus,' which is
normally not a hermaphrodite, is attached because it is 'unclean' ('omne
corvini generis'; Leviticus 11:15; Deuteronomy 14:14). As to the 'viperus'
(sic), whose sexual habits are well-known (see AR 12), we can only say that
one other mediaeval writer (1:i) also thought it was bisexual. For whatever

reason, the answer has a pattern of one bisexual animal each from land, sea, and air.

AR 25 Tell me why the sea is salt.
    I tell you, because Moses threw the ten commandments of the old law into the sea, when he made the tablets, because the people of Israel were worshipping idols.

See the commentary on ss 42.

AR 26 Tell me what are the two feet which the soul must have.
    I tell you, the love of God and man, and if it has neither of them it will be lame.

I
We have found no parallels in the question lists.

II
This statement on the two feet of the soul is an easy one to explain for medieval English specialists who have been repeatedly informed by Professors Robertson and Huppé that the Augustinian doctrine of Charity governs all medieval poetic creation. The two precepts of 'caritas' (charity), or as it is rendered in OE 'soð lufu' (true love), are the love of God and man. We may turn to Augustine for the identification: 'Pes animae recte intelligitur amor; qui cum prauus est, vocatur cupiditas aut libido, cum autem rectus, dilectio uel caritas' (*Enarr. in Ps.* IX 15 on vs 16, CCSL 38, 66; PL 36, col 124); but more pointedly for the form of our question, when exhorting his congregation to run to Christ, Augustine says: 'Pedes tui, caritas tua est. *Duos pedes habeto; noli esse claudus. Qui sunt duo pedes? Duo praecepta dilectionis, Dei et proximi.* Istis pedibus curre ad Deum,

accede ad illum' (*Enarr in Ps.* XXXIII, Sermo II.10 on vs 6; CCSL 38 289; PL 36, col 313; our italics).

AR 27 Tell me on how many wings the soul must fly if it is to fly to heaven.
I tell you, four, wisdom, concord, fortitude and righteousness.

I:i
Quod sunt qua euolant [animae] sanctorum ad caelum? Quattuor. Prudentia, fortitudo, sapientia, temperantia; McNally *Prebiarum* 26, *Scriptores Hiberniae Minores*, 163 (CCSL 108B).

II
Sometimes the two wings of the soul are the precepts of charity, love of God and one's neighbour, as in Ælfric on the Greater Litany (*CH* II, 318), and in *Spicilegium Solesmense* II 475–7. But the four wings of the soul are clearly the four cardinal virtues in the Hiberno-Latin of I:i, and very nearly these four virtues in AR 27, as Ælfric translates the Latin terms in his address on the Nativity (*Lives of Saints* I, 20): 'prudentia þæt is snoternysse,' 'iustitia þæt is rihtwisnys,' 'temperantia þæt is gemetegung,' 'fortitudo þæt is strængð.' AR 27 agrees with two of these, 'rihtwisnys' and strængð,' and 'snoternysse' (Ælfric) and 'glæwnisse' (AR) are synonyms which translate Latin 'prudentia.' But 'geþwærnisse' (AR) normally means 'agreement' and is often glossed 'concordia.' This item may have been a substitution from another group.

AR 28 Tell me which man died and was not born, and after death was later buried in his mother's womb.
I tell you, that was Adam the first man, because the earth was his mother and he was buried afterwards in the earth.

See the commentary on ss 15.

AR 29 Tell me the name of city where the sun rises.
     I tell you, it is called Iaiaca.
AR 30 Tell me what it is called where it sets.
     I tell you, it is called Iainta.

See the commentary on ss 26, 27.

AR 31 Tell me what command was first.
     I tell you, the Lord said: Let there be light.

See the commentary on ss 2.

AR 32 Tell me what is heaviest for men on earth.
     I tell you, his Lord's anger.

See the commentary on ss 48.

AR 33 Tell me how many kinds of flying birds there are.
     I tell you, fifty-two.
AR 34 Tell me how many kinds of serpents there are on earth.
     I tell you, thirty-four.
AR 35 Tell me how many kinds of fish there are in water.
     I tell you, thirty-six.
AR 36 Tell me who formed the names of all the fish.
     I tell you, Adam the first man.
ss 51 Tell me how many kinds of flying birds there are.
     I tell you, fifty-four.
ss 52 Tell me how many kinds of fish there are in water.
     I tell you, thirty-six.

I

Quod genera sunt volicribus [sic] pinnatis?
Quinquaginta IIIIor.
Quod genera sunt serpentium? Triginta IIIIor.
Quod genera sunt piscium? Triginta sex.
Qui illorum nomina posuit? Adam.
Wilmanns *Fragebüchlein* 15, 33, 35–6, 168–9.

II
The following chart illustrates some of the various answers to these questions attested in the dialogue literature.

	number of birds	number of serpents	number of fish	number of quadrupeds
AR 33–5	52	34	36	–
SS 51–2	54	–	36	–
Wilmanns, 15, 33, 35–6	54	34	36	–
Omont *Interrogationes* I, 52–5	54	34	36	56
Collectanea Bedae PL 94, col 544C	37	36	–	–
Lowe *Bobbio Missal*, 7	20	24	–	–
Suchier AE₂ 37, 45, 33	54	24	–	–
Suchier JM C 31–2, 49–50, 110	54	33	35	54
Suchier JM I 23–5, 121	–	33	33	62
Suchier *L'Enfant sage* I 28, 35, 267	54	24	–	–
Alfræði Íslenzk III, 39	46	36	–	–
Wölflinn-Troll 24–7, 110	54	–	64	22

The figures for the number of the various kinds of creatures do not represent an attempt to distinguish various species from nature. A lexicographical study of the OE bird names, for example, lists over a hundred names for distinct species of birds in OE and because of the nature of the extant OE literature, many terms of this sort were probably never recorded. See C.H. Whitman 'The Birds of OE Literature' *JEGP* 2 (1898) 149–98

These questions derive rather either from vocabulary lists, as Suchier suggests (p 38), or perhaps from entries in Isidore himself, under the various headings. Isidore, *Etymologiae* XII (PL 82, col 435f), lists over thirty kinds of serpents, over fifty bird names and more than thirty species of fish. Counting names in Isidore might seem a straightforward task, but the problem of determining when Isidore is concerned with a new species or when he is simply mentioning an alternative name is sometimes difficult.

Again Isidore's presentation is sometimes confusing – thus he lists the 'lacerti' (lizards) between two groups of serpents, a procedure which might cause some unwary readers to lump lizards together with serpents in their count and others to assume that Isidore was finished with serpents before he, in fact, was. At any rate, while the figures as we have them were probably influenced by such a compiler as Isidore, it is also possible that the question-master derived his figures direct from Latin vocabulary lists.

The final question on this topic in the AR sequence (AR 36) 'who named the fish?' is paralleled as a general question in Wilmanns (I) and in other dialogues, but it is somewhat surprising in its AR form since Bede comments: 'de piscibus adductis ad Adam ut eis nomina imponeret nil scriptura refert' (*In Genesim* I:ii.19–20, CCSL 118A, 55; PL 91, col 50) and, following Augustine (*De Genesi ad litteram* IX.xii, CSEL 28.1, 281–2; PL 34, cols 400–1), goes on to speculate that the fish were named by men over the years (55–6, cols 50–1).

Obviously two authoritative commentators were prepared to deny that Adam had named the fish. Genesis 2:19–20 (Vulgate) does say that Adam named 'cuncta animantia' with birds and 'bestias terrae' and a Vulgate reader could assume that fish could be included among the 'animantia.' But the Old Latin version of 2:20 is more precise in reading 'vocavit Adam nomina omnium pecorum' or 'imposuit Adam nomina omnibus pecoribus' in the place of the 'cuncta animantia' of the Vulgate. Fish seem to be deliberately omitted, which would explain the reaction of Augustine and Bede. Our question-master is unlikely, however, to disagree knowingly with such authorities and his question clearly derives from an unconscious adaptation of a dialogue sequence. It is easy to see how a final question 'who named them?' could be taken to refer to its immediate antecedent, which for example in I (Wilmanns) would be 'fish.'

AR 37 Tell me how many soldiers there were, who divided Christ's clothing.
I tell you, there were seven of them.

I:i
Quanti milites diviserunt vestimenti Christi? iiii; Suchier JM C 54, 110. See also Baesecke *Vocabularius* 6, 7; Omont *Interrogations* II 87, 69; Suchier *L'Enfant sage* I 32, 267; *Alfræði Íslenzk* III 40.

I:ii
Quantas sortes fecerunt milites de veste domini? Quattuor, unicuique militum parte una; stolam non divisam, et calciamenta non invenerunt; Wilmanns *Fragebüchlein* 45, 169.

II
The ordinary answer to this question in the dialogues (I:i, ii) accords with the scriptural text (John 19:23) in which four soldiers are specifically mentioned. It is probable that the 'seven' of our answer derives from a confusion of the usual form of the Roman numeral 'four' in the manuscripts of the period (iiii) with 'seven' (uii), both numbers being written with minim strokes.

AR 38 Tell me the four mute letters.
    I tell you, one is mind, the second [is] thought, the third is writing, the fourth is fear.

I:i
Quae sunt tria muta, quae docent sapientiam in corde hominis? Est mens, oculus et littera; *Collectanea Bedae* PL 94, col 545C.

I:ii
Quae sunt tertia [sic] muta [quae] dicunt hominem [sapientiam]? Id, mens, oculus, littera; McNally *Prebiarum* 79, *Scriptores Hiberniae Minores*, 167 (CCSL 108B). Bracketed words are editorially restored.

I:iii
H. Quid est epistola? E. Tacitus nuncius; Daly-Suchier AHE 2, 104. See also Daly-Suchier K 50, 120.

II
The question as it stands in the OE is incoherent and clearly is a corrupt version of an aphorism generally similar to the question we have cited from the *Collectanea Bedae* (I:i). The instance of this aphorism in *Prebiarum*

(1:ii) would also be incoherent, if it were not for editorial restoration of the text.

AR 39 Tell me what are the three things that no man can be without.
 I tell you, they are water and fire and iron.

See the commentary on ss 39.

AR 40 Tell me who first named the name of God.
 I tell you, the devil.

See the commentary on ss 47.

AR 41 Tell me how Christ was born from his mother Mary.
 I tell you, through the right breast.

1:i
Ri rogenair, ni bine / domulluch nah Ingine [The King was born without crime, from the head of the Virgin]; *Saltair na Rann* 7529–30

1:ii
When my Father thought to send me [Jesus] into the world, he sent his angel before me, by name Mary, to receive me. And I when I came down entered in by the ear and came forth by the ear; *Book of John the Evangelist*, James, 191.

II
We have no exact parallels for this question in the dialogue literature or elsewhere. There are, however, two kinds of traditional speculation which probably influenced its formulation. One is the folkloristic motif that a hero

is born in some extraordinary way. The theme of the hero 'born through the mother's side' (Caesarean birth) is widely attested (see Stith Thompson T 540.1 and A 511.1) in English balladry and elsewhere. Also Jerome records a god-figure Buddha being born from a virgin's side on the authority of the Gymnosophists: 'apud Gymnosophistas Indiae, quasi per manus huius opinionis auctoritas traditur, quod Buddam (*al* Buldam) principem dogmatis eorum, a latera suo virgo generarit' (*Adversus Jovinianum* I.42, PL 23 [1845], col 275). The Irish author of the *Saltair na Rann* (I:i above) was influenced, possibly at some remove, by the classical story of Minerva's birth from the head of Jove, although this could have been an acceptable adaptation of Christian mythography since Minerva was goddess of wisdom and Christ is the 'Wisdom' of God. Certain authors, taking a curiously literalistic approach to the description of the Virgin's conception in scripture when Gabriel came and spoke, had Christ conceived and born through the ear as in I:ii above (for other examples see Hirn *The Sacred Shrine*, 211).

But there may be another influence pertaining to theological discussion and heretical belief. A number of heresies remain in OE literature merely by the transmission of 'authoritative' texts. The sober M.R. James (*Latin Infancy Gospels* (Cambridge, Cambridge University Press 1927), xxv) sees a docetic belief about the birth of Christ in the infancy gospels, preserved in English manuscripts of the tenth and eleventh centuries, which are extensions on the *Protevangelium*. He notes that, in these, 'the birth is not a real birth at all,' and that 'here that which is born is a Light which gradually takes the form of a child. It has no weight, it needs no cleansing, it does not cry, it has intelligence from the moment of birth ... it is in short not a human child at all.'

If there is not some obtuse, and, to us, undetectable, error, the OE answer could be a crude attempt to emphasize the 'virginitas in partu' of Mary or be an echo of an heretical belief. But our writing around the topic above is a confession of our mystification.

AR 42 Tell me who caused the sun to stand still for one period of the day.
I tell you, Joshua did it in the battle of Moses; the hill which he stood on is called Gabaon.

I:i
Quis tres horas fecit sol stare? Jesu Nave, successor Moysen, in pugna;

mons autem in quo stabat Gabaon, et luna stetit in vale Elon; Wilmanns *Fragebüchlein* 11, 167.

I:ii

Quis tres horas solem fecit stare in celo? Iosue, minister Moysi, in pugna; Suchier AE₂ 55, 33. See also Suchier JM C, 12, 109 (with 'Ihesum Nave' for 'Iosue'); Omont *Interrogationes* II 79, 69 (with 'Jhesu filius Nave' for 'Iosue'); Suchier *L'Enfant sage* I 42, 267 ('Iosue' alone).

II

The Latin parallel questions and the ultimate scriptural source for AR 42 suggest that there is error in the OE statement. Scripture records that Josue prayed to the Lord and said: 'Sol contra Gabaon ne movearis, et luna contra vallem Ajalon' (Josue 10:12), and, 'stetit itaque sol ... et non festinavit occumbere spatio unius diei' (10:13).

The OE phrase 'an tid dæiges' could be a scribal error for 'tid anes dæiges' to translate the Latin 'spatio unius diei,' but it might be a rendering of the phrase 'tres horas' of the Latin questions, since the day was divided into a series of three-hour periods in monasteries and churches, and 'three hours' might reasonably be considered 'one period' of the day. OE 'tid' can also mean 'hour' (see Bosworth-Toller, Dict, sv 'tid' II, 2a), but if the word has that meaning here the OE question has no extant parallel.

Another probable error is the description of Josue's battle against the five kings of the Amorrhites as 'the battle of Moses.' The war, of which this was one battle, was instigated by Moses, but it is likely that our scribe or a predecessor saw a phrase in which 'Josue, minister [I:ii], ('successor' [I:i]), Moysi in pugna' (of the extant Latin answer) was miscopied as 'Iosue Moysi in pugna' and then 'corrected' to, or understood as, 'Iosue in pugna Moysi,' as in AR 42.

Finally, the implication in AR 42 that Josue stood on 'the hill ... called Gabaon' could derive a form of the answer as in I:i where it could be assumed that the subject of the verb 'stabat' was 'Iosue.' The 'Jesu Nave' of I:i is the Septuagint/Old Latin name for 'Iosue.'

AR 43 Tell me what is best and worst.
I tell you, the word of man.

See the commentary on ss 37.

AR 44 Tell me what is dearest to man in his life and most hateful after his death.
I tell you, his will.

I:i
Quod [sunt] quae amat homo, qui sit in peccatis et odit post mortem? Id, tres. Diligit longitudinem uitae et uoluntatem suam et diabulum in eo quod ei consentit; McNally *Prebiarum* 28, *Scriptores Hiberniae Minores*, 163 (CCSL 108B).

I:ii
Also the emperour hym demaunded wheder those ben happye that have theyr desyres and wyll in this worlde. And he answered that they be not happy, but those ben happy the whiche god ne letteth to do theyr wylles and desyres in this worlde, but correcteth them by adversyte; Suchier *L'Enfant sage* XVIII 21, 529.

II
The point of this question obviously relates to that (free) will which, according to Augustine, man lost at the Fall, but the Hiberno-Latin question (I:i), which defines the man as one 'in sins,' makes it very clear that the sinful man's will is going to cause suffering after death.

AR 45 Tell me what the sweet word does.
I tell you, it multiplies a man's friendship and appeases a man's enemies.

I
Verbum dulce quidem tibi multiplicabit amicos; Walther 33145.

II

This question and answer is a paraphrase of Ecclesiasticus 6:5 (Vulgate): 'Verbum dulce multiplicat amicos, et mitigat inimicos.' The conception of recasting a Biblical proverb as a question might have been suggested to a question-master by a text such as the *Collectanea Bedae* in which proverbs from the sapiential books of the Bible and questions from the dialogues occur together as items in the same miscellany.

AR 46 Tell me who is the false friend.
    I tell you, he is a man's companion at the table and none in necessity.

I

For summe ben at thi borde thi frende, ac at thi nede bihynde; *South English Legendary: OT History*, 83:31; cited by Whiting, F 659, who gives other examples.

II

This exchange apparently had some currency as a proverb, but it derives from Ecclesiasticus 6:20 (Vulgate): 'Est autem amicus socius mensae, et non permanebit in die necessitatis.'

AR 47 Tell me what the sick man detests which he loved before in health.
    I tell you, food is hateful to the sick man which was dear to him before, and light is hateful to his eyes which was dear to him before.

I

Lux gravis in luctu; Walther 14139.

II

There are no parallels to this question in the dialogues and it lacks the sharp focus of conception or expression which ordinarily characterizes a proverb. But it has the contact with reality which is often found in the forceful

images of the didactic Christian writers. We suggest that it derives ultimately from such a double image in Augustine's *Confessiones* on the
difficulty which a sinner has in accepting the truth: 'Et sensi et expertus non
esse mirum *quod palato non sano poena est panis, qui sano suavis est, et
oculis aegris odiosa lux, quae puris amabilis*' (VII.xvi.22; our italics).
Augustine's conclusion is 'so your justice (O Lord) displeases sinners.'

AR 48 Tell me in what can a man's death be seen.
        I tell you, two images of a man are in a man's eyes; if you do not see
    these the man will die and pass away before three days' time.

I
Pupilla est medius punctus oculi, in quo vis est videndi; ubi, quia parvae
imagines nobis videntur, propterea pupillae appellantur. Nam parvuli
pupilli dicuntur ... Physici dicunt easdem pupillas, quas videmus in oculis,
morituros ante triduum non habere, quibus non visis certa est desperatio;
Isidore *Etymologiae* XI.i.37.

II
There have been two attempts to discuss the content of this question within
our reading. Jacob Grimm linked the statement with the nineteenth-century
Scots folk belief that when the 'mannikins' can no longer be seen in a sick
person's eyes he is near death (*Teutonic Mythology* trans J.S. Stallybrass
(1882–8) III, 1181). The *Handwörterbuch des deutschen Aberglaubens*
('Auge' II.8; I, 696–7) discusses our question and refers to the belief
attested in the Talmud that a man will die within thirty days of the images
failing in his eyes. The idea of the fading reflecting power of the eye is
generally common also in the classical period. Pliny, for example, remarks
that 'augerim ex homine ipso est non timendi mortem in aegritudine,
quamdiu oculorum pupillae imaginem reddeant' (*Naturalis historia*
XXVIII.xvii.64). But the correspondence of significant detail with the Isido-
rean passage (I), and Isidore's importance as a transmitter of information
in the mediaeval period, indicates that he was a source for the OE question,
although he himself is citing Servius the grammarian (on the *Aeneid*
IV.244) for his last sentence. (See PL 82, col 402, footnote m).

PART THREE

Glossary
Proper Names
Latin Words

Glossary

The words are glossed alphabetically in the forms in which they appear in the texts. Words within brackets are alternative forms as recorded in the standard dictionaries. Forms marked † are editorial emendations. Grammatical abbreviations are those normally used for OE texts with the following exceptions:
- Arabic numerals following headword verbs indicate weak verbs by their class, ie, 1, 2, 3.
- Roman numerals following headword verbs indicate strong verbs by their class, ie, I, II, III, etc.
- Forms of verbs are in the indicative mood unless denoted as subj (subjunctive).
- Forms of adjectives are of strong declension unless denoted as wk (weak) except of those which are declined only as weak.
- After a headword noun n indicates neuter gender, but in description of nouns, pronouns, and adjectives n indicates nominative case. In such descriptions, where confusion might occur, neut indicates neuter gender.

Short titles used in the glossary are:

Campbell: A. Campbell *Old English Grammar* (Oxford, The Clarendon Press 1959).

Pope: John Pope *Homilies of Ælfric, a supplementary collection* EETS, nos 259, 260 (2 vols), 1967–8.

BT Dict. *An Anglo-Saxon Dictionary* J. Bosworth and T.N. Toller (Oxford, Oxford University Press 1898)

BT Supp: *An Anglo-Saxon Dictionary, Supplement* T.N. Toller (Oxford, Clarendon Press 1921)

abyrgan: 1 *to taste*; -de† 3 sg pt, SS 16

acennan: 1 *to bear, give birth to*; -ed: pp, SS 15, AR 28, 41

adder (ædder): f *vein, sinew*; addre: n pl, SS 59

æ: f *law*; here, *divine law, old and new, according to the two testaments*; d sg, SS 42, AR 13, 14; g sg, AR 25

æaldan: see eald

æfen: m n *evening*; a sg, or endingless locative, SS 27, 55, AR 8 (see SV on II)

æft: adv *afterwards, later*, SS 15, 45 (2 examples); eft, AR 2 (2 examples), 12, 28 (2 examples)

æfter: prep w d *after (temporal, subsequent to an event)*, SS 15, 17, 53, AR 28, 44

æfter: adv *afterwards*, AR 5

æftera: compar adj *next, second*; -n: d sg m, SS 5

ægesa (egesa): m *fear, dread*; n sg, AR 38

æht: f *possessions, goods*; -a: g pl, SS 43

ælc: adj *each, every*; -um: d sg. n, AR 9

æle (ele): m n *oil*; n sg, SS 54

ær: conj *before*, SS 13 (3 examples)

ær: prep w d *before (in time)*, SS 44, AR 13, 48

ær: adv *at an earlier time, before*, AR 2, 5, 12, 19, 21 (2 examples), 22, 47 (2 examples)

ærian (erian): 1 *to plough*; æriende, inflected infin, SS 35 (see textual note)

ærnemorgien: m *the twilight period before sunrise, dawn, daybreak*, AR 7. Pope, II, 509–10, ponders whether this should be taken as a compound or two separate words. If the latter, 'ærne' is a sg m of 'ær,' adj, *early*.

æror: compar adv *earlier, before*, AR 47

ærost: superl. adv *earliest, first*, SS 25, 47 (1 example, and 1†), 53, 58; ærust, SS 2, 25, 35; erost, SS 34, 46; ærest, AR 6, 12, 13, 15, 16, 17 (2 examples), 18, 31, 40.

ærosta: superl adj *first*; all forms here are wk; æresta: n sg m, AR 28, 36; ærustan: n sg m, SS 8; æroste: n sg f, SS 54; æroste: n sg neut, SS 9; ærostan: d sg m, SS 5; ærostan: a sg m, SS 5; ærostan: n pl m, SS 53

æðung (eðung): f *breath*: n sg, SS 9

agiltan: 1 *to sin*; agilte: 3 sg pt, AR 22

agitan (ageotan): II *to pour*; aget: 3 sg pt, SS 42

an: num pron *one*, SS 50, AR 38; on: SS 39

an: adj *one*; n sg neut, SS 13 etc, -ne: a sg m, SS 32; -e: a sg f AR 42; -an: a sg neut, SS 13 (5 examples); annes: g sg m, SS 36

ancra: m *hermit*; -n: n pl, SS 53

and: conj *and*, SS introd, etc

andworc (andweorc): n *substance, matter*; a sg, SS 8

apostol: m *apostle*; -um: d pl, SS 59

arian: 2 w d *to honour*; ara: imperative sg, ss 43

arke: AR 21; see earc

asettan: 1 *to place, put, set*; asette: 3 sg pt, ss 32

asweltan: III *to die*; asweolt: 3 sg pt, AR 2

aþencan: 1 *to think, think out*; aðohte: 3 sg pt, ss 35

atimbrian: 2 *to build*; -ode: 3 sg pt, ss 25

awacan: VI *to be born*; awocon: 3 pl pt, ss 14 (2 examples)

aweorpan: III *to throw, cast (away)*; awearp: 3 sg pt, ss 42

awyrgan: 1 *to curse*; awyrgeð: pp, ss 45; awirgeð: pp, ss 45

ban: n *bone*; -a: g pl, ss 59

be: prep w d *by*, ss 44

bearn: n *child, son*; a sg, ss 13 (4 examples); bæarn: ss 13; n pl, AR 12; a pl ss 13; -um: d pl, ss 14

bebeodan: II *to command*; beboden: pp, ss 56

bebod: n *command, decree*; -e: d sg, ss 42

bebyrgan, bebyrian, bibirigan: 1 *to bury*; bebyrged: pp, ss 15; bebyried, AR 28; bibiriged, AR 28

becuman: IV *to come, become*; becom: 3 sg pt ss 9

behelan: IV *to conceal, hide*; -að: 3 sg pr, ss 3

belifan: I *to remain, be left*; belyfon: pp, ss 17 (wesan belifen *to die*, BT Supp sv belīfan II)

beod: m *table*; -e: d sg, AR 46

beon wesan: anom vb *to be*; beon, AR 19, 39; ys: 3 sg pr (ss, 30 examples; AR, 1 example); is (ss, 1 example; AR, 11 examples); nys (neg, ss, 2 examples); byð (ss, 3 examples; AR, 9 examples); bið, AR 48; beoð: 3 pl pr (ss, 5 examples including 1†; AR, 3 examples); synt, ss 36; sint, AR 19, 39; syndon (ss, 9 examples); sindon (ss 14, 21, AR 26); sy: 3 sg pr subj, ss 3, AR 9, 10, 11; si (AR, 6 examples); wæs 3 sg pt (ss, 42 examples, including 2†; AR, 10 examples); was (ss, 11 examples; AR, 4 examples); næs (neg, ss 15); wæron: 3 pl pt (ss, 4 examples; AR, 1 example in AR 37); næron: neg, ss 50; wære: 3 sg pt subj (ss, 2 examples; AR, 6 examples); nære: neg, AR 28

beoð: see beon

beran: IV *to bear (sustain a burden), to bear (be fruitful)*; berende: pr part, ss 36; berende: inflected inf, ss 48 (see textual note)

betst: superl adj *best*; n sg f, ss 28, n sg neut, ss 37 (2 examples), 40, AR 43

betwinan (betweonan): prep w d *between*, ss 37

betwix (betweox): prep w d *between*, ss 37

beufan: prep w d *above*, ss 3

bisceop: m *bishop*; n sg, AR 13, 14

biðː see beon.

blæd: f *fruit*; -a: a pl, ss 16

blawan: VII *to blow*; bleow: 3 sg pt, AR 5

bletsian, gebletsian: 2 *to bless*; gebletsod: pp, ss 45 (2 examples)

blod: n *blood*; n sg, ss 9, 36; a sg, ss 45; -e: d sg, ss 41

blosma (blostma): m *blossom, flower*; blosmena: g pl, ss 9 (see AR textual note 16)

boc: f *book*; bec: n pl, ss 59

bockinn (boccynn): n *kind of books*; -a: g pl, ss 59

bocstæf: m *letter*; -stafas: *letters, literature, writing*; a pl, ss 58, AR 16

bragen (brægen): n *brain*; -e: d sg, ss 41

bred: n *table, tablet*; -a: a pl, AR 25

breost: n *breast*; a sg, AR 41

broðer (broðor): m *brother*; a sg, ss 36

burh (burg): f *city, stronghold*; n sg ss 25 (2 examples), 26, 27; buruh: ss 26; burge: g
  sg AR 29

butan, buton: adv *without*; -on: ss 39; -an: AR 39 (BT Supp sv butan B 2)

buton: prep w d *except for*, ss 59 (2 examples)

byrgen: f *grave, tomb*; n sg, ss 44

byrnan: III intrans *to burn*; -ende: pr part, AR 10

gebyrtid, (gebyrdtid): f *time of birth*; -e: d sg? ss 17

byð: see beon

cæaster (ceaster): f *city*; cæastræ: a sg, ss 25

kanon (canon): m *canon*; -es: g sg, ss 59

kempa (cempa): m *soldier*; -ena: g pl, AR 37

cennan: 1 *to bear, produce*; cende: 3 sg pt, ss 17

cigan: 1 *to call, invoke*; cig: imperative sg, ss 43

kining (cyning): m *king*; -es: g sg, ss 44

kiðan (cyðan): 1 here intrans with hu, *to tell, make known*; kið: 3 sg pr, ss introd

cnihthad: m *youth*; -e: d sg, ss 13 (2 examples)

culfre: f *dove*; n sg, ss 29

cuman: IV *to come*; cuma infin, AR 19; cymð: 3 sg pr, ss 30; kimð, ss 30; kymð, AR 7

cuð: adj *known, evident*; n sg neut, ss 38; superl cuðost: n sg neut, ss 38

cweðan: V *to say, speak*; cwæt: 3 sg pt, ss introd; cwæð, AR introd, AR 31; cweden:
  pp AR 6; cwæden, AR 18

cyngban (cin, cyne, *chin, jaw*): n *chinbone, jawbone*; -e: d sg, ss 36

kynn (cynn): n *kind, species*; -a: g pl, AR 33

dæg: m *day*; dæig: a sg, AR 2 (2 examples); -es: g sg, AR 5; dæiges, AR 42; -e: d sg AR 2
  (2 examples), ss 5 (6 examples); daga: g pl, ss 22, 59; dagena, ss 59; dagum: d pl, ss
  5, AR 48, dægum, ss 5

dæl: m *portion, part*; a sg, ss 32 (3 examples); -as: a pl ss 32

dælan: 1 *to divide*; dældon: 3 pl pt, AR 37

dead: adj *dead*; n sg m, AR 28; -e: n pl m, AR 19; g sg m wk as subst, deadan, AR 11

deað: m *death*; a sg, ss 38, AR 19, 48; -e: d sg, ss 15, AR 28, 44

deaw: m or n *dew*; n sg, ss 57, -es: g sg, ss 9

deofol, deoful: m *devil*; deoful: n sg, ss 47; deofol, AR 40

deofolgild: n *devil-idol, idolatry*; a pl, AR 25

deor: n *animal, wild beast*; a pl, ss 5

dohtor: f *daughter*; -ra: g pl. ss 24

dom: m *judgement, doom*; n sg, ss 49, -e: d sg, ss 44

domesdæig: m *doomsday, day of judgment*; a sg, AR 6

don, gedon: anom v *to do, cause, make*; deð: 3 sg pr, AR 45; dyde: 3 sg pt, AR 42; gedyde, AR 42

gedrif: n *tract, region*; a sg, ss 32; gedryf, ss 32

drihten: m *lord, the Lord*; n sg, AR 3, 4, 31

drincan: III *to drink*; dranc: 3 sg pt, AR 17

dry: m *magician, sorcerer*; n sg, AR 10

dumb: adj *dumb, mute*; -e: a pl m, AR 38

dun: f *hill, mountain*; n sg, AR 42

ea: f *river*; n sg, ss 31, -n†: n pl, ss 54

eage: n *eye*; -ena: g pl, ss 9; -um: d pl, AR 47, 48

eahta: cardinal num *eight*, ss 13; ehta, ss 59; as Roman numeral, ss 8

eahtoða: ordinal num *eighth*; eahtoðe: n sg neut, ss 9

eald: adj *old*; n sg f, ss 17; æaldan: g sg f wk AR 25; -an: d sg f wk, ss 42, AR 13; yldestan: superlative, d sg m wk, ss 14

eall: adj *all*; -um: d sg n, ss 59; -e: a pl n, ss 4, a pl f ss 5 (2 examples), AR 4; ealra: g pl neut, ss 40, g pl m, AR 36

eall: neut adj as subst, ss 3

ealles: g sg of eall as adv, *in all, altogether*, ss 13 (10 examples)

eall swa (eall adv w swa): *just as*, ss 59 (2 examples)

ealond: n *island*; as d sg (see sv on 1 f), AR 6

ealra: g pl of eall as adv, *in all, altogether*, ss 59 (3 examples)

earc: f *ark*; n sg, ss 23; -e: a sg, ss 18; arke: d sg, AR 21

eft: see æft

eft: adv *again*, AR 21

engel: m *angel*; engelas: n pl, ss 32

eondscynan (geondscīnan): I *to shine upon, illuminate*; infin, ss 56

eorðe: f *earth, soil*; n sg, ss 45, 50, AR 5 (2 examples), 9, 28; -an: a sg, ss 1, 5, 22, 57, AR 4; -an: d sg, ss 38, 48, AR 28, 32, 34 erost: see ærost

esol: m *ass*; -es†: g sg, ss 36 (see textual note)

fæder: m *father*; n sg, ss 13; feder, ss 13; a sg, AR 12 (2 examples); d sg, ss 43

fæðm: m *fathom* (the OE equivalent of the scriptural cubit); fæðema: g pl, ss 23 (3 examples)

farbodenan: see forbeodan

gefeallan: VII *to fall*; gefeoll: 3 sg pt, ss 36

fedan: 1 *feed, nourish, sustain*; -að: 3 pl pr ss 57; -de: 3 sg pt AR 22

fela: indecl pron and adj *many, much*; fala: as adj, ss 5; fela (fæla, ss 14) as pron w g, ss 12, 13, 33, 51, 52, 59 (2 examples), AR 33, 37; as pron, ss 59

gefeoht: n *fight, battle*; -e: d sg, AR 42

feond: m *enemy, foe*; a sg, AR 45

feorða: ordinal num *fourth*; feorðe, n sg m AR 38, n sg neut, ss 9, 50; ss 43†; n sg m or f, ss 54; feorðan: d sg m, ss 5

feower: cardinal num *four*, AR 27, 34, 38; also presented as Roman numeral

gefera: m *companion*; n sg, AR 46

feran: 1 *to go*; -de: 3 sg pt, ss 12

fersc: adj *fresh*; -e: n pl f, ss 33

fet: see fot

feðer: f *feather*, but, as pl *wings*; -um: d pl, ss 1; fiðerum, AR 4, 27

fettian: 2 *dispute*; -ode: 3 sg pt, ss introd

fictreow: n *figtree*; fictrewæs: g sg, ss 16

fif: cardinal num *five*; presented as Roman numeral

fifta: ordinal num *fifth*; fifte: n sg neut, ss 9; ss 43†; also presented as Roman numeral

fiftig: cardinal num *fifty*, AR 33; also presented as Roman numeral

fir: see fyr

fisc: m *fish*; n sg, AR 24; fixas: a pl, ss 5; -a: g pl, AR 36

fisccynn: n *species of fish*; -a: g pl, ss 52; fisckinna, AR 35

fleogan: II *to fly*; infin, AR 27 (2 examples): pr partic as adj, g pl, fleogendra, ss 51, AR 33

flesc (flæsc): n *flesh*; n sg ss 9

flod: m and n *flood*; n sg, ss 22; a sg, ss 17; -e: d sg, ss 17, 25

flowan: VII *to flow*; -að: 3 pl pr, ss 54

folc: n *people, tribe, race*; n sg, AR 5, 25

folde: f *earth, soil*; -an: g sg, ss 9

for: prep w d *on account of, because of, for*, ss 3, 45; for hwan: conj *wherefore, why*, ss 42, 55; for hwam, ss 36, AR 7, 8, 21, 22, 25; for þon, forðon: conj *for, because*, ss 3, 42, 55, 56; for þam, AR 2, 9, 28; for þy be: conj *for, because*; AR 21; for þon þe, for ðon þe; ss 28, 31, 36; for þam þe, AR 7, 12, 19, 25 (2 examples): for ðan þe, AR 8

forbeodan: II *to forbid*; farbodenan pp as adj wk, SS 16

for hwam, for hwan: see for

forma: ordinal num *first*; forme: n sg neut, SS 43

forð: adv *from that time, onwards (in time)*, SS 17

for þam, for þan: see for

forðgan: anom vb *to go forth, proceed*; forðeode: 3 sg pt, SS 2

for þy: see for

fot: m *foot*; fet: n pl, AR 26

fram: prep w d *from*, SS 6†, 17 (4 examples), 30 (2 examples)

freond: m *friend*; n sg, AR 46

freondscype: m *friendship*; a sg, AR 45

frigdæg: m *Friday*; a sg, SS 16; frydæig, AR 2

frimð (frymþ): f *beginning*; -e: d sg, SS 17 (2 examples, of which one is†)

fugel: m *bird*; n sg, SS 29, AR 24, fugelas: a pl, SS 5, fugela: g pl, AR 33

fugelcynn: n *species of birds*; -a†: g pl, SS 51 (see textual note)

full: adj *full, filled, satisfied*; -e: n pl neut, SS 50

fullian: 2 *to baptize*; gefullod: pp, SS 15, 31

fulluht n *baptism*; -e†: d sg, SS 45 (after þurh, see BT Dict sv þurh, B II. 1), 53 (after
æfter)

fyr, fir: n *fire*; fyr: n sg, SS 39, AR 39; fir, SS 50; fyres g sg, SS 9

gan: anom vb *to go*; gæð: 3 sg pr, SS 26, 27, AR 23, 30; eode: 3 sg pt, AR 5, 22

gast: m *spirit, ghost* (in Holy Ghost); a sg, SS 29

gear: n *year*; ger: a pl, SS 17; gear, AR 1; -a: g pl, SS 17 (2 examples) (after cardinal
numeral, cf, 'þrēo and þritig gēara,' *Christ and Satan* 501)

gif: conj *if*, AR 26, 27, 48

gigant, gygand: m *giant*; gygand: n sg, SS 58; gigant, AR 16

glæwnisse (glēawniss): f *wisdom, sapientia*; as n sg, AR 27

gleng: f *ornament, honour, glory*; n sg, AR 11

god: m *God*; n sg, SS 1, 4 (2 examples), 5 (2 examples), 13; a sg, SS 43; -es: g sg, SS 2,
42, 43, 47 (2 examples), AR 26, 40; -e: d sg, SS 32

grim(m): adj *severe, cruel, bitter*; grimme: a pl neut, SS 12

gyfu (gifu): f *gift, grace*; gyfe: g sg, SS 9

gytsian: 2 *covet, desire*; pr part as adj n sg m wk, gytsienda, SS 50

habban: 3 *to have*; infin, AR 26; hafað: 3 sg pr SS 4; nafað: neg, AR 26; hæfede: 3 sg pt,
SS 13 (9 examples), 24

hæman: 1 *to have sexual intercourse with, cohabit*; ... on unriht: *to commit
adultery*; hæm: imperative sg, SS 43 (see textual note)

hagol: m *hail*; n sg, SS 57

halig: adj *holy*; halegan: a sg m wk, ss 29: -an: a sg m wk, ss 43; -ra: g pl m, AR 6

hat: adj *hot*; n sg neut, ss 9; n s f, AR 9

hatan: VII *to call, name*; gehaten: pp, ss 3; hatte: sg *is called, was called*, ss 13, 19, 20 (2 examples), 21 (2 examples), 25, 26, 27, 28, 44, 54 (3 examples), AR 29, 30 (2 examples), 42; hætte, ss 13, 19, 26; hatton: pl, ss 7†, 9, 21

he: m; heo: f; hit: neut; pron 3rd person; he: n sg m, ss 1, AR 1, etc (49 examples); heo: n sg f, ss 17, AR 6 etc (32 examples, including 3 referring to wyf, wif: neut, ss 19, 20, 21); hit: n sg neut, AR 10, 30, 45 (including 1 referring to sunne: f, AR 10, and 1 referring to burh: f, AR 30); hine: a sg m, ss 13, hyne, ss 36; hyg: a sg f, ss 44; hit: a sg neut, AR 42; his: g sg m, ss 9 only, AR 12 etc (8 examples); hys, ss 4 etc (13 examples), AR 12 only; him: d sg m, ss 9 etc (4 examples), AR 22 etc (4 examples); hym, ss only (8 examples); hyre: d sg f, ss 31, 56, (2 examples, 1†); hi: n pl, AR 19 (2 examples), hy; AR 19, 20; hyg; ss 21 (2 examples), 32†; heora: g pl, ss introd, 54, AR 37. With relative particle as relative, þe heo, AR 42

heafod: n *head*; heafde: d sg, AR 23

heaftnod (hæftnēod, hæftnȳd): f *captivity*; -e: d sg, AR 5

heah: adj *high*; n sg f, ss 23

heahfæder: m *patriarch*; n sg, ss 46

healden: VII *hold, support, contain*; -að: imperative pl, ss 43; -að: 3 pl pr, ss 5

healt: adj *halt, lame*; n sg f, AR 26

hefig: adj *heavy, burdensome*; hefogost: superl, ss 48; hefegost, AR 32

hell: f *hell*; n sg, ss 50; -e: g sg, ss 32; -e: d sg, ss 12, 16, 55, AR 6, 8

heo: see he

heofon: m *heaven*; n sg, ss 3 (2 examples); a sg, ss 5, 13; heofonæs: g sg, ss 5; -as†: a pl, ss 1; -a: g pl, ss 32; -um: d pl, AR 27

heofone: f *heaven*; -an: a sg, AR 4

heora: see he

heorte: f *heart*; -an: d sg, ss 41.

her: adv *here*; ss introd

hi, him, hine, his, hit: see he

hlaf: m *loaf*; -a: g pl, ss 59 (2 examples)

hlaford: m *lord*; -es: g sg, ss 48, AR 32

hrefen (hræfn): m *raven*; n sg, hrefen, AR 22, 24, hreuen AR 21.

hregel (hrægl, hrægel): n *garment, robe*; a sg or pl, AR 37

hu: adv *how*; (a) modifying a verb, ss introd, AR 41; (b) modifying an adj or adv, ss 5 etc (18 examples), AR 1 etc (5 examples).

hund: m *dog*; a sg, ss 34

hund: n *a hundred*, ss 12 (2 examples), 13 (12 examples), 59 (2 examples); hunð, ss 13; also as Roman numeral

hundred: n *a hundred*, ss 13

hundseofontig: cardinal num *seventy*, ss 59
hundtwelftig: cardinal num *one hundred and twenty*, ss 25†
hunig: n *honey*; n sg, ss 54.
hus: n *house*; -e: d sg ss 44.
hwa: m (f); hwæt: neut; interr pron *who, what*; n sg m, ss 46†, etc, AR 16 etc (10
   examples); n sg neut, ss 4 etc (26 examples); hwæt: w g *how many*, ss 24, 59, AR
   34, 35; hwam: d sg neut, AR 48; hwan, hwan, see also 'for hwam' under 'for'
hwader (hwæder): adv *whither, where ... to*; ss 32
hwær (hwar, hwer): adv *where*; hwar, ss 27, 41; hwær, ss 44, AR 4, 5, 6, 20, 23; hwer,
   ss 1
hwæðer: conj *whether*; ss 56
hwæðer: pron decl as adj *which (of two)*; -e: d sg f, AR 3
hwal (hwæl): m *whale*; hwales: g sg, AR 6
hwanon: adv *whence, where ...from*; ss 6, 30
hwi: adv (instrumental of hwæt) *why*; in question ss 56
hwilc: interrog adj and pron; (a) as adj *what, which*; hwilc: n sg, ss 2, 25, 28, 29, 31,
   34, 35, 40, 53, AR 12, 13, 14, 15, 28, 31; hwylc, AR 46; -ne: a sg m, AR 2; -um: d sg
   neut, ss 3, 45; -ere: d sg f, ss 10; -e: n pl, AR 24; (b) as pron, hwilc, AR 10
gehwirfan (gehwyrfan): 1 *turn, return*; -de: 3 s pt, AR 21
hwit: adj *white*; n sg m, AR 21
hy, hyg, hyre, hyne, hys, hym: see he
gehyrsumniss: f *obedience*; -e: a sg, AR 22

ic: pron 1st pers *I*; n sg ss 1 etc, AR 1 etc (106 examples); me, ss 1 etc, AR 1 etc.: a (d)
   sg (105 examples)
in: prep I w d of position or location: *in, within*; in worulde, ss 13; in sæ, AR 5; in
   innoðe, AR 28; in eorðan, AR 28; in gefeohte, AR 42; in æ, ss 42 (metaphorical).
      II w a indicating motion to or towards a position: *to, into*; up in heofon, ss 13, in
   sæ, ss 42 (2 examples)
innoð: m *inside* (of a body), *belly*; -e: d sg, ss 15, AR 6, 12, 28
in to: prep w d *to, into*; in to arke, AR 21; in to westenne, AR 22
is: see beon
isen: n *iron*; n sg, AR 39; ysen, ss 39

k: See under c

læce: m *doctor, physician*; n sg, AR 18
længu, lengu, f *length, height*; længe: d sg, ss 11; lenge, ss 23
land: n *land, country*; -e: d sg, AR 9
lang: adj *long, tall* n sg m, ss 11 (2 examples); n sg f, ss 23 (2 examples)

lange, longe: adv *long* (temporal); lange, ss 16, 18, 22, AR 1; longe, AR 19

lað: adj *hateful, displeasing*; n sg m and neut, AR 47 (2 examples); superl laðest n sg m, AR 44

leas: adj *false*; -a: n sg m wk, AR 46; -e: a sg f, ss 43

lengu: see længu

leof: adj *dear, desirable, pleasing*; n sg m and neut, AR 47 (2 examples); superl leofust n sg m, AR 44

leofode: see lifian

leoht: n *light*; n sg, AR 31, 47; a sg, ss 5

leornyngcniht: m *disciple*; -a: g pl, ss 59

libban: 3 *live*; lyfde: 3 sg pt, ss 13 (10 examples), 16

lician: 2 impers w d *to please, be pleasing to*; licyge: 3 sg pr subj, ss 49

lif: n *life*; -e: d sg, AR 44; lyfe, ss 59

lifian, leofian: 2 (see Campbell § 762) *to live*; lufian: infin, ss 39 (see textual note); pr part as adj liuigendan, AR 11; leofode: 3 sg pt, ss 12 (2 examples), 13 (as scribal correction)

ligetu: f *lightning*; n sg, ss 30

lilige: f *lily*; n sg, ss 28

locian: 2 *look, gaze*; -að: 3 sg pr, ss 55; lokað, AR 8

gelomlice: adv *often, frequently*; AR 19

lufian: 2 *to love*; lufa: imperative sg, ss 43; -ode: 3 sg pt, AR 47

lufian, ss 39, see lifian

lufu: f *love*; n sg, AR 26

lychama (lichama): m *body*; n sg, lychaman, ss 41 (see textual note); lychaman: d sg, ss 13

lyf: see lif

lyfde: see libban

lyft: m n *air*; -es: g sg, ss 32

magan: pret -pres vb *to be able*; mæg: 3 sg pr, ss 39, 56 (2 examples), mæig, AR 39, 48

gemanifealdian: 2 *to multiply*; -að: 3 sg pr, AR 45

manig: adj *many*; manegum: d pl f, AR 27

manlica: m *man-likeness, image of a man*; -n: n pl, AR 48

mann, man: m, I *man*; n sg man, ss 8 etc (12 examples); man: a sg, ss 5; mannes: g sg, ss 41 etc (7 examples), AR 11 etc (8 examples); men: d sg, ss 38, 59, AR 44, 47; men: n pl, AR 19; manna: g pl, AR 6, 26; mannum: d pl, AR 32; mannon, ss 37 (2 examples), ss 38.

II *man, one*; nan man, *no man, no one*, ss 39, 44, AR 39; man *one*, ss 43, AR 48; men as sg? ss 18; see wyrcan mara: see micel

me: see ic

gemen: m pl *men*; -manna: g pl, ss 25

meolc: f *milk*; n sg, ss 54

mete: m *food*; n sg, AR 47

micel, mycel: adj *big, large, great*; mycel n sg f, AR 9; micclan a sg m wk, ss 17; miclan d sg m wk, ss 44; mara compar *more*; mare n sg f, AR 9

mid: see myd

middangeard: m *earth, world*; a sg, AR 19; myddaneard, ss 56; myddaneardes: g sg, ss 17 (2 examples); myddaneardde: d sg, ss 17

mod: n *spirit, mood, intellect*, anima (?), see commentary; n sg, AR 23, 38; -es: g sg, ss 9

moder: f *mother*; n sg, AR 12, 28; a sg, AR 12; g sg, ss 15, AR 12, 28; meder: d sg, ss 43, AR 41

mona: m *moon*; n sg, AR 5

monað: m *month*; monðum†: d pl, ss 59 (3 examples)

morgemette (morgen-mete): m *morning-meal, breakfast*; morgemetten†: d pl, ss 59

morgen: m *morning*; on morgen, ss 26; on morgene, ss 56; on morgien (see ærnemorgien), AR 7. [Historically 'morgen' without inflectional ending is thought to be an endingless locative (Campbell §572), but the 'e' inflection in 'morgene' seems to indicate location by means of the dative ending.]

muð: m *mouth*; a sg, AR 23; -e: d sg, ss 2

mycel: see micel

myd (mid): prep I w d *with*; (a) denoting association of some kind, ss 13 (2 examples), 17, 43; (b) denoting instrumentality, ss 36.

    II w a denoting instrumentality, ss 35

myddaneard: see middangeard

mynster: n *monastery*; a sg, ss 53

myslycian: 2 w d *to displease, to be displeasing to*; myslycige: 3 sg pr subj, ss 49

myssenlicnys: f *variety*; n sg, ss 9 (see illustrative note)

nædderkinn: n *species (kind) of reptile, serpent*; -a: g pl, AR 34

næddre: f *serpent, snake*; n sg, AR 24; næddran: g sg, AR 12

næfre: adv *never*, ss 50 (2 examples), AR 5 (2 examples)

nænig: adj *no, not any*; nænygum: d sg m, ss 38

næs, næron, nære: see beon

nafað: see habban

nama: m *name*; n sg, ss 6; -n: a sg, ss 43, 47 (2 examples), AR 29, 40; nama: a pl, AR 36; -n: d pl, ss 21 nan: pron, adj *not one, none, no*; as adj, n sg m, SS 39, 44, AR 39; -e: a sg f, AR 5

nang (nænig): pron *none, no-one*, AR 46

nanwyht: as subst *nothing*, SS 38

naðer (nahwæðer): pron *neither*, AR 26

ne: particle *not*; in sequence, *nor ... nor*, SS 39 etc, AR 5 etc

nemnan: 1 *to name, call*; nemde: 3 sg pt, SS 47 (2 examples); nemnede, AR 40; genemned: pp, SS 18; nemned, AR 6, genemnede: pp pl, SS 21

neodþærf (neodþearf, nidþearf): f *necessity, need*; -e: d sg, AR 46

neorxnawang: m *paradise*; on neorxnawang, AR 19; on neorxnawange, AR 1; on neorxenawange, SS 16, 54. [Normally 'on' takes the dative when indicating position or location so, in view of AR 1, AR 19 may be an error. But 'on' can take the accusative, see below 'on' III d.]

neowelnyss: f *abyss*; -e: a sg, SS 32 (see below 'on' IIId)

niht: f *night*; a sg or endingless locative, AR 6 (on niht); -a: g pl, SS 22

niman: IV *take*; nam: 3 sg pt, AR 3

geniman: IV *take*; genam: 3 sg pt, SS 13

niwe: adj *new*; niwan: d sg f wk, AR 14

non-mette: m *noon-meal, afternoon meal*; nonmettum: d pl, SS 59

nygon (nigon): num *nine*, SS 13 etc (6 examples); also as Roman numeral

nys: see beon

nyten: n *cattle, beast*; -u: a pl, SS 5

of: prep w d *of, from, out of* (a) indicating the thing, place, person from which anything moves (literal or figurative) *out of, from*; of muðe, SS 2; of Egyptum, SS 17; of heaftnode, AR 5; with adv, up of sæ, AR 7. (b) indicating a limit from which time or space is measured, *from* (BT Dict sv 'of' X); of frimðe, SS 17. (c) indicating origin or source, personal or impersonal, *from, of*; *out of*, of bearnum, SS 14; of Seme, of Cham, of Iafeðe, SS 14; of meder, AR 41. (d) indicating the material or substance from which anything is made, *from, out of*; of treowcinne, SS 18; of viii punda gewihte, SS 8 (with vb 'to make' understood); of ðam, SS 9. (e) with verb of saying, *about* (BT Dict sv 'of' VIII); Saga me of ylde, SS 17. (f) indicating the means by which something is done, *by, from*; of ðam wordon, SS 42. (g) with relative þe, *from which*; þe ... of, of þe, SS 8, AR 3, 17, 21

ofer: prep w d or a (the distinction between rest (d) and motion (a) is not always maintained)

I w d (a) above and in contact with, *above, on*; ofer feðerum, SS 1, AR 4. (b) marking time, *after, beyond* (BT Dict sv ofer I 8); ofer flode, SS 25 (see textual note). (c) with the idea of movement, where the accusative might be expected, *over*; ofer þære (sæ), AR 5

II w a (a) *over, on*, ofer stan, SS 36; ofer eorðan, SS 22 (see BT Dict sv ofer II 2).

(b) denoting degree, *beyond, besides*; ofer me, ss 43 (BT Supp sv ofer II 8); cf Old Latin Scripture, præter me.

oferfar (oferfær): n *journey over*, here, *exodus*; a sg (after oð), ss 17

ofermodigniss: f *pride, arrogance*; -e: a sg, AR 22

ofslean: VI *to kill*; -sleað: 3 pl pr, AR 12; -sloh: 3 sg pt, ss 36, AR 12

on: prep w d or a or endless locative

I w d (a) of position or location, *on, upon* (above and in contact with or above and supported by); on eorðan, ss 38, 48, AR 32, 34; *in, within*; on worulde, ss 12, 13, 17; on innoðe, ss 15, AR 6, 12; on neorxenawange, ss 16, 54†, AR 1; on helle, ss 16; on myddanaeardde, ss 17; on hyre, ss 31; on rice, ss 32; on stowum, ss 41; on bragene, on heortan, on blode, ss 41; on sæ, AR 24, on heafde, AR 23; on wætere, ss 52, AR 35; on hwam, on eagum, AR 48; on sidan, on winstran, AR 3; on simfelda (?), on sceanfelda (?), AR 20; on lande, AR 9; *in, within* (metaphorical); on æ, AR 13, 14; on gewealdum, ss 4. (b) (of temporal relations) *on, at, in, a point of time*, eg a particular day; on þam ... dæge, ss 5 (6 examples), AR 2 (2 examples); on þam, ss 16. *in, within, during, a period of time*; on hu fala dagum, ss 5; on VI dagum, ss 5; on xii monðum, ss 59 (3 examples); on hys lyfe, ss 59; AR 44; on cnihthade, ss 13 (2 examples); on morgene, ss 56 (see morgen). (c) (marking size, measure etc) *in, of*; on længe, ss 11; on lenge, ss 23; on hwilcere ylde, ss 10; on xxx wintra yldo, ss 10; on gerime, ss 59 (2 examples); on getal gerimes, ss 17 (see getal). (d) (indicating state, condition) *in*; on geswince, on yrmðe, ss 12. (e) (marking the means or instrument) *with, on*; on fiðerum, AR 27. (f) with the verb scinan (*to shine*), *on, in*; on stowum, on innoðe, on helle, on þam ealond, AR 6

II w endless locative, probably in certain temporal phrases although these may have come to be regarded as a; on niht, AR 6; on æfen, ss 27; ss 55; AR 8; on morgen, ss 26 (cf on morgene under I (b) above); on ærnemorgien, AR 7 (see ærnemorgien above).

III w a (a) (indicating motion to or towards a position, actual or figurative) *to, into*; on sæ, AR 25; on sætl, AR 30; on ðisne middangeard, AR 19. (b) (in certain temporal expressions; perhaps to be taken under II above, on a specified day, time etc) *on*; on Frigdæg, Frydæig, ss 16, AR 2; on hwilcne dæig, AR 2; on þone dæig, AR 2; on oðre tid, AR 6. (c) in certain set phrases; on ydel, ss 43; on unriht, ss 43 (2 examples). (d) (marking position) *on*; on gedryf, gedrif, ss 32 (2 examples); and thus probably: on neowelnysse, ss 32; on neorxnawang, AR 19. (e) (with a verb indicating division: BT Dict sv 'on' B. I 5) *into*; on þri dælas, ss 32. (f) (as an object of sight: BT Dict sv 'on' B.III 5) *on*; locað, lokað, on helle, ss 55, AR 8.

on: adv (elliptical use of the prep) *on*; AR 5 (2 examples)

on: num pron *one*, ss 39: see an

onscunian: 2 *to abhor, detest, loathe*; -scunað: 3 sg pr, AR 47

onstandan: VI *to stand on*; -stod: 3 sg pt, AR 42

oð: prep w a referring to a temporal limit, *until*; oð(†) flod; oð tid, ss 17; oð(†) ðrowunge, ss 17; oð domesdæig, AR 6; w d oð† gebyrtide ss 17

oðer: pron, adj, strong declension only. (a) pron as numeral, *second*; n sg, ss 9, 39, 50, 54, AR 38. (b) adj as numeral, *second*; n sg n, ss 43; -ne: a sg m, ss 32; oðre: a sg f, AR 6. (c) adj, *other, another*; -ne: a sg m, ss 43; oðres: g sg m, ss 43 (2 examples); oðrum: d pl m, ss 21. (d) in the phrase, oðer ... oðer, *one ... another, some ... others*; oðre ... oþre: a sg f, AR 24; oðrum ... oðrum: d sg, or pl. ss 49

oððe: conj *or*; ss 41 (2 examples), 45

plantian: 2 *plant*; -ode: 3 sg pt, ss 46

pund: n *pound* (of weight); n sg, ss 9 (8 examples); -a: g pl, ss 8

read: adj *red*; n sg n, ss 9; n sg f, ss 55, AR 8; -an: d sg f wk, AR 5

reade: adv *red*; ss 56, AR 7

restan: 1 *to rest, remain*; -eð: 3 sg pr, ss 41; -að: 3 pl pr, AR 6

restendæg: m *day of rest, Sabbath*; a sg, ss 43

ribb: n *rib*; a sg, AR 3

rice: n *kingdom*; d sg, ss 32

rihwisnisse (rihtwisniss): f *righteousness, justice*; as n sg, AR 27 (see textual note)

gerim: n *number*; -es: g sg, ss 17; -e: d sg, ss 59 (2 examples)

sæ: f where distinguishable *sea*; n sg, ss 42, AR 25; a sg, ss 5, 42, (2 examples), AR 25; d sg, AR 5, 7, 24; n pl, ss 33

sætl, (setl): n *seat*; a sg, AR 30; -e: d sg, ss 27; gan on, to, s: *to set*, ss 27, AR 30

sawul: f *soul*; n sg, ss 41, AR 26, 27; sawle, d sg, ss 13; saula†: n pl. AR 6

gesceaft: f *creature, creation*; -a: a pl, ss 5 (2 examples), AR 4

Sceanfelda: AR 20; see Proper Names

gesceap: n *creature, form*; -u: a pl, ss 5

gescieppan: VI *to create, make*; -sceop: 3 sg pt, ss 5 (7 examples); -sceope: 3 sg pt subj, AR 36; -sceapen: pp, ss 6, AR 2; -seapen, ss 10, 11 (see textual note)

sculan: pret pres vb *shall*; w infin *shall, must*; sealt: 2 sg pr, ss 59 (see textual note); sceal: 3 sg pr, ss 38, AR 26, 27, (2 examples); sceole: 3 pl pr, AR 19

scynan (scinan): 1 *to shine*; scyneð: 3 sg pr, ss 56; scynð, AR 6 (2 examples); scyne: 3 sg pr subj, AR 6, 7; scean: 3 sg pt, AR 5

se: m; seo: f; þæt: neut; pron, adj, def art *that one, that, the* [One example of each form in each text is given, unless the form needs special note when all examples are cited.] se: n sg m, ss 8 etc, AR 10 etc; seo: n sg f, ss 9 etc, AR 5 etc; þeo, AR 26, 42; þæt: n sg neut, ss 9 etc, AR 45 etc; þone: a sg m, ss 5 etc, AR 19 etc; þane, AR 12; þa: a sg f, AR 6 etc; þæt: a sg neut, ss 8, AR 3; þæs: g sg m and neut, ss 32 etc, AR 11; þas, AR 11; þære: g sg f, AR 12 etc; þam, ðam: d sg m and neut, ss 5 etc, AR 2 etc;

þære: d sg f, ss 42, AR 5 etc; þere, ss 41; þare, AR 13; þa: n and a pl, ss 5 etc, AR 19 etc; ðæra: g pl, AR 26; þære, AR 37.

Used as relative pronoun with or without relative þe, *who, which, that*; se, ss 13 (2 examples); se ðe, ss 15; þæt, ss 3, AR 6; þære, AR 5; þa (pl), AR 26.

Used as 3rd pers pron se, AR 18

Idiom with the neuter pron þæt is, ys *that is*; ss 54, 57, AR 20, 24.

Definite article used where it is not in NE, w deað, ss 15, AR 19, 28; w heofon, ss 13

sealt: n *salt*; -es: g sg, ss 9

sealt: adj *salt*; n sg, ss 42 (2 examples), AR 25; -e: n pl, ss 9, 33

secgan: 3 *to say, tell*; saga: imperative sg, ss 3 etc, AR 1 etc, the most common form; exceptions are: sage, ss1†, 2; sæge, ss 43; sæga, AR 18, 19; secge: 1 sg pr, ss 1 etc, AR 1 etc, the most common form; an exception is: sæcge, ss 16; sæde: 3 sg pt, AR 10

sefa: m *understanding, mind*; n sg, ss 9

selust: adj superl, *best*; n sg f, ss 28, 29, 31; n sg m, ss 29; n sg neut, ss 31

sendan: 1 *to send*; gesend: pp, AR 21

seoc: adj *sick, ill*; seoca: n sg m wk, AR 47; seoca: d sg m wk, AR 47

seofon: cardinal num *seven*, AR 37

seofoða: ordinal num *seventh*; seofoðo: n sg neut, ss 9; also as Roman numeral

geseon: v *to see*; infin, AR 48; gesihst: 2 sg pr, AR 48

settan: 1 *to establish, make, set up*; sette: 3 sg pt, ss 58, AR 17

si, sindon, sint: see beon

side: f *side*; sidan: d sg, AR 3

Simfelda: AR 20; see Proper Names

gesingian: 2 *to sin*; -ode: 3 sg pt, AR 2

sittan: v *to sit, be*; sæt: 3 sg pt, AR 4; sætt, ss 1; sete: 3 sg pt subj, ss 1

six: cardinal num *six*, AR 35

slæpan: VII *to sleep*; slepð: 3 sg pr, ss 41

slean: VI *to kill*; sleh: imperative sg, ss 43

snaw: m *snow*; n sg, ss 57

gesomnian: 2 *to collect, gather*; -ode: 3 sg pt, ss 42

sprecan: v *to speak*; sprecende: pr participle, ss 34

stæf, stef: m *letter, writing*; n sg, AR 38; stafas: a pl, AR 38

stalian: 2 *to steal*; stala: imperative sg, ss 43

stan: m *stone*; n sg, AR 10; a sg, ss 36; -as: n pl, ss 36

standan: VI *to stand* (as opposed to 'move'); stod: 3 sg pt, AR 42

steorra: m *star*; -um: d pl, ss 6

stillan: 1 *to appease*; -eð: 3 sg pr, AR 45

stow: f *place*, -um: d pl, ss 41, AR 6

stream: m *stream*; -as: n pl, ss 54

strengþe (strengþ): f *strength, courage, fortitudo*; as n sg, AR 27

strinan, gestrinan l *to beget, produce (children)*; strinde: 3 sg pt, ss 13 (2 examples); gestrinde, ss 13 (11 examples)

sul, sulh: normally f *plough*; sul: a sg, ss 35

gesund: adj *healthy, sound*; n sg m, AR 47

sunne: f *sun*; n sg, ss 26, 27, 55, AR 5, 6, 7, 8, 9, 10, 29, 42

sunu: m (also wk m forms) *son*; n sg, ss 13, 35, AR 12 (2 examples); suna: d sg, ss 14; sunu: g pl, ss 24 (after hwæt); sunena: g pl wk, ss 24

swa: adv and conj *so, as*; ss 21, 56 (2 examples), AR 7, 8, 21; swa ... swa, enclosing adj cuð, *as ... as*, ss 38; in combination, eall swa fela, *just as many*, ss 59 (2 examples)

swat: n *blood*; n sg, AR 11; *sweat*; n sg, ss 9

sweart: adj *black*; n sg m, AR 21

sweltan, swiltan: III *to die*; swilt: 3 sg pr for future, AR 48

swete: adj *sweet*; n sg neut, AR 45

geswinc: n *hardship, toil, affliction*; -e: d sg, ss 12

swiðra: compar adj *right* (as opposed to *left*); swiðre: a sg neut, AR 41

sy: see beon

sylf: pron adj *self*; in n sg agreeing with subject but preceded by reflexive d pron, hym sylf, ss 13

syllan (sellan): l *to give*, infin, ss 59; geseald: pp, ss 9 (4 examples)

syndon: see beon

synn: f *sin*; -a: n pl, ss 48

synt: see beon

syððan: adv *afterwards*, ss 12

syxsta: ordinal num *sixth*; syxste: n sg neut, ss 9; also as Roman numeral

syxtig: cardinal num *sixty*, ss 17

getacnian: 2 *to signify, betoken*; -að: 3 sg pr, ss 28, 29

getal (getæl, getel): *reckoning, count*; getal, ss 17 (prob for d sg; see examples of d after 'on' in BT Supp sv getæl IV ff)

tear: m *tear*; -as: n pl, ss 9; a pl, ss 42

tid: f *time, hour*; a sg, ss 17, AR 5, 6 (2 examples), 24 (2 examples), 42; tyda: g pl, ss 59 (2 examples)

getimbrian: 2 *to build*; -ode: 3 sg pt, ss 53; getymbrod: pp, ss 25

tin (tyn): cardinal num *ten*, AR 25

to: prep w d *to*; (a) with verbs expressing motion towards; to helle, ss 12; to sætle, ss 27; to Noe, (in) to arke, AR 21; to westenne, AR 22; to heofonum, AR 27. (b) with words denoting address (BT Dict sv 'to' 4e); to Ritheus, AR introd; to Salomane, ss introd. (c) with inflected infin; to æriende, ss 35; to berende, ss 48 (see textual note); to witanne, ss 38. (d) marking purpose fulfilled by the object, with a verb of being, *to*, *as*; to beode, to neodþærfe (BT Dict sv 'to' I 5 f), AR 46.

todælan: 1 *to divide* (intrans); -don: 3 sg pt, ss 32

tokyme (tocyme): m *coming*, *advent*; d sg, AR 13

toð: m *tooth*; -a†: g pl, ss 59

treow: n *tree*; n sg, ss 40; -a: g pl, ss 40

treowcinn (treowcynn): n *kind of tree*; treowcinne: d sg, ss 18

tungol: n or m, weak forms occur in n and a pl as here; *heavenly body*, *light*; tunglon: a pl, ss 5

twegen: m; twa: f, neut: *two*; twegen: n m AR 19, 26; twege, AR 48; twa: n f, ss 33 (2 examples), 59; neut, AR 33; twa: a neut, ss 12; also as Roman numeral

twynian (tweonian): 2 impers w d *to doubt*; -að†: 3 sg pr, ss 56

þa, ða: adv *then*, ss introd, 13 etc; conj *when*, ss 1 etc

þær, þar: adv *there*; þar, ss 12, AR 6; *where*; þær, ss 26, AR 29, 30

þæt: conj *that*; introducing (a) a substantive clause, AR 10; (b) a clause of purpose, *so that*, AR 42

þæt: adj, pron, definite article: see se

þæt: relative pron, *that*, *which*; ss 3, AR 6, 22 (þæt he)

þage (þæge): pron *these*, ss 7, 9 (see textual note)

þam, þan: see se

geþanc: m, n *thought*; n sg, AR 38; geþang, ss 9

þanne: adv, conj; see þonne

þanon, ðanon: adv *thence*; or conj; *whence*; þanon, ss 9 (6 examples); ðanon, ss 9

þarin: adv *therein, in there*, ss 25

þa ða: conj, *when*, AR 25

þe, ðe: indecl relat particle, *that, who, which*; ss 4 etc, AR 3 etc; with demonstrative, as relative, se ðe, ss 15; with personal pron, as relative, þe heo, AR 42

þe: conj *or*, ss 56 (BT Dict sv þe III.3)

þe: 2 pers pron: see ðu

þeah: conj *although*, AR 19

þenian (þegnian): 2 w d *to serve, minister to*; -ode: 3 sg pt, AR 22

þeo: see seo, under se

þeod: f *nation, people*; -a: g pl, ss 14 (2 examples); ðeoda, ss 59†

ðeow: adj *serving*; -an: d sg m wk, ss 59 (ðeow man, *servant*, ss 59)

þes: m; þeos: f; þis: n; demonst pron and adj *this*; (a) as adj, þeos: n sg f, ss 45; þisne: a sg m, ss 5, 56, AR 19; þas: a sg f, ss 41; ðissere: d sg f, ss 13; þissere, ss 12, 13; þas: a pl, ss 57. (b) as pron þas: n pl, AR 19

þin: poss adj *thine, your*; þinon: d sg m, ss 43, 59; þinre: d sg f, ss 43 þing: n (i) *thing*; n pl, ss 39, 50; ðinc, AR 39; (ii) *creature, thing*; a pl, ss 4; (iii) *reason, cause*; -um, ðingum: d pl, ss 3, 45

geþingian: 2 *to atone*; -ode: 3 sg pt, AR 22

ðolian: 2 *to suffer, endure, undergo*; -ode: 3 sg pt, ss 12

þonne, þone, þanne: adv *then*; conj *when*; þonne, AR 12, 48; þanne, AR 26; þone, ss 41; with comparative, *than*, þonne, AR 9

þri: m; þreo: f and n; cardinal num *three*; ðreo: n f or neut, ss 21; þreo, AR 39; þri: a m, ss 32; þrim: d f, ss 41, AR 6; d m, AR 48; also as Roman numeral

þridda, þridde: ordinal num *third*; þridde: n sg m, AR 38; ðridde: n sg neut, ss 9, 39, 43†, 50; þriddan: a sg m, ss 32; ðridda: a sg f, AR 6; þriddan: d sg m, ss 5; also as Roman numeral

þrittig: cardinal num *thirty*, AR 34, AR 35

þrittine: cardinal num *thirteen*, AR 1

þrowian: 2 *to suffer*; infin, ss 38; -ede: 3 sg pt, AR 2

ðrowung: f *passion*; -e: a sg, ss 17

ðu, þu: pron 2 pers *thou, you*; n sg, ss 43 etc; þe, ðe: d sg, ss 1 etc

þurh: prep w a *through*; (a) in a physical sense, þurh, AR 23; ðurc, AR 41. (b) figuratively, indicating means, agent, cause, *through, because of*, ss 16, 45 (3 examples, 2†), AR 22 (2 examples). (c) as (b) but with d, ss 45, see sv fulluht

þusend: n *thousand*; n or a pl with partitive g, ss 12, 59; ðusend, ss 16, 17 (2 examples); -a, ðusenda: g pl, ss 25

geþwærnisse (geþwærnyss): f *concord, agreement*; as n sg, AR 27

ufan: adv *down, from above*, AR 8

unriht: n *wrong, injustice, evil*; -e: d sg, ss 43; as adverbial phrase, on unriht, *wrongly*, ss 43 (2 examples); see 'on' III c

unrot: adj *sad, sorrowful*; -e: n pl m, AR 19

unscildi (unscyldig): adj *innocent*; -ne†: a sg m, ss 43

unstaðelfæstnes: f *instability*; n sg, ss 9

up: adv *up*, ss 13, 26, AR 7

upgan: anom vb: see gan *to go up*; upgæð: 3 sg pr, AR 29

ure: poss adj *our*; n sg, AR 3, 4

ut: adv *out*, ss 17, AR 23

wæpnedkinn (wæpnedcynn): n *male*; -es: g sg, AR 24

wæs, was, wære, wæron: see beon

wæter: n *water*; n sg, ss 39, 57, AR 39; water, ss 31; wateres: g sg, ss 32; wætere: d sg, ss 52, AR 35; watere, ss 30; wætera: g pl (prob, after cardinal number), ss 57; watra? (after fela), ss 33, or compound woruldwatra sv

geweald: n *power, control*; -um: d pl, ss 4

wearð: see wurþan

wela: m *wealth, riches*; -ena: g pl, ss 50

weorpan: III *to throw*; wearp: 3 sg pt, AR 25

wepan: VII *to weep*; -að: 3 pl pr, AR 19 (2 examples)

westenn: n or m *wilderness*; westenne†: d sg, AR 22 (see textual note)

wid: adj *wide, broad*; n sg f, ss 23

wif, wyf: n *wife, woman*, wif: n sg, ss 20; wyf, ss 19, 21; wif: a sg, AR 3; wyfes: g sg, ss 43

wifkinn: n *female*; -es: g sg, AR 24

wiht: (here) f *creature*; -a: n pl, AR 24 (hwilce wihta)

gewiht: n *weight*; -e: d sg, ss 8

willa: m *will, desire*; n sg, AR 44

gewilnian: 2 w g *desire*; -myd unrihte, on unriht, *to covet*; gewilna: imperative sg, ss 43 (2 examples)

win: n *wine*, n sg, ss 54; a sg, AR 17†

wind: m *wind*; n sg, AR 5; -es: g sg, ss 9; -e: d sg, ss 30; -a: g pl, ss 1†, AR 4

wingeard: m *vineyard*; a sg, ss 46†; wineardas: a pl, AR 17

winstra (winestra): adj *left*; -n: d sg f wk, AR 3

winter: m *winter, year*; -a: g pl, ss 12 etc

wintreow: n *vine*; n sg, ss 40

wisdom: m *wisdom, knowledge*; a sg, ss introd

witan: pret pres vb *to know*; wite: 3 sg pr subj, ss 44; inflected infin witanne, ss 38

gewitan: I *to go, depart*; -on: 3 pl pt, ss 32; -en: pp (*gone*, euphemism for *dead*), AR 48

wite: n *punishment*; -u: a pl, ss 12

witega: m *prophet*; n pl, ss 53 (see textual note)

witegian: 2 *to prophesy*; -ode: 3 sg pt, AR 15

gewitnyss: f *witness*; -e: a sg, ss 43; lease-, *false witness*

wolcen: n *cloud*; wolcnes: g sg, ss 9

word: n (i) *word, command, commandment*; n sg, ss 2, 43 (7 examples plus 2†), AR 31; wurd, AR 45; worð, ss 43; worð: n pl, ss 43; a pl, ss 42, AR 25; -on: d pl, ss 42. (ii) *word, speech*; n sg, ss 37, AR 43

woruld (weorold): f *world*; -e: g sg, ss 50; -e: d sg, ss 12, 13 (2 examples), 17.

woruldwæter (?): n *waters of the world*; as compound (?), woruldwatra: g pl, ss 33

wrecan: V *to avenge*; wræce: 3 sg pt subj, AR 12

writan: I *to write*; wrat: 3 sg pt, AR 16

wucu (wicu): f *week*; wucena: g pl, ss 59

wunian: 2 *to dwell, live*; wuniað: 3 pl pr, AR 20

wurðan (weorðan): III *to become, be*; wearð: 3 sg pt, ss 42; geworden pp, ss 42

gewurðan: III *to be*; gewurðe: 3 sg pr subj, AR 31

wurðian, (weorðian): 2 *to honour*; -edon: 3 pl pt, AR 25

wyrcan, gewyrcan: 1 *to make, build*; worhte: 3 sg pt, SS 18, AR 25; geworhte, SS 1, 5, AR 3, 4; geworht: pp, SS 8, 9; men worhte, SS 18, illustrates either a lack of grammatical concord, or 'men' is in place of 'man.'

wyrst: superl adj *worst*; n sg neut, SS 37 (2 examples), AR 43

wyrt: f *plant*; n sg, SS 28 (2 examples)

wyð (wið): prep w a *with* (marking conversation), SS 34

wyðsacan: VI w d of what is rejected, *to reject, forsake*; wyðsocon: 3 pl pt, SS 32

ydel (idel): n *emptiness, vanity*; here only in phrase 'on ydel,' *in vain*, SS 43

yld(u) (ield(u)): see Pope, Glossary sv; yld: f *age*; yldo: d sg, SS 10; ylde, SS 10, 17

yldan: 1 *to delay*; -on: 3 pl pt, AR 19

yldestan: see eald

ymbe: prep w a *about*; SS introd

ynce: m *inch*; -a: g pl, SS 11

yrmð(e) (iermð(e)): see Pope, Glossary sv; f *misery*; yrmðe: d sg, SS 12

yrre (ierre): n *anger*; n sg, SS 48, AR 32

ys: see beon

ysen: see isen

Proper Names

This index includes all the proper names in the forms in which they occur in the OE texts. The headword is the name in the nominative singular, according to the Vulgate usage for Biblical names, and according to the usage of the OE dialogues otherwise. Case is given, often by function and context, although it is evident that the copyists were often not conscious of case in less common names. Cross-references are provided where appropriate, and explanation where necessary.

Chanan: See Cainan

Christus (Christ): Crist, n sg, ss 31, AR 2,
41; Crist, a sg, ss 17, 28; Cristes, g sg,
ss 17, AR 13, 37

Coruus: Coruus, n sg, AR 24 (see commentary)

Dalila: Dalila, n sg, ss 19 (see commentary)

Dux: Dux n sg, ss 7 (cardinal point in
Greek, Dysis)

Egipta, Egyptum: See Aegyptus

Elias, Helias (Elijah): Elias, n sg, ss 53;
Helias, AR 19; Heliam, a sg, AR 22

Eliseus: Eliseus, n sg, ss 53

Enoc, Enoh: See Henoch

Enos: Enos (son of Seth), n sg, ss 13 (3
examples); Enos (son of Cain), n sg,
ss 25

Euphrates: Eufraten, n sg, ss 54

Fegor: See Phogor

Fison: See Phison

Gabaon: Gabaon, n sg, AR 42

Garita: Garita, n sg, ss 27 (see commentary)

Geon: See Gihon

Gihon: Geon, n sg, ss 54

Gliŏ: Gliŏ, n sg, AR 6 (see textual notes
and commentary)

Ham: See Cham

Helias, Heliam: See Elias

Henoch: Enoc, n sg, AR 19; Enoh, n sg,
ss 13 (2 examples); Enoh, a sg, ss 13

Hierusalem: See Ierusalem

Iacobus: Iacobus, n sg, AR 14

Iafet: See Iaphet

Iaiaca: Iaiaca, n sg, ss 26, AR 29

Iainta: Iainta, n sg, AR 30

Iaitarecta: Iaitarecta, n sg, ss 20

Iaphet (Japhet): Iafet, a sg, ss 13;
Iafeŏes, g sg, ss 21; Iafeŏe, d sg, ss 14

Iared: Iared, n sg, ss 13 (2 examples);
Iared, a sg, ss 13

Ierusalem (Jerusalem): Hierusalem, n
sg, ss 25

Intimphonis: Intimphonis, n sg, AR 20

Iordanes (Jordan): Iordanem, n sg, ss 31

Ioshue: Iosue, n sg, AR 42

Israel: Israela, g p (people for place), ss
17, AR 5, 25

Lamech: Lamec, n sg, ss 13 (2 examples); Lamec, a sg, ss 13

Leuiathan: Leuiathan, n sg, AR 6

Malaleel: Malaleh, n sg, ss 13 (2 examples); Malaleh, a sg, ss 13

Malifica: Malifica, n sg, AR 20

Maria: Maria, g sg, ss 17; Maria, d sg, AR
41

Mathusalem: Mathusalem, n sg, ss 13;
Matusalem, n sg, ss 13; Matusalem, a
sg, ss 13

Melchisedech: Melchisedech, n sg, AR
13

Mercurius: Mercurius, n sg, ss 58, AR 16

Moses: Moyses, n sg, AR 25; Moises, n
sg, ss 42, Moises, g sg, ss 17; Moyses,
g sg, ss 44, AR 42

Mynsymbrie: Mynsymbrie, n sg, ss 7
(cardinal point in Greek, Mesembria)

Ninive: Niniuem, n sg, ss 25

Noe: Noe, n sg, ss 13 (2 examples), 46,

AR 17; Noe, a sg, ss 13, 45; Noes, g sg, ss 17, 18, 19, 22, 23, 25, 35; Noe, d sg, AR 21

Olla: Olla, n sg, ss 21

Ollibania: Ollibania, n sg, ss 21

Ollina: Ollina, n sg, ss 21

Paulus: Paulus, n sg, ss 53

Petrus: Petrus, n sg, ss 34, AR 14

Phison: Fison, n sg, ss 54

Phogor: Fegor, n sg, ss 44

Ritheus: Ritheus, d sg, AR introduction

Saloman: Saloman, n sg, ss introduction; Salomane, d sg, ss introduction

Samuel: Samuel, n sg, AR 15

Saturnus: Saturnus, n sg, ss introduction (2 examples)

Sceanfelda: Sceanfelda, d sg?, AR 20

Sem: Sem, a sg, ss 13; Seme, d sg, ss 14; Sem (for sethim), n sg, ss 18 (see commentary)

Seth: Seth, n sg, ss 13 (2 examples)

Simfelda: Simfelda, d sg?, AR 20

Tigris: Tygres, n sg, ss 54

Viperus: Viperus, n sg, AR 24 (see commentary)

Latin Words

These words are merely listed in the form in which they appear in the text, but corruptions are noted.

adsumes ss 43
alienos ss 43
concupiscens (for concupisces) ss 43
  (2 examples)
deos ss 43
domini ss 43
est ss 2
et ss 2, 43
facta ss 2
fiat ss 2
habeos (for habeas) ss 43
in ss 43
lux ss 2 (2 examples)

mechaberis ss 43
nomen ss 43
non ss 43 (6 examples)
occides ss 43
omnia ss 43
proximi ss 43 (2 examples)
rem ss 43
sancta ss 17
sanctus ss 34
tui ss 43 (2 examples)
uanum ss 43
uxorem ss 43

McMaster Old English Studies and Texts